Infamy and Revolt:

The Rise of the National Problem in Early Modern Greek Thought

Dean J. Kostantaras

East European Monographs, Boulder
Distributed by Columbia University Press, New York
2006

EAST EUROPEAN MONOGRAPHS, NO. DCLXXXIII

ISBN: 0-88033-581-5
(978-0-88033-581-2)

Library of Congress of Control Number: 2006923385

Printed in the United States of America

To my parents

Table of Contents

Glossary of Terms

Diaphotismos: enlightenment; used here to denote the Neohellenic (modern Greek) Enlightenment, signifying the participation of Greek thinkers in the speculations of the Early Modern era.

Emboros/oi: merchant/s.

Ethnos: nation and also ethnicity.

Genos: race; could also be used to denote one's family or religious affiliation.

Klephtos/oi: bandit/s.

Logios/oi: men of high learning/letters, often assumed to have an enlightening role in Greek society.

Patrida: fatherland. Usually signifies the village of one's birth but also used occasionally to refer more generally to 'Greece'.

Phanariot: class of Greek nobles inhabiting the Phanar or lighthouse district of Constantinople.

Philike Etairia: 'Friendly Society.' Secret revolutionary organization founded in Odessa in 1814.

Progonoplexeia: ancestor-fixation.

Tourkokratia: term used by Greek historians to identify the period of Turkish rule (1453-1821).

Vlach: term used by Greeks over the period studied to identify modern day Romanians, as well as the Balkan peoples who are still referred to by this name.

Stasis:	discord.
Xeniteia:	foreign parts/lands.
Zetema:	question, debate, issue. Used here in the context of the language debate.

Preface

It hurts me now that I have met you and that I don't have work, since when someone has work he is more esteemed among men and better listened to. Me, if I had work and were at sea, I could win many good and beneficial patriots (for the Fatherland) .[1]

This study, which sets out to analyze the emergence of the 'Greek Enlightenment' and independence movement over the century and a half preceding the 1821 revolution, was first coaxed along its way by the melancholy words of individuals such as the above. He is an aspiring merchant, still young, only thirty years old, whose hopes nonetheless for quick fortune have met with failure. We encounter him here in the midst of a daring and desperate act of self re-invention: his application for membership into a secret society of patriots dedicated to the revolutionary overthrow of Ottoman rule in the Balkans.

Such tales of profitless wandering, repeated in conspicuous detail by others who like this young merchant found a salve for their battered ambitions in the revolutionary 'Society of Friends,' were among the first voices that suggested to me the ideas that underlay this study. What they suggested, and in a form more explicit than most, was how closely mingled feelings of nationalism could be with self worth. Moving farther back from the 1821 Revolution, the crowning achievement of the Society of Friends, back into the history of the Ottoman period, new examples steadily emerged of just how closely and in what a variety of contexts this 'mingling' can take place.

It was among the logioi, the men of letters, that the notes of revolt were first raised, aimed in this case against the plight and infamy of the fallen 'ethnos' (nation). The intense preoccupation of these scholars with cultural degeneration was such a fixture of the Neohellenic Enlightenment that it soon posed to my mind the question of vintage; such a discourse had clearly attained maturity long before the arrival of those later luminaries, Adamantios Koraes (1748-1833) and Regas Velestinlis (1757-1798). How old was it? The research led me back into the seventeenth century, to logioi such as the Metropolitan Meletios Metros (1661-1714) and the rector John Patousas (1677-1712), and the discovery that their writings contained a similar stock of themes and images. So does one find Fragkiskos Skouphos (1644-1697), born a hundred years before Koraes, thanking God for "providing me with a little learning that I may benefit my race (genos), once wealthy in every virtue, and wisdom, and now for the pitilessness of chance naked, and deprived."[2]

It became clear that this discourse was much older than I had first assumed, was much older than the Enlightenment, though to trace it back too far would greatly exceed the intended scope of this project. Nonetheless, the Greek reaction to the Enlightenment is only understandable if one first recognizes the tradition of thought that came before. Surely one of the most prominent features of the chapters that follow is the eager appropriation of Enlightenment philosophy by the logioi. And yet this outcome becomes less surprising when critical matters of context, such as the historical posture of the Greek world toward the West, are taken into consideration.

The efforts of the logioi to restore the nation to a respectable place in the world cannot be said to have been greatly rewarded by their homeland. Returning to the East after periods of study in Europe—an interaction that had been taking place since Byzantine times—they might find their careers inconstant, given the paucity of schools, or confront resistance to their attempts at innovation. The frustrations engendered by these experiences occasionally surface in the sources, often sounding very much like those expressed by the thwarted merchants of the Etairia. Such was the case of the logios Neophetos Doukas (1760-1845), who, though advanced in age when approached, consented to lend his own fading energies to the militant nationalists of the Society of Friends. "Since I departed from Zagori, my beloved fatherland, until now I have been occupied in studies," Doukas wrote in his dedicatory letter from Bucharest. "I lead a layman's existence, giving lessons to a few students, not having the strength any longer for great labors, being already over fifty-five years in age. I plan to return to my fatherland, perhaps to raise up again the school where I took my first lessons... if only I can move myself in old age for such a journey."[3]

Whether the revolutionary nationalism of Doukas and the Society of Friends was in truth a work of sublimation borne of personal hardship or the yearning for "redemption" is an intriguing question and one that has been the subject of other studies.[4] These speculations notwithstanding, the declarations of the revolutionary generation do at least reveal the influence of a much older national discourse upon their consciousness, for they drew heavily upon images of ruin and infamy that had long ruled the intellectual culture of the Greek world.

Studies of early modern Balkan nationalism will always face one great obstacle: the peasants who formed the vast majority of these largely agrarian societies have mostly passed mute and silent through history. The sources are dominated by the writings of a few scholars, quite often in the form of exhortations directed at these very same peasants. It was upon the rehabilitation of the people, after all, that the logios's dream of national revival (and his own escape from the stigma of backwardness) depended. Indeed, "five educated people don't make a nation," the geographers Konstantas and Philippides complained. "From these no one could say such a nation was educated, but that it was barbarous and ignorant."[5] No doubt such men were especially grieved by the retinue of picturesque if degenerate natives that filled the pages of Western travelogues, or strolled aloofly through the ruins of Athens, according to Gibbon, so "debased" in character "that they are incapable of admiring the genius of their predecessors."[6]

The works of the logioi offer the testimony therefore of a group of men who took a very different path from the norm, and one that often led them into alien cultures. To understand these texts is to try as well to understand the social circumstances of those who wrote them. In this regard, the logios's experience of life in a foreign society must certainly have been an enlightening experience, if often too a troubling one. As the influential scholar Iosepos Moisiodax (1720-?1800) observed in his first book, "All of Europe deplores and deems Greece in misery, not so much for its captivity, as for its illiteracy."[7] If occupying unique positions in their home society, the logioi were, in Europe, simply 'Greeks', and automatically subject to the images associated with this term. Such an experience was bound to have a heightening influence on one's sense of group identity, even if the individual response to this stimulus could take a variety of forms.

The old Hellenic discourse of the fallen nation seeking redemption found special reinforcement in the Enlightenment's optimistic vision of human perfectability, no matter that the original intent was often cosmopolitan in nature. But this was not the Enlightenment of the logioi. It was upon their own national program of renewal that the 'men of learning' expended so much ink and energy. Their encounter with the Enlightenment was only the latest episode in a larger pattern of encounter and response that appears to have been set far in the past. Certainly the Enlightenment was a phenomenon of rare power in this sequence and one that seemed to lose nothing of its potency in the diffusion of its works. And yet for the Greeks these remained the works of 'others,' best understood in relation to their own experience. No surprise then that the cosmopolitan element should fade in the ensuing exchange. This was an admirable vision, but, again, it was not their Enlightenment. Absent in them was the self-satisfaction that gave rise to such projections of a similarly enlightened world; such a premise could only strike those in darkness with the force of an indictment. No surprise indeed that the Enlightenment project of the logioi was an intensely private one, or that the 'heavenly city' of their imagination was to lie again, God-willing, somewhere on the shores of the Aegean Sea.

Notes

1. Emmanuel Glykoudes of Ithaca from the collection of 'Devotional Letters' in Ioannes Philemon, *Dokimion Historikon peri tes Hellenikes Epanastaseos*, 4 Volumes, (Athens: P. Soutsa, 1859-61), I: 334. Such letters were required as part of an initiation ritual in which each new member was asked to make a financial contribution to the Society. This contribution was disguised as an act of national philanthropy, such as the restoration of a school or publication of new books, described by the donor in his letter. However these 'devotional' letters often acquired a confessional character, as the examples here indicate.

2. Fragkiskos Skouphos, 'Texne Rhetorike,' in *Skouphos, Meniates, Voulgaris, Theotokes*, edited by Basile N. Tatakis, (Athens: Vasike Vivliotheke, 1953), 50. Skouphos's 'Rhetorike' was first published in Venice in 1681.

3. Neophetos Doukas, 'Devotional Letter,' in Ioannes Philemon, *Dokimion Historikon peri tes Hellenikes Epanastaseos*, I: 337-8.

4. See for example George Frangos, The Philike Etairia: A Premature National Coalition, in *The Greek Struggle for Independence*, edited by Richard Clogg, (London: Archon Books, 1973).

5. Gregorios Konstantas and Daniel Philippides, *Geographia Neoterike*, (reprint, edited by Aikaterina Koumarianou, Athens: Hermes, 1988), 76. This work was first published in 1791.

6. Edward Gibbon, *The Decline and Fall of the Roman Empire*, (Franklin Center, Pennsylvania: The Franklin Library, 1983), VI: 231. As will be shown later, such narratives as these became so common they ultimately inspired a Greek parody literature.

7. Iosepos Moisiodax, 'Prologue, Ethike Philosophia,' in Appendix I of Paschalis Kitromilides, *Iosepos Moisiodax, Hoi syntetagmenes tes Balkanakes Skepses ton 18o aiona*, (Athens: Morfotiko Idroma Ethnikes Trapezes, 1985), 339. Moisiodax's *Ethike* was first published in Venice in 1761.

I. General Features of Greek Intellectual Culture In the Time of the Enlightenment

In the early spring of 1821 a revolutionary war burst out in several provinces of the Ottoman Empire and most seriously among the Greek populated lands of 'European Turkey.'[1] After nearly twelve months of violence and confusion, and with the fate of the revolution still much in doubt, delegates were gathered to create a constitution for the newly liberated 'nation' and announce its intentions to the world. The ensuing 'Proclamation of Independence' began with a bold declaration:

> We, descendants of the wise and humane peoples of Hellas, we who are the contemporaries of the enlightened and civilized nations of Europe, who seeing the advantages they enjoy under the protection of the unbreakable auspices of the law, find it no longer possible to endure without cowardice and self-contempt the harsh yoke of Ottoman power that has fallen upon our heads for more than four centuries.[2]

This very brief fragment of revolutionary rhetoric contains, nevertheless, some important points of interest for the historian of nationalism. No doubt the ideological character and foundations of the Proclamation are among its most curious features. The authors have in fact dressed their demands for independence in language lifted straight from the Western liberal canon, a tendency that becomes even more recognizable as the address continues. The Greeks seek no less than to acquire the "rights" due to them, "of individual liberty, of property and honor—rights which the civilized people of Europe, our neighbors, enjoy today."[3] The legitimacy of the revolution rests therefore on the authority of principles that had circulated in Europe since the days of Locke.[4]

The presence of so much Western thought in the Proclamation has great implications for the history of the Greek revolution. In the first case, such facts have been wielded to judge not only this event, but eighteenth and nineteenth century national movements in general, as instances of ideological mimicry, calling into question the pre-existence of purely native notions of 'nation' or independence. These sentiments either did not exist or were not felt very widely by the subject peoples, so the argument goes, until made so by their exposure to foreign ideas—ideas that had come to the East through the various agencies of history and the Enlightenment.

These are formidable arguments and there is no disputing the fact that the Enlightenment was a phenomenon of great reach and influence. However previous studies have not sufficiently depicted the full nature of the cultural exchanges taking place within it.[5] Ideas were surely bartered and borrowed, but the laws of selection guiding this exchange are far from self-evident.[6]

As described in the ensuing chapters, Greek intellectuals had long brooded over the declining status of their world in relation to western Europe. These concerns were raised substantially during the eighteenth century, partly as a result of social and political changes that elevated the level of Greek exposure to the West just as the Enlightenment hit its stride. Vital structural confluences such as these were reinforced by the appeal to progress that Greek scholars were prone to deduce from the Enlightenment, a message that related quite well to issues that had shaped their own tradition of thought.

The Enlightenment was not therefore an object of incidental notice among Greek intellectuals, but was a matter of vigorous speculation and activity. When the sources surrounding this activity are taken into account, the 'native quotient' of the intellectual exchange rises to the surface. The reflexive nationalization of certain Enlightenment ideals by the logioi is itself a striking exhibition of the existence of preoccupations that had animated Hellenic intelligentsia for centuries. It was from the Enlightenment that these intellectuals found new tools for addressing old problems.

In summary, speculations over the role that the Enlightenment may have played in the arousal of nationalism in the eastern lands of Europe during these times must account for the interplay of all the elements sketched above.

Enlightenment, the National Problem and Revolt

The 'national problem' is a term used here to refer to a long running dialogue within Hellenic culture dating back to the late Byzantine era, a dialogue centered around the theme of civilizational decadence and decline. This dialogue steadily gathered momentum over the succeeding centuries of Turkish rule, even if, according to most historians, it articulated no clear course of political action. Such ambiguity would remain true up to the very eve of the revolution itself. Education was the most common answer given by the Greek Enlightenment, or Diaphotismos, to the question of renewal, and in this it evoked the intellectual inclinations of its predecessors. But was this enough? As C.M. Woodhouse once pointed out, "The learned Greeks abroad might insist that education was the right road for the new generation... but to what goal would education carry them? The intellectuals had no precise answer."[7] If the logioi truly had no clear vision of 'whither Enlightenment?', they seemed at least agreed on the need to bring Greek society to a recognition of its plight—and thus the pervasive self-critique intimated by the title of this study. The Enlightenment appears in fact to have supplied a fresh impetus to this activity.

To speak of the Enlightenment as of a uniform canon of thought emanating out from (western) Europe would be of course to greatly misjudge its scope and complexity.[8] This inner complexity in fact was not lost on the logioi, who followed the intellectual movements of the times very closely. However it could well be said that their most immediate reaction to the Enlightenment occurred on an entirely visceral level, as if so much talk of progress and civilization were fresh indictments of their predicament. Such fears were not completely unfounded. As Dena Goodman observed, there was a tendency among French philosophes to "mutually identify" Enlightenment with the best of French culture.[9] Nor did this attitude go unnoticed by intellectuals from other lands. Johann Gottfried von Herder's critique, for example, of Enlightenment cosmopolitanism appeared to cloak a personal antagonism to what he perceived as a quest for French cultural hegemony.[10]

Herder (1744-1803) surely qualifies as one of the most unique voices of the Enlightenment and it is natural to ask whether there exist any parallels between his thought and the Diaphotismos. It must be said from the start that the prideful nativism of Herder only dimly evokes the merciless national self-critique of the logioi. These scholars were oppressed by the awful figure of modern Greek society, and more oppressed still by the numberless charges of barbarism lodged against it by Europeans fixated on its golden past.[11] Although Herder experienced a bout or two of cultural self-consciousness himself when exposed to the national prejudices of his time, it appears to be a mild form of the condition afflicting the logioi; another consequence perhaps of the attitudes their respective societies were prone to elicit from the Western republic of letters. As other scholars have shown, Herder's thought cannot be said, finally, to have exerted much of an influence on Greek intellectuals before the 1821 revolution.[12] This conclusion precludes what may otherwise have been a fruitful source of inspiration behind the increasingly radical Greek national movement that emerged toward the close of the eighteenth century.[13] However the path taken by the Diaphotismos conforms more closely to what Woodhouse suggested above: an impulse toward regeneration that had no articulate sense of where it was leading. History supplied its own force to the resolution of these ambiguities, although ambiguities certainly remained, as noted later, up to the very outbreak of the revolution itself.

Did the Greek Enlightenment cause the 1821 revolution? Dorinda Outram considered a similar question in the context of French history. Her thesis, that it would be more correct to see revolution and enlightenment as simultaneous phenomena, does not completely dismiss the problem.[14] However this point is essential in conditioning the view of the Diaphotismos as an exhibition of ideological mimicry often proffered by Western scholars. War and revolution were steadily transforming the Balkans and we should expect these events to have had a serious effect on the development of Greek thought. To what extent the Diaphotismos *caused* the Greek Revolution or was itself a product of revolutionary times therefore remains in question. My own analysis of the Philike Etairia in Chapter Four, the secret society that ultimately led the Greek revolt of 1821, attempts to demonstrate the ambiguity of these connections. It cannot simply be said that the ideas of the Diaphotismos moved the men of the Etairia to revolt, although their sources are permeated with its imagery and language. The weakening of Ottoman power, the victories of Austria and Russia in their conflicts with the Turks, the Orlov Revolt of 1770—these and other events were defining precedents, and may well have stimulated the growing emphasis we find in the sources on political action. The important lesson that this suggests regarding the relationship between ideology and history is instructive for understanding future developments. Perhaps nowhere is this more true or more significant than in the Greek conception of 'nation-state.' As discussed below, this entity can claim only a shadowy existence in the literature preceding the Revolution.[15] When a Greek nation-state ultimately did emerge, it was an object determined more by default than design.

The Sociology of Enlightenment

To what extent had the Greek people as the Proclamation of 1822 claims, or for that matter the Serbs, Vlachs or Bulgarians, viewed themselves as suffering under the 'harsh yoke' of the Turks? To what extent had they yearned for independence? National or ethnic self-consciousness in pre-independence Greece certainly existed on some level, as later events made shockingly clear. The most vivid example was furnished by the Greek peasants, who apparently required little prompting to identify who their 'enemies' were once the revolution broke out: the first days of the uprising witnessed a slaughter of the Turkish population in the Peloponnesus and Rumeli that left European observers aghast.[16]

But these events occurred within a unique and revolutionary-charged atmosphere and for the most part historians are left with little means to determine the national consciousness of Balkan peasantry in the pre-revolutionary epoch.[17] It does not appear from the sources, in any case, that peasants represent the starting point for nationalist movements. Assumptions such as these have furnished the critics of 'primordial' nationalism with their most damning weapons in the battle for history.[18]

The first blows fell before the nineteenth century had ended, delivered by historians such as Lord Acton, who dismissed the adherents of nationalism as promoters of a 'fictitious unity.' Benedict Anderson's 'imagined community' at once comes to mind, but to say that Anderson's celebrated thesis has simply returned us to the former view doesn't suffice. If the modern scholar presents the nation as a 'fiction' he is obligated to tell us also who felt most compelled to embrace this fiction, and why.

A study of the Neohellenic Enlightenment would certainly be incomplete if it did not address such a question by considering the promoters of its discourse. The chapters that follow therefore describe the history of early modern Greek thought with due attention to social context, recognizing that to some extent a movement of ideas is a social phenomenon. The experiences of people like the young merchant, or the elder logios Doukas, belong to that vast mosaic composing the fall of Ottoman power in the Balkans and the rise of the new states that appear in its wake. One confronts immediately the dimension of the phenomenon, the universe of personalities and events that go into its making. Fortunately, the intellectual history of the early modern Greek world does yield itself to a socially-oriented analysis. This method assumes that the forces of enlightenment and revival, consolidated for the moment under the title of nationalism, appeal more readily to some social groups than others.

As noted above, there had long existed a tradition of thought in the Greek world concerning the 'national problem.' The creators of this tradition were a class of native scholars and intelligentsia known to Greek history as the logioi. As Anthony D. Smith, has written of other movements, "The intelligentsia always contributes representatives out of proportion to its numbers."[19] But what makes this group of Greek intellectuals more intriguing is the fact that the great majority of them belonged to the Orthodox Church, an institution most commonly regarded as a bastion of conservatism. And yet the Neohellenic Enlightenment is in fundamental ways the work of Orthodox clerics. Later, over the course of the second half of the eighteenth century, accompanying economic and social developments within the Greek world and without, secular intellectuals also emerged and began to exert their influence on events.[20]

The stock of images surrounding the 'national problem' was remarkably consistent over the early modern period. As we approach the end of the eighteenth century the sources acquire a more radical character, a result that parallels the dissemination of the discourse from a small circle of 'patriots,' to borrow the terminology of Miroslav Hroch, to a wider and more diverse spectrum of Greek society.[21] No doubt the factors behind this development are somewhat complex. One may assume however that steady social change, leading to the participation of larger numbers of people in the national dialogue, in company with the strikingly altered European political landscape of the late eighteenth century, were fated to exert a powerful influence on the course of Greek thought in the decades preceding 1821.

Nonetheless commonalities do appear among the original and late groups of 'patriots.' It would not be premature to say that many of the participants in the dialogue surrounding the 'national problem' were Greeks who were estranged or separated from their native lands.[22] Although the status of these people as outsiders was usually voluntary, a result of the desire to study or trade in the West, the situation does recall Lord Acton's remark that "exile is the nursery of nationality."[23] Why should this be so?

One possibility is that as outsiders they could be exposed to ideas and attitudes that had a novel consciousness-shaping influence, or perhaps even find themselves swept up, like Adamantios Koraes, in seminal events such as the French Revolution. But there may be more fundamental conditions in the exigencies of life as an 'outsider' that inclines one more readily to extreme forms of group identification.

Questions such as these lead the historian to consider the forces of identity that operate just below the surface of ideology. The rhetoric of nationalism has often, after all, provided rich opportunities for its critics. "Generally speaking," Ernst Gellner once observed, "we shall not learn too much about nationalism from the study of its own prophets."[24] Not when taken literally perhaps, but what of the deeper motives operating beneath the surface of their rhetoric?[25]

This is certainly no easy task, however the historiography of nationalism has featured approaches of this kind in the past. Roger Chickering, for example, has written of the arch-nationalist 'Pan-Germans' of Imperial Germany:

> the evidence suggests that the Pan-Germans ... were lonely men whose attempts to establish close contacts among their fellow patriots betokened psychological needs deeper than the desire to assure unanimity for the sake of impressing the public.[26]

The Pan-Germans saw themselves as 'custodians' of German society and their highly charged awareness of the dangers confronting it derived as much from personal or psychic causes as any other. George Frangos writes similarly of the early members of the Philiki Etairia, in this case men of "low economic status" who "found a solution to their alienation in the promise of a nation-state that would recognize them as redeeming sons."[27] Elements of Chickering's method could well be applied to the study of the Greek movement over the period in review. This implies a careful analysis of symbolism, imagery and language to reconstruct the motivations that lay behind the rhetoric of these groups.[28]

Chickering's emphasis on the role of 'cultural custodians' is another item that may have special application to the Greek case. Early modern Greek society possessed its own classes of men naturally disposed to fill this role. The Greek clergy represented one such class. The sources often depict the worried thoughts of these men as they confronted the spectacle of illiteracy and superstition that reigned among the peasants and even the priests of the rural lands within their fold. Their view of the national problem therefore could not be universally characterized as having a secular meaning, though it very often did. The Neohellenic Enlightenment would seem in fact hardly to exist without the persistent contributions of Orthodox deacons, priests and Metropolitans. Such men filled the ranks of the 'logioi,' the learned or lettered, who were the motive force behind the push for cultural revival. Nor was this a late phenomenon. Educational reform of the Greek world, often influenced by Western precepts, was primarily transmitted throughout the centuries of the Tourkokratia within the channels of the Greek church. These efforts were admittedly rather meager in the early period of Ottoman rule, but began to show impressive vigor by the middle of the eighteenth century. Of course, as champions of new learning, the activities of the cleric-logioi might not always harmonize with their roles as Orthodox churchmen, obedient to the strictures of the Patriarchate. This conflict only became more apparent with time. Ultimately, in its late stage, the Diaphotismos presented a conflict of loyalties to this segment of Greek society that was as critical as that confronted by any other.

The national question presented a similar dilemma to the Phanariots, a class of Greek nobility centered around the Phanar or lighthouse section of Constantinople. Another group of men who could be expected to see themselves as cultural custodians, the Phanariots actually supplied the Greek Enlightenment with some of its leading figures. They too were outsiders in a sense, educated Greeks who had frequent dealings with the West while maintaining formidable positions within the Ottoman state. But as the Diaphotismos gathered force, the paradoxes of Phanariot life became increasingly more apparent and perhaps untenable. Untenable because the deepening crisis seemed to confront them with a choice. To put themselves on the side of the "new ideas," as Cyril Mango writes, implied the end of a whole world of status and power. In the end, Mango concludes "those Phanariots and Patriarchs who implacably opposed French philosophy and revolution had perhaps a clearer understanding of what was about to happen."[29]

One additional group requires mentioning, outsiders to be sure, but not necessarily of the kind that would at first glance be identified as 'custodians': the Greek merchants or emboroi of the diaspora. And yet as the eighteenth century progressed some of these merchants became intense advocates of educational revival and enlightenment. The young people who benefitted from their philanthropy represent the final generation of pre-revolution emigre intellectuals to be studied here, including the 'secular' intellectuals Koraes, Regas and Sakellarios.

It is not difficult to trace the path taken by the 'national problem' as it was carried afresh from generation to generation of Greek thinkers. As will be discussed shortly, there existed purely native agencies for transmitting this message, as well as external ones; this latter channel is perhaps a unique aspect of the Greek case.[30] The considerable quantity of all this thought, finally, invested by Greek intellectuals into the issues surrounding nation, culture and status, serve to make the Greek Enlightenment a unique medium for exploring the subject of early modern European nationalism.

What is Nationalism?

Like the Enlightenment, the meaning of nationalism has hardly met with a consensus. This study addresses some of the dilemmas surrounding this subject by offering a fuller picture of the Greek conception, at least, of the meanings associated with the term 'nation' over the centuries preceding the 1821 Revolution. Tracing the Greek discourse back to the declining years of Byzantium serves, on one hand, to disabuse historians of the notion that peoples pass through periods of total darkness where all contact with the past is lost; this is only one of the failures of imagination that modern thought has fostered. To be sure, this discourse took place on a social plane that was quite narrowly circumscribed. It was also one that produced no definite view of what it always meant by the term 'nation,' nor was the Western Enlightenment able to supply the answer. To put the following discussion in context, it seems necessary to survey the historiography surrounding these questions.

One of the modern trends in the study of nationalism is to regard the nation as an invented entity. It follows from this view that nationalism itself, the feeling of attachment *to* the nation, can be explained by a host of factors, some historical to be sure, but also intellectual, sociological and psychological. Since a Greek nation-state had never existed in history, the idea of such an entity had likely been encouraged by European concepts of nationhood. Greek 'outsiders,' whether they be merchants, emissaries, or scholars, were exposed to these ideas of nationhood just as they had been exposed to earlier European ideas of natural rights or popular sovereignty. They in turn produced a variety of national prototypes themselves, or if nothing as definite as a prototype, at least a significant amount of literature concerning the 'nation.'

The considerable presence of Western ideas in documents such as the Proclamation of 1822, as well as the timing of the revolution itself, have given historians a basis for questioning the national pedigree of the uprising. As noted earlier, however, nationalism was not so inherently a fixture of Enlightenment thought as is typically assumed, nor was it at all self-evident to people at the time that new nations could be made or politically constructed.[31] Eugenios Voulgaris's (1716-1806) own conception, for example, of a future, independent Greek state represented little more than a return to the past.[32] Nonetheless, the line of reasoning advanced above settles on national consciousness as the central historical problem, and as we see here it is a problem that is virtually inseparable from the study of the Greek independence movement. In the terminology of the influential scholar Benedict Anderson, the Greek Revolution serves in fact as an example of ideological 'piracy.'[33]

'Piracy' clearly opposes a more romantic view of nationalism and the revolutions waged in its name. This version holds that peoples are historically distinct and carry inside them a reflexive desire for national self-determination. Nationalism was thus as organic, instinctive and self-evident as any other sensation. Furthermore, only through independence could the nation's 'genius' as Herder famously declared be realized. To Greek patriots and philhellenes alike this appeared especially true. How else to explain the awful erosion of their civilization, as reflected so well in the plight of Athens? Once the cultural center of the ancient world, it had become by 1821 an inconsequential village of seven or eight thousand inhabitants.[34] If the nation needed an 'awakener' it was not because the people had lost their national consciousness, but because their spirits had been broken by centuries of tyranny.

This view was (and remains) most common among historians of newly independent states. Such scholars would certainly object to the characterization of the very dearest events of their history as products of false sentiment or pirated ideology.[35] And yet this is the path that modern scholarship has tended to tread, as witnessed by the publications of Eric Hobsbawm, Elie Kedourie, Ernest Gellner, and Benedict Anderson. Not surprisingly the Greek Revolution, labeled by Gellner himself as the "first nationalist rising", comes periodically under review and reinterpretation.[36] There is cause to argue however that previous approaches to the subject have suffered from that general malady of comparative history, oversimplification.[37] No doubt language has figured into this state of affairs. A special benefit of this subject is in fact to work with documents that are virtually unknown in the West. Neither Smith, Gellner, nor any of the other authors cited above use Greek sources in their books, even when writing on Greek nationalism.[38] This simple fact alone is cause to treat their assertions with some caution. This is meant as no slight to earlier Anglo historians of modern Greece, Dakin, Clogg and Woodhouse, who largely introduced the subject to English readers. However these writers do not deal with the subject of nationalism as it has come to be addressed today.

Confronted with the complexity of the subject as well as the poverty of materials in translation, it is probably not surprising that Gellner himself once confessed that "it would be idle to deny that some of its (the Greek Revolution's) features present a problem for my theory."[39] Certainly this is one of the hazards of attempting to consolidate numerous incidents of nationalism into a single historical scheme.

Turning to Greek historiography, we find that some of the most prominent historians of the Turkish period employ a synthesis of the early and modern views described above. Aikaterina Koumarianou, for example, sees the encounter with the West as having a clarifying influence on Greek thought. In this case, events such as the French Revolution "not only acted as an inspiration to the peoples of Europe, and in particular to the subject peoples, but it also provided the political and ideological content for movements which, until then, had been unable to express in concrete terms even their immediate aims, or to organize their activities coherently."[40] Historians may in fact find that the Greek sources provide an interesting and largely untapped testimony of the events unfolding in the West over these years. The reaction of Greek intellectuals to these developments could take many forms and was often the occasion for fanciful judgements on the contemporary world, though it very often reflects too the "clarifying" influence Koumarianou describes above.[41] Here again, for example, we meet the geographers Konstantas and Philippides, drawing below on French ideas to assess the Islamic architecture of Constantinople:

> Its mosques... though great in number and scale are really nothing but copies of Aghia Sophia; since in such a people invention fears to show itself, so says Morvilliers, and when they have an idea they multiply it, they stretch it, perpetuate it, reproduce it, without stretching themselves out to find a second; such are the results that despotism brings about in the arts and thought.[42]

Western learning is used here not only to clarify but also to legitimate views that exhibit a native political or cultural bias.

As we will see in the following chapters, the geography of Konstantas and Philippides is a 'late' source from an old tradition of discourse devoted to the degenerated 'ethnos.' This national critique was accompanied with an impulse to reform however that often sought its model in the West, as the geographers do above. On a deeper level this discourse also articulated the wish to be 'considered worthy' by the West. No doubt these impulses affected some more than others and perhaps those most of all who were exposed to the human universe outside their native lands.

The 'Hideous Spectacle': Self-Contempt as Discourse

The Greek preoccupation with national degeneration is surely the most immediate feature of the Diaphotismos, and one that became ritualized over time within its intellectual culture. One of the aims of the present study is to demonstrate the primacy of this critique as a unifying force in Greek thought from late Byzantine times. The image of the 'wretched nation' was in fact so imbedded in Neohellenic culture that it came to acquire a remote quality in the literature. Nonetheless, it is difficult at least for this researcher to entirely discount as 'custom' the energy given to the tireless recapitulation of the 'wretched nation,' as well as the devotion of the logioi to its rescue, without assuming the existence of some essential ego predicament.

As discussed above, tradition had long before cast the logios into the role of cultural custodian. The ceaseless fixation in the works of these men with the 'national problem' could thus have functioned as a means to reaffirm their status in Greek society. It could also, and here we enter into more theoretical territory, have 'masked' the resentment they felt toward what might be conceived as their chief antagonists: Enlightened Europe, the heroes of antiquity, and of course the simple Balkan folk who aroused so much ridicule. Certainly all collaborated in magnifying the predicament of that somewhat oppressed creature, the diaspora logios. In this case, the Greek intellectual's high praise of Europe, like his devotion to the rude masses in his charge, could have camouflaged more compelling if morally inadmissible sentiments.[43]

From the voluminous writings of Max Weber comes a more conventional approach to the problem of group identification, one which links the strength of national consciousness to the presence of 'prestige' elements. In words that recall Herder, though imbued now with a quality of the intellectual self-consciousness that characterizes the Modern, Weber proposed that one attained a certain level of self-worth by belonging to a group with a particular "culture mission." This identity marked the subject off as special in some way and thus sealed his association to the nation through the force of ego.[44] But why should one cling to such an association if it is not a source of prestige, but its very opposite, infamy and contempt? The answer to this important question can only be the object of speculation, but there are some important factors to consider.

The Greek situation was of course vastly more complicated than the scenario posed above. For all the ugly criticisms lodged against contemporary Greece by European observers, there was yet the ancient and Byzantine heritage, a cultural possession of inestimable value, and one that would have to be relinquished in any identity renunciation. The logioi were especially attached to this possession and no doubt conceived themselves as its custodians. Certainly they enjoyed great satisfaction in the praise lavished upon their heritage by Europe. The ancients had also featured, of course, as the centerpiece of Greek education throughout Byzantine times and into the Tourkokratia. This tradition cultivated the assumption of the grandeur of their ancestors and thus contributed its own force to the preoccupation with inadequacy that appears in the Greek texts. We encounter here in fact the source of the 'progonoplexeia' or 'ancestor-fixation' that continues to find expression in Greek society today.

One also wonders to what extent the people in question believed that their identity was 'mutable,' given the intimate communal attachments of a traditional society. The historian must try to imagine the shaping influence of a small village upbringing dominated by relations to family and kin, to which so many of the logioi were subject. The notion of identity renunciation may well have been foreign to their consciousness.

And yet, these considerations notwithstanding, it does appear that such renunciations were occasionally attempted by emigre students and merchants—much to the consternation and ridicule of their former co-nationals. Could one really expect to be accepted by a foreign society as one of its own? Such was the charge made, in the most belligerent terms, by the anonymous author of the *Hellenike Nomarchia.* The question applied as well to certain 'Vlach' intellectuals, men like Iosepos Moisiodax and Demetrios Darvares, who tended to present themselves as Greeks and even became avid Hellenizers. But to what extent were these conversions 'accepted' by their Greek peers? Moisiodax's own 'Greekness' was not self-evident, as witnessed by the statements made against him during the language debate.

We note finally, that if the logioi were prone to dwell upon the 'national problem' and all its troubling implications, it was partly an outcome of their unique position. Living in 'foreign parts,' they were exposed in an elevated way to the assumptions regarding Balkan life and perhaps even felt personally accountable for the charges of barbarism made against it.[45] Certainly they found their own 'worth' as individuals in some way conditioned by the ideas associated with their nation in the European imagination.

Such visceral reactions to the perception of cultural and moral decay are in fact a staple of nationalist rhetoric. A late example is presented by the twentieth century Spanish intellectual Ortega y Gasset (1883-1955), who Robert Wohl tells us was deeply affected by his experiences as a young emigre philosophy student in Germany. "There is every reason to believe," writes Wohl, "that the discoveries about Spain and what it meant to be a Spaniard that Ortega made while in Germany were extremely painful."[46] Returning to Madrid, Ortega revealed his wounds to his countrymen in words that bear a striking resemblance to those found in Neohellenic texts. Ortega speaks below for those Spaniards who feel:

> ...at every hour, during every minute an ethnic shame that burns their entrails and tortures their fantasy. The young men of my time who have traveled outside the country have learned a terrible lesson, ominous and discouraging, that must be revealed without fear and without equivocation: outside Spain, to be Spanish is to be an object of ridicule.[47]

Like its opposite self-love, which Rousseau famously described as an outcome of man's passage from nature to civil society, self-contempt too is encouraged by exposure to a wider reality.[48] Ortega's bitter ethnic-self-reproach, his consciousness of the spectacle of the 'nation,' helps to reveal how such afflictions are very often a disorder of the outsider.

It is easy to spot the discomfort felt by Greeks similarly exposed to foreign assumptions and biases. The sting of these affronts is quite visible in the writings of Adamantios Koraes (1748-1833), the most influential figure of the late Greek Enlightenment.[49] In a famous speech from 1803 entitled the 'The Present State of Civilization in Greece,' delivered in Paris to a gathering of French intellectuals, Koraes sought to persuade his audience that Greek society, despite its fallen condition, showed signs of revival. At one point he makes the telling remark:

> For the first time the nation surveys the hideous spectacle of its ignorance and trembles in measuring with the eye the distance separating it from its ancestors' glory. This painful discovery, however, does not precipitate the Greeks into despair: We are the descendants of Greeks, they implicitly told themselves, we must either try to become again worthy of this name, or we must not bear it.[50]

As the language above suggests, the 'hideous spectacle' of Greece struck Koraes deeply and he took great pains in this and other writings to convince his Western readers that appearances sometimes deceive, that beneath the rot were stirrings of regeneration. The rehabilitation of Greece was not only a matter of education, of building schools and libraries, it was also a matter of rehabilitating the image of Greece, of reclaiming its place and dignity in the world, which of course meant the Western world.

The considerable influence, as we see here, of the West on the Greek imagination, or the extent to which intellectual activity surrounding the subjects of identity and civilization was conditioned by the 'presence' of the West, has given contemporary scholars cause to view Neohellenic literature as a species of post-colonial studies. "Reading Greece and Neohellenism as national-imaginary institutions," as Stathis Gourgouris writes, means "to read them as succinct expressions of the interceding sociocultural relations between Europe and the Balkan or eastern Mediterranean region from the mid-eighteenth century to the present."[51] Certainly Koraes, like the logioi who preceded him, expressed the basic impulse to see the nation reborn in the eyes of and in the image of the advanced European societies of his day; his 'nationalism' coveted their power, wealth and works, their standing in the world. So was his predecessor Iosepos Moisiodax moved to declare in his remarkable *Apologia* of 1780: "I am not a bit shy to say that Greece has a need, it has a need for Europe, for while Greece goes without everything, Europe abounds with everything. Given the paucity of works that circulate among us, philosophy, history, theology and others, how can we not need Europe?"[52]

But perhaps most of all, more than even her works, which he held no less dear than Moisiodax, Koraes coveted Europe's respect. This evident desire to be respected by the West counters the often repeated and somewhat facile notion that philhellenism inflated the pride of Greeks imbuing them with an exaggerated notion of who they were and their proper place in the world.[53] More accurately, the pressure to be true Hellenes as Vassilis Lambropoulos has written, and as we see reflected very much in the words of Koraes, "was presented to the Greeks as their only way or chance to define an acceptable identity and justify their political claims."[54] In Koraes's desperate attempts to live up to these romantic images and earn the respect of his European peers, we see the force of an even greater power on his psyche, a deep and troubling cognizance of inferiority. To be sure, philhellenism was a fixture of the eighteenth century, but there was another more pervasive understanding present among Westerners of the Balkans and its inhabitants. Indeed, the diaspora Greek could not hide from the terrible images of degeneracy that largely constituted enlightened Europe's view of the contemporary East.

From time to time works of self reflection appear that reveal with disarming clarity the effect of these images on the psyche of those exposed to them. Following is an excerpt from the revolutionary pamphlet, *Hellenike Nomarchia, etoi logos peri Eleftheras* (the Greek Rule of Law, or a word about Freedom) published anonymously in Italy in 1806. In this sharply written passage the author derides the lengths taken by emigre Greeks seeking to escape the sting of these affronts by blending into their new surroundings:

> So many there are that don't bother themselves about our fatherland and with every effort attempt to mimic the ill manners of the other races in order that none recognize that they are Greeks. And if there was a way to change fatherlands they would buy for themselves a foreign one though it cost them one of their own eyes. ... But what can I say of them, to our misfortune not a few, who, in order to separate themselves forever from Greece and to forget even her name, decide with extreme stupidity to take as spouse a woman of another race?... O shameless and in truth goat-headed apostate from the motherland. You think, perhaps, that they will praise you the other races? You deceive yourself, unfortunate one, again in your own deception. They hate you, they despise you and everywhere mock you. Each of them says 'See that pig, that vulgar Greek, to lessen his worthlessness he thought to take a wife of our race. But he always remains the same. He has not changed the barbarous ways of his country....' Do you think, you true unfortunate, that your wife truly loves you? Do not deceive yourself, I say again! She mocks you, she dishonors you, she robs you and often prepares for you an untimely death.[55]

The language is severe, as befits a pamphleteer, nonetheless in such words, especially those that dwell on ethnic infamy and inadequacy, the operations of the human ego appear to express themselves with special immediacy. Do the comments above articulate feelings widely shared among diaspora Greeks? Certainly Koraes often exhibited this type of acute ethnic self-consciousness, as an earlier biographer once observed.[56] Why then did he not take the path of the merchant vilified in the *Nomarchia*? This would have been the natural response according to Anthony Smith, who argued once that "emigrants do not generally make good nationalists."[57] As a man who would come to spend the vast majority of his life in Paris, why was Koraes so preoccupied with the state of Greek society? Why did it not cease to matter to him?

Unfortunately, such a question can only alert the historian to what must remain one of the mysterious properties of Koraes's personality. Although he constructed for himself the model life of an emigre-intellectual, a professional writer who consorted with Jeremy Bentham, Thomas Jefferson and other great figures of his time, Koraes withdrew from fully exploiting the opportunities presented him in order to better devote himself to the 'national problem.' No doubt the preoccupation of his era with antiquity was a source of pride for him and perhaps even of ultimate value in guiding his activity. But it was a preoccupation too that one could enjoy only with reservation, for such glorifications of the past often contained a silent, and sometimes not so silent, condemnation of the present.

In *Imagining the Balkans* Maria Todorova surveys the images of Greece's degeneracy one commonly finds in European travel literature from the period, particularly among French and English authors. The philhellenes themselves, as Todorova observes, frequently suffered a sharp and troubling crisis at the sight of modern Greek society.[58] It was consequently to the rescue of ancient Greece—so dear to the enlightened European's image of himself—that the philhellenes were driven and inspired, more than any impulse to save the regrettable Greeks, who were, if anything, simply interfering with that image.[59]

One of the most spectacular literary exhibitions of this attitude is Friedrich Holderlin's *Hyperion* (1792), a work that vividly illustrates both the philhellene's worship of classical Greece and his terrible disappointment with its degenerate offspring. *Hyperion* describes the coming of age of the young Greek of the title, who, inspired by his readings of antiquity, throws himself into the work of national emancipation. Hyperion's revolt is doomed however from the start by the moral failure of his own people. Living now as an exile in the West, the protagonist begins his tale with the melancholy lines: "Fortunate the man whose native country flourishes to rejoice and strengthen his heart! For me, it is if I were cast into a swamp ...if anyone reminds me of mine, and whenever I hear myself called a Greek, it is as if I were being bound with a dog collar."[60] Here we have a

European imagining the consciousness of a modern Greek, confirming in the process the most pessimistic declarations of the *Nomarchia*. 'Do you not find your predicament a humiliating one?' Holderlin intimates in this passage, 'collared to a nation that is the object of the world's contempt?' True to form, Hyperion's efforts must end in disaster, the revolution collapsing on account of the barbarism of the Greek soldiery.[61] His companion Diotima, who bears more than a passing resemblance to the character in Plato's famous Eros, attempts to console him, but with words that recall again the bitter reproaches of a disillusioned philhellene: "You are too proud any longer to concern yourself with this villainous race. And you are right. You led them to freedom, and they thought of robbery. You led them victoriously into their ancient Lacedaemon, and these monsters fall to plundering..."[62] It is a hard truth, but one Hyperion had kown since his schoolboy days in Smyrna. It was here that he first became aware of the distance separating the immortal ancients from their all too earthbound progeny: "As I went now here, now there, among these people, it seemed to me that human nature had resolved itself into the multifarious species of the animal kingdom," Hyperion observes gloomily. "As everywhere, so here, too, the men were especially demoralized and corrupted. Some animals howl when they hear music. But my more mannerly humans laughed when the conversation turned to beauty of spirit and virtue of heart."[63] Finally, in lines that echo what Woodhouse described as the not so subtle wish that the modern Greeks, the ruin of all the dreamy idylls of Western philhellenes, be simply made to disappear, Holderlin delivers a murderous verdict:

> I will take a shovel and throw the dung into a pit. A people among whom spirit and greatness no longer engenders any spirit and any greatness has nothing in common with other peoples who are still men, has no more rights, and it is an empty farce, sheer superstition, to go on honoring such will-less corpses as if a Roman heart beat in them. Away with them! The withered, decaying tree shall not stand where it stands, it steals light and air from the young life that is ripening for a new world!.....Oh! Let someone light a torch for me, that I may burn the weeds from the field, let someone lay me the mine with which I can blow the dull clods from the face of the earth![64]

One can anticipate the feelings such writings must have aroused in the proud Koraes.[65] Confronted with these images and no doubt the social biases that must have accompanied them, one might well take the path of the condemned Francophiles of the *Nomarchia*. For those like Koraes, who were for one reason or another precluded from such a course, the way ahead was dim at best. In this case Koraes's stubborn willingness to confront the reality of his predicament "without equivocation," in Ortega y Gasset's words, was admirable, and perhaps especially so in light of the uncertainties surrounding the prospects for change.[66]

In summary, much has been written of how the celebration of the Greek past aroused in intellectuals such as Koraes a sense of pride and nationalism, but it was just as likely to arouse feelings of extreme discomfort and inadequacy. The present study emphasizes as well the shock that exposure to the modern West itself inflicted on the minds of these individuals, seeing in their words the battered psyche, recoiling like Koraes from the 'hideous spectacle' of his homeland. A spectacle which, if he had acquired a sense of it before, could only have been enormously amplified by personal encounter. "Imagine a city much larger than Constantinople," Koraes wrote to a friend in 1788 of his first impressions of Paris, "with 800,000 people, all sorts of academies, public libraries, where science and art have been developed to perfection, where learned men are to be seen all over the city in boulevards, market places, cafes, etc." Against this image of physical and intellectual grandeur he contrasts Greece, a land ruled by "ignorance, malice, force, wickedness, insolence and shamelessness... governed by scoundrels and stupid men as well as by an ignorant clergy who are even worse than our foreign tyrants the Turks."[67] The following chapters describe how impressions such as these fit into a larger and much older cultural discourse between Greek intellectuals and Europe. It is particularly well expressed in the earliest Greek works of the eighteenth century, works for example of geography, that often seem to have no greater purpose than to articulate the vast gulf separating these two worlds, one advanced and vital, the other withered and obsolete.

Nationalism functioned in the case of Koraes on something much more immediate than ideas. The persistent cultural self-critique in his works appears to illuminate the operation of the human ego, which experiences, perhaps to its misfortune, inadequacy more dearly than success. The talented Koraes was yet an outsider, and thus subject to the assumptions of the society in which he lived. His name, his accent, functioned as a kind of passport, a means of identification, that accompanies one through the world. They specify a place of origin that marks the carrier, and as a mark, adds to or diminishes one's standing in the world. It cannot be a 'hideous spectacle.'

To be an outsider meant to be associated, via a process of cultural or cognitive shorthand, with a group, as the diaspora Greeks surely discovered, and consequently to find one's value in the world conditioned by the relative rank of that group. Clifford Geertz describes how these forces produce the essential features of a nationalist discourse:

> ...it is a demand for progress... and beyond that of ...'exercising influence among the nations.' The two motives are... most intimately related, because citizenship in a truly modern state has more and more become the most broadly negotiable claim to personal significance, and because what Mazzini called the demand to exist and have a name is to such a great extent fired by a humiliating sense of exclusion from the important centers of power in world society.[68]

An early testament to the existence of the kind of feelings Geertz describes above is furnished by Ioannis Voulgaris (1686?-?), a teacher at the Flaggineio Schole of Venice.[69] Voulgaris's poem "In Praise of Greece' was published in the school's anthology of 1708, *Anthe Eulaveias*. Reflecting on the triumphs of ancient Greece and lamenting how the difficult years had 'benumbed her children' to virtue, the poet suddenly feels a surge of hope. He imagines the youth of these lands awakening to her lights and renewing her glory in the world. His spirits restored, Voulgaris now rejoices when he anticipates the 'majestic height' that she will rise to. "And it is so majestic," he writes of his ecstatic vision, "that gazing up at it I become dizzy. And if it grows larger, her greatness, she will become grandest of all and the envy of the world."[70] Unfortunately for Koraes, a man surrounded by the prejudices and assumptions by which he himself came to measure Greece's station in the world, there was no such fanciful escape from reality.

This study will occasionally bring into view questions surrounding the themes of modernization, secularism, and Westernization that have wielded a powerful influence on the evolution of Greek history and culture down to the present. Indeed enlightenment and independence were not sufficient of course to restore the Greeks to their former place in the world. Succeeding generations of Greek intellectuals were thus destined to experience the same culture shock and bouts of self consciousness we find in the works of the old 'logioi'.

Most of all this section has attempted to suggest the self-consciousness that afflicted those Greeks who managed to roam beyond the pale of their eastern homelands. The words of the 'philhellene' Holderlin, expressed the assumptions they encountered in a particularly unforgettable form: "Whenever I hear myself called a Greek, it is as if I were being bound with a dog collar," he wrote, as if incredulous that one could bear the weight of contempt he aroused from the civilized world. The national consciousness of the Greeks, stung by these experiences, expressed itself in the vigorous renovation efforts spearheaded by the intellectuals of the Diaphotismos. These forces of course continued to exert their influence on Greek society after the Revolution, they may perhaps have even been amplified.

Clifford Geertz's attempt to describe the universal pattern of this phenomenon holds interesting possibilities for the Greek situation, as when he writes of the will of nascent nations "to be noticed: it is a search for an identity, and a demand that that identity be publicly acknowledged as having import, a social assertion of the self as 'being somebody in the world.'"[71] It could well be that the forces of ego-group correlation helped shape the archaizing spirit that featured so prominently in the pre and post revolutionary decades of Greek culture. The most visible outcome of this was the gradual Atticization of the Greek language that took place over the nineteenth century. Here after all was an object of group identity that served to elevate the status of Greeks, being as it was a property of the old and admired Greece.[72] Such a phenomenon may not be wholly consistent with the 'modernizing' campaigns that equally galvanized the founders of the new state, but perhaps this serves to demonstrate very well the torturous culture wars that are the lot of the 'new' nation.

And yet 'civilization' gaps are difficult to close, the path to modernization and respect, however they may be defined, a project of monumental proportions. We see the tensions aroused by these dilemmas, expressed in alternating voices of contempt and defiance, in the declarations of Greek intellectuals from the eighteenth century to the present. In a revealing essay from the 1930s, Nikos Kazantzakis articulated sentiments for example that would not have seemed out of place in a work of Koraes. A lifelong wanderer, Kazantzakis's re-experience of his homeland after each protracted foray into 'xeniteia' aroused in him that complicated array of emotions endemic to the diaspora intellectual of whatever time or place. From time to time Kazantzakis was even given to episodes of despair that could match in intensity those of the most disenchanted philhellene. Here we find him again in Greece, traveling through the Peloponnesus and ruminating somewhat bleakly on the mores of its inhabitants. At such moments it seems that he too must fall back on the fortifying stuff of antiquity, as appears to happen during a conversation with a village elder:

> I listened to him and held back with difficulty my emotion and joy. Here are the living spirits of Greece! Pass through the cities and villages, speak with thousands of people and your heart becomes upset from indignation and shame. These wingless bipeds are our race? Is this how far our blood has sunk? Small merchants, dunces, schemers, enviers, and crooks. And suddenly a spirit flies up in front of you that reached the peak of the Greek mission—to join daring with intellect, passion with play. And then you take a deep breath. The confidence in your blood returns, the deep conviction that this race does not easily perish.[73]

Here in Kazantzakis's words, much closer to us in time, are a vivid recreation of the feelings and images that animated his eighteenth century predecessors. And if the challenges they confronted in seeing their goals realized appeared almost too great to overcome, the predicament of the modern Greek had complications of its own. Unlike the men of the Diaphotismos, intellectuals of Kazantzakis's time lived in the era of Greek independence; there was no clear enemy for them to vent their indignation upon.

One final note: Cultural self-consciousness is the term most favored in this study for describing much of the intellectual history and activity being addressed. It might be said from the start that it is exceedingly difficult to determine from the sources when 'modern nationalism' began, but not so difficult to identify the ethnic self-consciousness that appears to be so essential to it. It is older than the Enlightenment, older than the eighteenth century. We see it in these earlier eras in the posture of the Greek world toward the West and the urgent efforts at appropriation described in the ensuing pages. What we find in these sources is the reverse effect of what Edward Said famously depicted in *Orientalism*, a discourse of some vintage that seeks to demonstrate in an almost wholly unscrutinized way the superiority of the 'other,' in this case the European world, through a standardized repertoire of images and language, indeed the erection of an entire intellectual culture on the foundation of this assumed knowledge. If 'Orientalism,' the *mission civilisatrice* or white man's burden of Todorova's romantic voyeurs, expresses in one fashion the national consciousness of the 'advanced' society, it finds its inverse in the numberless allusions to infamy, and the insistent appeals for rehabilitation and respectability that feature so prominently in the pages ahead.

Notes

1. This is only one of the terms used to describe the fairly extensive territory in question, encompassing not only present day Greece but also much of Macedonia and Romania, where the army of Ypsilantes began its ill-fated campaign.

2. 'Tes en Epidauro a ethnikes ton hellenon syneleuseos,' in Apostoles Basileiou Daskalakes (ed.), *Keimena pegai tes historia tes Hellenikes Epanastaseos*, Volume I, (Athens: Typois Adelphon, 1966), 176-178.

3. The Proclamation especially reflects the contribution of Alexandros Mavrocordatos, a member of one of the preeminent Phanariot families, and a man quite familiar with the thought of the West. Like Koraes, Mavrocordatos was also an acquaintance of Jeremy Bentham and other Western luminaries. It was in fact to

Mavrocordatos that Shelley dedicated his remarkable work of revolutionary philhellenism 'Hellas' "as an imperfect token of the admiration, sympathy and friendship of the author." Some know this piece by the poet's famous declaration in the Preface: "We are all Greeks. Our laws, our literature, our religion, our arts have their root in Greece." 'Hellas' was written in the autumn of 1821. See *The Complete Poetical Works of Percy Bysshe Shelley*, edited by Thomas Hutchinson (London: Oxford University Press, 1952), 446-7.

4. The resemblance of the language in the Proclamation cited above to Locke's Second Treatise of Government, written in 1690, is actually quite remarkable. Paragraph 192 of the Second Treatise declares: "Who doubts but the Grecian christians, descendants of the ancient possessors of that country, may justly cast off the Turkish yoke, which they have so long groaned under, whenever they have an opportunity to do it?" John Locke, *Second Treatise of Government*, (Indianapolis: Hackett, 1980), 98. Despite these similarities Kitromilides argues, with reason, that Locke's influence among the Greek intelligentsia had been eclipsed by European thinkers of more recent vintage. See 'John Locke and the Greek Intellectual Tradition: An Episode in Locke's Reception in South-East Europe' in *Locke's Philosophy, Content and Context*, Edited by G.A.J. Rogers, (Oxford: Oxford University Press, 1994), 217-236. For a discussion of the influence of later intellectuals such as Bentham on the political thought of the Greeks, see Sterios Phasoulakes, ed., *Praktika Synedriou 'Koraes kai Chios', Chios, 11-15 Maiou, 1983*, (Athens: Omerion Pnevmatikon Kentron, 1984). See especially Kitromilides's own contribution to the collection, 'Jeremy Bentham and Adamantios Koraes', 285-308.

5. The works of the historians in question, Elie Kedourie, Benedict Anderson, Ernst Gellner, etc, are discussed below. Note also the use of the terms 'East' and 'West' as a means of distinguishing Greek writers from those of France, England, Italy, etc. Such terms do appear in the texts from these times, as does 'Europe.' The latter must be defined by the context of its use, as noted in the relevant sections below.

6. In this case, the problem of 'exchange' parallels those difficulties surrounding the very conception of the Enlightenment itself. The perennial question, 'What is Enlightenment?', is more directly addressed here, however, in its national context. That is, how was the Enlightenment perceived by those non-Western intellectuals drawn into its orbit? An earlier model of such an approach is presented by Roy Porter and Mikulas Teich, eds., *The Enlightenment in National Context*, (Cambridge: Cambridge University Press, 1981).

7. C.M. Woodhouse, *Modern Greece*, (London: Faber and Faber, 1986), 127. But even these observations can only be advanced with reservation, for it is difficult to ascertain whether the intense cultural reform project of the logioi was accompanied by a more far-reaching political one. The fact remains that scholars such as Daniel Philippides, Neophetos Doukas and Benjamin of Lesbos all became members of the revolutionary Philike Etairia. Earlier logioi, such as Meletios and Moisiodax produced critical works similar to those of the men above, but we have little means to confirm the political motivations that lay behind them. One recalls too, of course, that the earliest figures lived in the time before the rise of Austria and Russia had transformed the balance of power in the East, an event that had enormous influence on Balkan attitudes; to some degree political thought and activity must be contingent upon political realities.

8. Outram advances a subtler view of the Enlightenment's 'unity,' calling it a "capsule containing sets of debates, stresses and concerns, which however differently formulated or responded to, do appear to be characteristic of the way in which ideas, opinions and social and political structures interacted and changed in the eighteenth century." Dorinda Outram, *The Enlightenment*, (Cambridge: Cambridge University Press, 1995), 12. As this passage attests, it is doubtful that the 'founders' of the Enlightenment were themselves agreed on 'where it was leading.'

9. Goodman used the term "French cultural boosterism" to describe this phenomenon. "By the middle of the eighteenth century," she explains, "French men of letters had merged the discourses of sociability to forge the

commonplace that France was the most civilized because it was the most sociable and polite of nations. By implication, moreover, it was also the most moral. French men of letters saw themselves as the leader of a project of Enlightenment that was both cultural and moral, if not political." Dena Goodman, *The Republic of Letters*, (Ithaca: Cornell University Press, 1994), 4-5.

10. For Herder's reaction to the French see Isaiah Berlin, *Three Critics of the Enlightenment: Vico, Hamann, Herder*, (Princeton: Princeton University Press, 2000), 177-79, 207. Note also this very revealing passage from the same text: "...the voyage to Nantes and Paris depressed Herder acutely. He met some of the most distinguished of the philosophes, but evidently failed to achieve any degree of communication with them. He suffered that mixture of envy, humiliation, admiration, resentment and defiant pride which backward peoples feel towards advanced ones... Wounded national feeling—this scarcely needs saying—breeds nationalism, but it is important to realize that Herder's nationalism was never political." Ibid, 205.

11. The Greek impulse to return to this past or rehabilitate themselves in its image, would similarly have been rejected by the German philosopher. Herder's uncompromising position on cultural "belonging" and his strict view of historical relativity precluded him from the kind of worship of antiquity practiced by his peers: "Authoritative decisions of praise and blame which we heap, from a discovered favorite people in antiquity at which we stared until we fell in love with it, onto the whole world—what is your legitimacy!" Johann Gottfried Von Herder, *Philosophical Writings*, translated and edited by Michael N. Forster, (Cambridge: Cambridge University Press, 2002), 295. Critiques of this kind do occasionally appear among the 'demoticist' sources surrounding the Neohellenic language 'zetema,' as we will see below.

12. See Konstantine Demaras, 'Ho J.-G Herder kai he parousia tou sten diamorfose tou neoellenikou pnevmatos,' in *Neohellenikos Diaphotismos*, (Athens: Philippos Eliou, 1977), 283-99. The absence of Herder in the Greek sources is true of German philosophy and the Neohellenic Enlightenment in general. However Herder's influence on later nineteenth century Greek thought, as Demaras shows, was considerable.

13. Even here however it must be said that Herder's own appeal for cultural preservation, or what Berlin calls "populism," was shorn of any strident demand for national self-determinism as it has come to be understood today; he was in fact hostile to such a concept. See Berlin, *Three Critics of the Enlightenment: Vico, Hamann, Herder*, 208-10. Historians commonly speak, finally, of nationalism as finding its ideological roots in the treatises of intellectuals such as Rousseau. However such works, with their emphasis on popular sovereignty, offer only the palest glimpse of what was to come. See E.H. Carr, 'Three Phases of Nationalism,' in *Nationalism*, edited by John Hutchinson and Anthony D. Smith, (Oxford: Oxford University Press, 1994), 243-45.

14. "A peaceful period called 'Enlightenment'," Outram writes, "was not ended by a sudden upheaval called 'Revolution.' For most of Europe it is far truer to say that Enlightenment and Revolution proceeded side by side for much of the century." Outram, *The Enlightenment*, 120.

15. As noted in the Proclamation of Independence, the Greeks were fluent in Western conceptions of 'civic nationalism'; however the Enlightenment was much less clear on the matter of 'ethnic nationalism' (that every nation must be a state). This was not, after all, a problem for the philosophes. There are exceptions, such as Rousseau's notes on Poland, the oblique criticisms of Montesquieu against empire, Voltaire's odes to Greece during the Orlov Revolt, and the earlier sympathy for the Greek cause in Locke. However if Easterners were to infer ethnic nationalism from civic, they apparently brought something of their own to the process. Note, finally, that Greeks did not themselves think first of 'nation-states.' They surely thought of independent states as we see from Koraes's correspondence with Thomas Jefferson and Jeremy Bentham. The latter in fact busied himself in drafting a constitution for such a future state—interestingly, it was one led by Greeks but not a nation-state. Bentham assumed the political co-existence of Greeks and Turks within the borders of the new Greece. The same was true of the earlier Hellenic Republic envisioned by Regas Velestinlis. See Jeremy Bentham, *Securities Against Misrule and Other Constitutional Writings For Tripoli and Greece*, (Oxford:

Clarendon Press, 1990), 181-276.

16. More astonishing still, this wave of violence was not accompanied by confiscation of the now masterless Turkish lands, nor demands for land redistribution (these demands do develop later). This phenomenon suggests intriguing questions regarding the primacy of national consciousness viz a viz class consciousness. See William W. McGrew, "The Land Issue in the Greek War of Independence,' in *Hellenism and the First Greek War of Liberation (1821-1830): Continuity and Change*, edited and with and Introduction by John A. Petropulos, (Thessaloniki: Institute for Balkan Studies, 1976), 111-130.

17. And yet this has not prevented historians from making the case, often strenuously, that the early modern Balkan peasantry were entirely absent of national consciousness. Mark Mazower's *The Balkans*, (New York: Modern Library, 2002) must be said to represent a recent example of this tendency.

18. Compilations of the membership of the Philike Etairia indicate for example an insignificant level of peasant participation. This subject discussed in great detail in Chapter 4 below.

19. Historians and sociologists cite the almost universal role intellectuals play in the founding and early histories of nationalist movements. This phenomenon has been discussed by Anthony D. Smith in *Theories of Nationalism*, Ch. 6, especially p. 124, 133-150. Note also Weber's comments below on the intelligentsia and their "inevitable" attraction to nationalism.

20. Note that it cannot be simply concluded that the 'secular' intellectuals represent a more radical class of thinkers than the clerical. Intellectuals, both clerical and secular, lined up on both sides of all the cultural and political debates surrounding the revival of 'Hellas'. There could be rather radical cleric-logioi such as Konstantas and Philippides, and conservative secular ones such as Kodrikas and Perdikares.

21. Miroslav Hroch, *Social Preconditions of National Revival in Europe*, translated by Ben Fowkes, (New York: Columbia University Press, 2000).

22. It is important to note however that those who traveled to the West for educations were going to *complete* their studies. They had already received some instruction in their homelands, and a kind of instruction that would have dwelled heavily on native traditions of thought, the old luminaries of the Hellenic past, etc. This process, even if limited to a very small number of people in the first centuries of the Tourkokratia, was the basis for the 'internal transmission' of the native tradition that continued through the Diaphotismos. Greek scholars did not 'discover their past' upon emigration to the West as it is sometimes asserted. This subject given greater discussion in the following chapters.

23. Lord Acton, 'Nationality' in *Selected Writings of Lord Acton:, Volume I: Essays in the History of Liberty*, (Indianapolis: Liberty Fund, 1985), 422.

24. Ernst Gellner, *Nations and Nationalism*, (Ithaca: Cornell University Press, 1983), 125.

25. This is in fact closer to the approach taken by Gellner himself. For all their sound and fury, he argued, nationalists, "almost without exception, fail to understand what it is they do...the movement is.... the external manifestation of a deep adjustment in the relationship between polity and culture." Gellner, *Nations and Nationalism*, 35.

26. Roger Chickering, *We Men Who Feel Most German*, (Boston: George Allen & Unwin, 1984), 164.

27. George D. Frangos, 'The Philiki Etairia: A Premature National Coalition,' 95.

28. Raymond Pearson takes a similar approach in 'Fact, Fantasy, Fraud: Perceptions and Projections of National Revival' in *Ethnic Groups* 10, (1993): 43-64.

29. Cyril Mango, 'The Phanariots and the Byzantine Tradition' in *The Greek Struggle for Independence*, 59.

30. To explain the source of this energy, Henderson could do no more than suggest a "sense of apartness." See *The Revival of Greek Thought 1620-1830*, (Albany: SUNY Press, 1970), 10.

31. As David Bell writes in a recent monograph: "...until the eighteenth century age of revolutions, the idea of actively *constructing* a nation through political action lay beyond the mental horizons of Western Europeans." David A. Bell, *The Cult of the Nation in France*, (Cambridge: Harvard University Press, 2001), 5. (author's italics)

32. See Eugenios Voulgaris, *Stochasmoi eis tous parontas krisimous kairous, tou kratous tou Othomanikou*, (Athens: Vivliophilika Tetradia Ergasias, 1996). This essay written during the Russo-Turkish War of 1768-74, contains Voulgaris's proposals for the creation of a new 'Greek Empire' to be raised upon the remains of the Ottoman state. In this case, Voulgaris's assumptions reinforce the conclusions of historians Robert Forster and Jack Greene. Writing in *Preconditions of Revolution in Early Modern Europe*, the latter authors noted that revolutionaries of this period "like most human beings... (they) were drastically limited in their behavior and their objectives by traditional patterns of thought, patterns so repressive in character as to make it extremely difficult for the men who held them to break through ancient and deeply engrained conceptions of society and the polity..." The Greeks of this study, men like Skouphos, Regas and Voulgaris, were similarly prone to be guided "by a passion, not for innovation, but for renovation..." Robert Forster and Jack P. Greene, *Preconditions of Revolution in Early Modern Europe*, (Baltimore: The Johns Hopkins Press, 1970), 15.

33. Benedict Anderson, *Imagined Communities*, (New York: Verso, 1991), 81.

34. Thomas Gallant, *Modern Greece*, (London: Arnold, 2001), 108. The Neohellenic geographers Konstantas and Philippides used the larger figure of 15,000 in their 1791 text: Gregorios Konstantas and Daniel Philippides, *Geographia Neoterike*, 84. Of course the cause of Athens' plight was not simply the Ottoman conquest; Constantinople had long before supplanted her as the first city of 'Greece.'

35. Interesting essays on this theme can be found in Dennis Deletant, ed., *Historians as Nation-Builders: Central and South-East Europe*, (Basingstoke, UK: Macmillan, 1988). See especially Clogg's short piece in this volume on the great nineteenth century Greek historian Konstantinos Paparregopoulos.

36. Ernst Gellner, *Nationalism*, (New York: New York University Press, 1997) 41.

37. While conceding, for example, that the case of pre-revolutionary Greek nationalism is a "complex one," Anthony Smith tends to promote the type of oversimplification fatal to a clearer understanding of the subject. He asserts that Greek nationalism was "at once a 'rational' and westernizing movement of merchants and intelligentsia for a revived Hellas along the lines of ancient Athens, and a yearning for an ethno-religious revival of the Orthodox Byzantine empire in Constantinople among the clergy and peasant communities." Smith, *Nationalism*, 7. The author has fallen here into a number of common pitfalls, even betraying a certain modern prejudice in his conception of intellectual sociology. In the first case the Greek intelligentsia were overwhelmingly clerics and secondly, the most fully-formed prototype of a restored Byzantium was the brainchild of Regas, who happened to be a secular intellectual. Smith's reference finally to 'peasant communities,' is utter conjecture. As in the case of Gellner, Smith overlooks the single most important element complicating (and perhaps even preventing) the Greek conception of a 'nation-state': the dispersion of the Greek population around the Eastern Mediterranean (in the words of Plato, as relevant in 1821 as they were in the fifth century B.C.E., 'we are like frogs around a pond.') Once again, historians must consider how

the creation of 'nation-states' was influenced by the ethnic strife and dislocation that accompanied each revolutionary spasm; these human calamities did as much to foster the concept of the nation-state as any legion of nationalist-minded intellectuals.

38. Adamantios Koraes's 'Memoire sur l'etat actuel de la civilisation dans la Grece' (1803) is a rare exception. Kedourie published an English translation (Report on the Present State of Civilization in Greece) in his *Nationalism in Asia and Africa*, (New York: Meridian, 1970), 153-188.

39. Gellner, *Nationalism*, 41. More will be said below regarding Gellner's efforts to resolve the theoretical difficulties raised by the Revolution.

40. Aikaterina Koumarianou, 'The Contribution of the Intelligentsia towards the Greek Independence Movement, 1798-1821,' Translated by E.J.W. King in *The Struggle for Greek Independence*, 72.

41. Writing for example upon the immediate outbreak of the French Revolution, the geographers Konstantas and Philippides mused that "the character of the ancient Athenians resembles very much that of the French today; obstinate, quick-tempered, forgiving, sentimental, vigorous in their works, eager to make a big splash in the world..." Konstantas and Philippides, *Geographia Neoterike*, 82.

42. Ibid, 149. N. Masson de Morvilliers (1740-1789) was a French geographer and contributor to the venerable Encyclopedia of Diderot and D'Alembert.

43. See for example Freud's thoughts in 'Mourning and Melancholia' regarding how a "melancholic's self-accusations... are hardly at all applicable to the patient himself." One modifies or shifts negative feelings toward some object, Freud explained, in order to avoid the reproach of the superego. These interesting observations, for which I am indebted to Professor Andrew Zimmerman of George Washington University for suggesting, are put forward nonetheless with caution. The historian of the Greek Enlightenment is often deprived of the source material that would permit deeper psychological enquiries. Sigmund Freud, *The Freud Reader*, edited b Peter Gay, (New York: W.W. Norton & Company, 1989), 584-89.

44. National identity drew upon the status conferred by belonging to a group with a particular "culture mission" that was "anchored in the values that are to be preserved." It was thus inevitable according to Weber, that the intelligentsia, the culture workers, should identify themselves so closely in the "mission" that lay at the heart of nationalism. See Max Weber's essay, 'The Nation' in *Nationalism*, 25.

45. For the close association of 'self worth' with group identity see Michael Horowitz's classic *Ethnic Groups in Conflict*, (Berkeley: University of California Press, 1985). Writing on the experience of national movements and their leaders Horowitz has noted for example that"ego identity depends heavily on affiliations." Ibid, 181.

46. Robert Wohl, *The Generation of 1914*, (Cambridge: Harvard University Press, 1979), 128.

47. Quoted in Wohl, 128-9.

48. "The savage man lives within himself; social man always lives outside himself; he knows how to live only in the opinion of others, it is, so to speak, from their judgement alone that he derives the sense of his own existence." Jean-Jacques Rousseau, *A Discourse on Inequality*, Translated and with an Introduction by Maurice Cranston, (London: Penguin Books, 1984), 136.

49. Such a judgement is based on the formidable volume, the relatively coherent program and the widespread distribution of Koraes's writings and translations. Koraes was furthermore the most well known of all the

Greek 'enlighteners' in the West. In addition to his French works and collaborations Koraes was quite competent in English and carried on a correspondence with such leading figures as Jeremy Bentham and Thomas Jefferson, both of whom he queried on the subject of the political and constitutional formation of the new Greek state. A sample of the Koraes-Jefferson correspondence is contained in Adrienne Koch and William Peden (eds.) *The Life and Selected Writings of Thomas Jefferson*, (New York: The Modern Library, 1972). See 'To Monsieur A. Coray,' 711. See also Athanasios Moulakes, 'He allelographia Korae-Jefferson,' in *Praktika Synedriou 'Koraes kai Chios'*, 269-284.

50. Adamantios Koraes, 'Report on the Present State of Civilization in Greece,' in Elie Kedourie, *Nationalism in Asia and Africa*, (London, 1971), 183-4.

51. Stathis Gourgouris *Dream Nation; Enlightenment, Colonization and Modern Greece*, (Stanford: Stanford University Press, 1996), 5. The author writes of his own work as an effort to engage "...the project of post colonial theory, by reflecting on a nation...ideologically constructed by colonialist Europe without having been, strictly speaking, colonized." Ibid, 6.

52. Iosepos Moisiodax, *Apologia*, (Reprint, edited by Alkhes Aggelou, Athens: Nea Hellenike Vivliotheke, 1976), 153. Note: this work originally published in Venice in 1780.

53. Benedict Anderson, for example, writes that "young Greek speaking Christian intellectuals," in the "last quarter of the (eighteenth) century," were "exalted by the philhellenism at the centres of Western European civilization." He further cites Koraes 1803 Address on 'The Present State of Civilization in Greece' as emblematic of a dramatic "change in consciousness." *Imagined Communities*, 72. As discussed later, the Greek students who traveled to the West to finish their educations, including Koraes, were already well acquainted with the 'luminaries' of the Hellenic tradition. The works of ancient and Christian Greeks had been taught in Greek schools and academies, including the Patriarchal Academy of Constantinople, since the days of Byzantium. See Runciman, *The Great Church in Captivity*, 120.

54. Vassilis Lambropoulos, *Literature as National Institution; Studies in the Politics of Modern Greek Criticism*, (Princeton: Princeton University Press, 1988), 8.

55. Anonymou tou Ellenos, *Hellenike Nomarchia, etoi logos peri Eleftherias*, (Reprint, edited by Tasos Vournas, Athens: Aphon Tolide, 1982), 157-161.

56. "He (Koraes) sought to excel in his studies so that the French might form a better opinion of the modern Greeks; he never lost an opportunity to boast to them of his compatriots; and he carefully concealed anything which might place the latter in an unfavorable light. His moral behavior was impeccable... because he believed his conduct would redound to the advantage of his people." Stephen George Chaconas, *Adamantios Korais, A Study in Greek Nationalism*, (New York: Columbia University Press, 1942), 27.

57. Smith, *Theories of Nationalism*, 109. Smith later cites in support the following passage from Hector St. Jean de Crevecoeur's *Letters of an American Farmer*: "What can a poor European immigrant have for a country where he had nothing? The knowledge of a language, the love of a few kindred as poor as himself, were the only cords that tied him: his country is now that which gives him land, bread, protection and consequence." Ibid, 119.

58. "Even when they embraced the ideal of Greek liberty," Todorova writes, "the French would not shed the air of *mission civilisatrice* of culturally superior Europeans." Maria Todorova, *Imagining the Balkans*, (Oxford: Oxford University Press, 1997), 78.

59. Todorova, *Imagining the Balkans*, 94. See also Christopher M. Woodhouse's important work *The*

Philhellenes, (London: Hodder and Stoughton, 1969).

60. Friedrich Holderlin, *Hyperion and Selected Poems*, Translated by William R. Trask and adapted by David Schwarz, (New York: Continuum, 1990), 2.

61. The poem itself was apparently inspired by the failed revolution of 1770, the notorious Orlov affair, incited by Catherine II to coincide with the Russo-Turkish War of 1768. (See editor's note on *Hyperion and Selected Poems*, 77) The 1770 revolution ended not only in failure, but a prolonged period of devastation and atrocity in the Peloponnesus, committed by Albanian irregulars, whom the Turks themselves were eventually moved to suppress.

62. Holderlin, *Hyperion and Selected Poems*, 108.

63. Ibid, 15.

64. Ibid, 20-21.

65. "To be judged unworthy, again, I detest," declared the great logios in his autobiography. Adamantios Koraes, 'Autoviographia' in Konstantine Demaras, (ed.), *Ho Koraes kai he Epoche Tou*, (Athens: Vasike Vivliotheke, 1974), 244.

66. No doubt the French Revolution supplied a certain impetus to those who did; it crossed the line separating ideals from activism, and helped set a precedent for revolutionary change. As discussed below a number of other historically essential elements helped to encourage the sense of expectation evident in these years. These expectations of course conflicted with the conservative post-revolutionary European settlement, persuading some Greeks to abandon their hopes of delivery from foreign benefactors; no doubt for such thinkers the arrest of Regas in 1798 by Austrian authorities provided sufficient evidence of the new European order. Note also that Koraes did undergo himself a brief 'revolutionary period' as the Napoleonic Wars appeared to be heading toward a conclusion favorable to the Greeks.

67. Cited in Chaconas, *Adamantios Korais, A Study in Greek Nationalism*, 28. These remarks bring to mind the words of another young Greek apostate, Nikos Kazantzakis, on traveling to Paris to study in the first decade of the twentieth century. His youthful reactions of bewilderment and admiration are characteristic of the startling nature, even at this late date, of that first contact with the West: "How the long haired wild youth of Greece was cut down here in the outside world!" wrote Kazantzakis, "Here, even the sun had changed, it goes to say the very face and soul of the earth had changed....'This is the new face of God,' I thought looking about with rapacity at the trees, the houses, the made-up women, the dark churches,'I kneel and worship its grace!' It was an intoxication, my first contact with this new face of the earth, lasting for days and weeks. The streets, the parks, the libraries, the museums, the Gothic churches, the men and women at the theaters and in the streets, they too were intoxicated, reeling before my enraptured soul until the intoxication finally faded and the world became steady and firm again." Nikos Kazantzakis, *Anaphora ston Greko*, (Athens: Eleni Kazantzakis, 1982), 313.

68. Clifford Geertz, 'Primordial and Civic Ties,' in *Nationalism*, 30. Guiseppe Mazzini (1805-1872) was of course a powerful advocate of these very same principles, as Geertz mentions above; he was also a popular figure among Greek intellectuals of the nineteenth century, especially those absorbed in the rhetoric of the Megale Idea. Mazzini's own writings are highly reminiscent of the themes and even the language of Herder, as when he declared that each people requires 'unity,' "the only security for equality and the due development of the life of the people." Mazzini, 'On the Unity of Italy,' in *Nationalism: Its Meaning and History*, 120.

69. The school, named after its tireless advocate, the Venetian-born son of Greek immigrants Thomas

---

Flaggineis (1578-1648), was founded in 1665. The activities of the school and its educators will be discussed further in the following chapter.

70. Voulgaris's sonnet 'In Praise of Greece' was originally published in Italian (In lode della Grecia), as were several other pieces in the anthology. The passages above were taken from a Modern Greek translation of the poem included in a recent reprint of the original volume. Ioannes Patousas (ed.), *Anthe Eulaveias*, (Reprint, edited by Athanasios Karathanases, Athens: Hermes, 1978), 44.

71. Clifford Geertz, 'Primordial and Civic Ties,' in *Nationalism*, 30.

72. One notes the revealing comments on this theme made by Moses Mendelssohn (1729-86) when advancing his own view of 'What is Enlightenment?': "The Greeks had both culture and enlightenment. They were an educated nation, just as their language is an educated language. Overall the language of a people is the best indicator of its education, of culture as well as enlightenment in both breadth and intensity." The author was obviously referring here to the ancient idiom. Moses Mendelssohn, 'What is Enlightenment?' in James Schmidt (ed.), *What is Enlightenment*? (Berkeley: University of Berkeley Press, 1996), 54. Mendelssohn made these remarks in 1784.

73. Nikos Kazantzakis, *Taxidevontas*, (Athens: Eleni Kazantzakis, 1969), 300.

II. Roots of Discourse

> *And now has fallen all of the nobility of the Hellenes, Hope has taken flight, Shame and Nemesis have abandoned men for Olympus. Now even the race of barbarians and all our enemies are exultant... and we are brought down by fear.*[1]

The passage above is taken from a letter written by the late Byzantine scholar Ioannes Argyropoulos (1415-1487) to the newly crowned Emperor Constantine (1449-1453). It surely expresses the distress that must have been felt by many inhabitants of Constantinople in these final years of Byzantium's existence. Argyropoulos might well have added that like the pagan spirits Shame and Nemesis he too could not bear the spectacle of the Empire's final act, seeking refuge himself in the Olympus of the West.

Looking back on these words from the distance of time, the historian recognizes images that suggest a strong thematic contiguity between past and present. The bleak, self-conscious mood of the piece, the author's nostalgia for antiquity, even his flight to Europe, strike many of the notes so characteristic of Hellenic intellectual culture during the ensuing Turkish era.

This section surveys the pre-Enlightenment period in Greek thought, focusing mainly on the seventeenth and very early eighteenth centuries, as the sources from this era reveal especially well the cultural self-consciousness that characterizes the larger discourse. The urgent appeals to reform raised by the scholars of these times were themselves echoes of a dialogue that could be traced farther back in the past, as we see above, to times as distant as the Fall of Constantinople. It was from the struggles surrounding this event that the pre-occupation with cultural and moral decline became securely rooted in Greek thought; a phenomenon of great significance, for it was the basic premise on which the posture of the Greek world toward the West was founded. Here we have the political and intellectual developments that ultimately set the path of Greek learning on a course that led through Europe. The other outstanding pattern-setting feature of this era concerns the people who set out on this path. And here we note the virtual supremacy of the clerical element in the perpetuation of a Greek high culture over the first centuries of the Tourkokratia. This too was a phenomenon that owed its development to the changing political order in the East.

Looking Into the Abyss: The Struggle For a New Byzantium

> ...came a voice from the heavens, from the mouth of an angel:
> 'Send word to the Franks to bring three ships,
> to take the gold crucifix and the holy gospel
> and the holy altar, that it not be defiled.'
> And when the Virgin heard it, the icons wept.
> 'Quiet now, Virgin lady, don't cry, don't weep,
> again with years, with time, again it will be yours.'[2]

The lines above come from a famous piece of folk literature entitled 'The Taking of the City,' of unknown authorship and vintage. The tale begins with the disconsolate lament: 'They took the City, they took her, they took Salonika! They took too Hagia Sofia, the great monastery..." The events depicted refer of course to the fall of Constantinople and the destruction of the Byzantine Empire. Nonetheless hopeful words appear at the end of the piece that someday, "...with years, with time," these agonies would be redeemed. Such hopes were the basis of strange prophecies that circulated throughout the Greek world in the centuries preceding the 1821 revolution, prophecies that referred vaguely to liberation via the forces of a 'blond race,' widely assumed to be the Russians.[3] However obscure, these literary relics from late Byzantium and the early Tourkokratia offer evidence nonetheless of a new cultural discourse in the East.

The events surrounding the fall of Constantinople ushered in an animated, some might even say chaotic chapter in Greek intellectual history, and it should come as no surprise that the decline of the Empire and the specter of imminent destruction upset its doctrinal equilibrium no less than its political. Byzantine intellectuals, grasping for a means to avert the final disaster, found themselves intensely occupied in movements and disputes that add their own dramatic essence to the failing Empire's final years. One of the conflicts unearthed in this strenuous enquiry into the sources of decline and renewal concerned the highly-charged issue of identity. In Argyropoulos's letter we cannot escape his own bleak awareness that he was, like the emperor, presiding over something rare and momentous, the ending of an era, a historical epoch, a civilization. But behind this profound sense of 'ending' trailed a question of an even more esoteric nature: what was this thing that was ending, this Byzantium? What had it been, and who were its people? It is a question that appears to move all the late Byzantine intellectuals at some point in their writing lives.

And yet there were those who still hoped for a reprieve. They turned to the West for deliverance, even if a reunification of the Churches was necessary to win its support. Such a course raised questions of identity and tradition that were certain to prove divisive. Others searched elsewhere for salvation, seeking not allies but a new morality to erect Byzantium's recovery upon, perhaps even a 'new man.' They found him in the past, in the Hellenes of old. Fixing upon elements of cultural contiguity that appeared to them, at least, unbroken by time, advocates of this school asserted that the inhabitants of Byzantium were the descendants of these heroic peoples; their strength still lay dormant inside them waiting to be rekindled, perhaps through the genius of their laws and customs, now to be revived. Could the salvation of the Empire, as these men claimed, lay in a neo-Hellenic renaissance? Here too was a thesis that was sure to elicit powerful reactions.

And yet for all the emotions this appeal stirred up, it does appear that the late Byzantine world, telescoping with each Turkish victory into an ever narrowing perimeter around the 'Greek' lands of the Balkans and the immediate environs of Constantinople, began to experience a 'fashion' for Hellenism.[4] The expressions of this 'Hellenistic idea,' which implied a revival of interest in the thought and history of the ancients, or a renewed emphasis on this past as an element of identity, obviously conflicted with the culture of Orthodox Christianity that largely defined Byzantine life.

In addition to providing an insight into the tense political environment of the Empire's final years, these nationalistic-sounding declarations of 'Hellenism,' of cultural distinctiveness, have all the sound and form of those we have come to recognize in our own day. Such is the verdict of no less an authority than Steven Runciman, marshaling as evidence the activities and writings of Byzantine intellectuals such as Argyropoulus, whom we encountered above, and perhaps the most famous and enigmatic of all, George Plethon (1360-1450). Plethon's often-quoted remarks on the 'Hellenic nation' include the one taken below from his 'Address to Emperor Manuel' (1416):

> We are Hellenes by descent. That is proved by our language and culture. The Peloponnesus and adjacent islands have been the home of the Hellenes and no one else since time immemorial. Many Greek achievements were initiated from the Peloponnesus... Byzantium was founded by the Dorians... and the Romans who later developed Byzantium into Constantinople were related to the Peloponnesians, since the Sabeans, who helped in the foundation of Rome, were Laconians from the Peloponnesus.[5]

Runciman considered the "fashion" for Hellenism contained in these declarations as a product of the escalating political crisis, suggesting once that in its final stages, the conflict with the Turks had become a "struggle for the freedom of Hellas."[6] Harvard historian Deno Geanakoplos offered a similar explanation, observing that "intellectual activity might offer a temporary escape from the hard realities of life and perhaps spur the flagging courage of the people through contemplation of the glories of ancient Greece."[7]

The subject of the emergence of a 'Hellenistic consciousness' among late Byzantine intellectuals is an intriguing one as these brief glimpses intimate. But another subject was raised above that was to have a similarly profound influence on the future of Greek thought: the changing character of East-West relations.

Geanakoplos once described the Christian civilizations of the East and West during the Middle Ages as 'siblings.'[8] Theirs was a relationship between equals, he contended, with the cultural edge resting on the side of the East by virtue of its age and historical contiguity.[9] However it is reasonable to assume that the nature of this relationship changed with the setbacks suffered by Constantinople in its ceaseless wars with rival states.[10] The power balance shifted over the course of time, the West rising in status, defacto in some measure, by virtue of Byzantium's decline. Larger and larger numbers of Greeks began emigrating to the West, including considerable numbers of Greek scholars. It was also during this time that Western culture began to exhibit a tremendous surge in vitality, rapidly closed the gap between itself and the East, and ultimately leapt ahead in brilliance. From this point to the end of the Renaissance, Geanakoplos observes "...the situation was reversed, with Latin culture in certain respects surpassing the Greek. Contacts now occurred primarily in the West, to which many Greek figures fled to escape the Turkish occupation."[11] By 1453, therefore, the pattern was set that would shape the path of Greek scholarship for the next four hundred years. Significantly, this redefinition of the geography of power and civilization was readily acknowledged by the social and intellectual elites of the Greek world, as symbolized by the acts of appropriation that become such a conspicuous fixture of the cultural exchanges of succeeding centuries.

We should note one final episode in the waning years of the Empire that helps to illuminate the changing power relations between East and West, as well as the effect this was to have on the questions surrounding cultural identity. It has been alluded to briefly above. As the curtain descended on Byzantium, the prospect of annihilation moved some within the Orthodox Church to consider reconciliation with Rome, an initiative considered necessary to enlist the aid of western Christendom in the defense of the City. This dramatic change in course represents very well the altered power relationship between the two worlds of East and West. However it was not effected without great cost to the internal unity of Byzantium's religious estate. Reconciliation became in fact the occasion for serious conflicts over the future of Greek Orthodoxy and even national identity.[12] Ultimately, the reunification movement elicited so much protest within the Church that the final settlement could claim only a dubious legitimacy.[13]

In summary, fear, defeat, insecurity, all dominant elements of the historical setting of late Byzantium, proved fertile ground for new directions in thought and sometimes dramatic reversals of tradition. Later chapters will focus on the acts of appropriation that characterized the Greek contact with the Enlightenment, but we can see already in the times surrounding the decline and fall of Constantinople the emergence of ideas and assumptions that were to incline Greek intellectuals in this direction. For some, of course, the 'Frankish' West would continue to serve as an object of contempt and distrust; for others, an object of supplication, a material and moral force of growing dimension in the world.

After 'the Fall': Together but Apart

The long feared Armageddon finally descended on the 'City' in 1453 and ended forever the Empire of the Byzantines. This event became the source of gloomy songs and prophecies as we have seen. However, with the passage of time, the initial destruction and displacement of the Turkish conquest gave way to a new settlement that did leave some room for the continued development of Greek culture. The Patriarchs of Constantinople, who had watched their ecclesiastical domains pull free of central control over the course of Byzantium's long decline, received a surprising reprieve. The fall of Constantinople would have in fact a uniting effect on the Orthodox Churches of the Balkans, which found themselves tethered again to the Patriarch through the well known millet system of Turkish administration.[14]

The Greeks therefore retained their own church, indeed a church whose power and authority was elevated to the status of national guardian by the Ottoman state; they retained too their language, which also gained in prominence as a medium of culture and education with the revived authority of the Greek church in the Balkans.[15] The relationship between the Ottoman Empire and the Orthodox Church is too large a story to be sufficiently discussed here, although its presence seems to intrude everywhere in the ensuing history. It is a relationship that represents so well the ambiguities, pliancy and perhaps even the contradictions of Ottoman rule. Of the latter, certainly there can be no greater exhibition of the considerable powers that non-Turkish, indeed raya or infidel institutions, might acquire within the Empire. The bond between Sultan and Patriarch was one born of conquest and expedience, but characterized to its very end by questions of trust, as might be expected of two parties among whom existed a basic disaffection that neither time, tradition, nor even expedience could fully extinguish. It seems in fact that the expedients of good tragedy required that the play have a violent end; such an end was furnished by the hanging of Patriarch Gregorios V on the very gates of the Patriarchal enclave in the weeks following the outbreak of the Greek revolution in 1821.

The original compact between the Empire and the Patriarchate occurred in the years immediately succeeding the conquest. It was the work in fact of two intriguing and remarkable men, the Sultan Mohammed II and the monk whom he elevated to a Patriarch, George Scholarios.[16] The Sultan's selection of Gennadios, as Scholarios now came to be called, was influenced by the widespread reputation he had earned as a vehement anti-Unionist, a faction within the Orthodox Church that opposed any gesture of reconciliation with Catholicism. An anti-Unionist Patriarch was deemed beneficial to the political interests of the Empire as it might serve to widen the distance between Eastern and Western Christendom.[17] Gennadios served as Patriarch until 1456, retired, then served at least one more term before withdrawing again into monastic life. He devoted much of his time in these later years to writing and rumination, producing works that express an unredeemable grief over the events he had witnessed and his fears for the way ahead. "I am terribly sorry for the destruction of the race," he writes in a characteristic passage, "a race than which there has been none finer on earth, resplendent in its erudition, fortunate in its wisdom, distinguished for its excellent laws, and adorned with all manner of beautiful things. Who is there who will not admit that the Hellenes were the most singular people of all?"[18] Nonetheless, it cannot be said that Gennadios simply identified himself as a 'Hellene.' Though a "child of the Hellenes," as he writes in one passage, by virtue of the fact they shared a common language, he could never overlook their paganism. "Though I am a Greek by speech I would never call myself Greek because I do not think like the ancient Greeks. On the contrary I want to be known by my faith and if someone should ask me who I am I will answer that I am a Christian."[19]

Well, an Eastern Orthodox, arch anti-unionist, Greek-speaking Christian, would seem a more revealing answer. Gennadios's words suggest a complex sense of identity, touching upon elements of culture such as language and religion, along with vague musings over a past and legacy that he evidently took some pride in. 'Christian' serves therefore to distinguish him from the pagans of earlier times, but does not indicate the cultural and historical elements of identity by which Gennadios separated himself from other Christians.

One certainly encounters in Gennadios's words at least a quotient of that cloudy nostalgia for 'Hellenism' that is much more extravagantly manifested in Plethon or the younger Argyropoulos. This is not a surprising outcome, as, like all educated men of his time and place, the ancient heritage of the Greek world had figured largely in Gennadios's schooling. He came himself to be eminently learned in the intricacies of Aristotelian and Platonic thought. We may not necessarily agree with Vacalopoulos that "Gennadios's orientation towards Hellenism marked the beginning of the alliance between Orthodoxy and Greek nationalism," or that "the word 'Hellene' held a national connotation for him."[20] However his efforts to explain what he 'is' reveal something of the existence in his times of a dialogue concerning this very question; a dialogue that appears to have been shaped and encouraged in no small part by the melancholy awareness of an epoch ending.

In the villages and provinces of now 'European Turkey', in places far removed from the imperial capital and its intrigues, the social consequences of the conquest were given to a certain degree of variation.[21] In many parts of the Empire the Greeks continued to live by and large in the villages and towns they had inhabited before the Turkish conquest, although a steady process of Greek depopulation becomes evident in Asia Minor over the intervening centuries.[22] Turks and Greeks mixed to some degree in the European domains of the Ottoman Empire as well, although this was a process too that was slow to develop. In many places the two peoples were very much 'together but apart,' as geographies indicate. A passage from the *Geographia Neoterike* of 1791 describes for instance the town of Elassona in Macedonia, where: "The inhabitants are Turks and Greeks, the Greeks have three churches, the Turks five mosques; the Greeks live on the right side of the river that divides the city, the Turks on the left."[23] William McGrew estimates that at the time of the 1821 revolution, an event occurring nearly four hundred years after the fall of Constantinople, there was a Turkish minority of perhaps 65,000 people living in Rumely and the Peloponnesus (lands that would constitute the original Kingdom of Greece). The Greek population of this area was perhaps 635,000, the majority of whom were probably tenant farmers, often of Turkish landlords, who though representing only ten percent of the population held over half of the arable land.[24]

It is possible to speculate therefore that some of the essential consciousness raising or preserving mechanisms of ethnic distinction and awareness—church, language and culture—remained intact over these centuries (indeed some experienced a dramatic revival) and continued to function despite the destruction of the Byzantine Empire. In addition to these, the conditions of Ottoman rule served to heighten social tensions within the Turkish-raya relationship. The land issue presents one obvious source of tension, but there were others. As Runciman writes, "The Christians were not allowed to forget that they were a subject people."[25] The dreaded paidomazoma, or 'child-gathering,' undertaken to fill out the elite force of janisseries was perhaps the most notorious condition of Turkish rule.[26] There were also dress and legal customs, such as those preventing Christians from testifying in court proceedings involving themselves and Muslims. Christians were also subject to special and sometimes heavy taxation.[27] As in the case of Hagia Sophia, the largest non-Muslim places of worship in the conquered lands were typically converted to mosques, often simply by affixing a minaret to the existing structure; such a sight was no doubt a powerful and enduring symbol of conquest for the now subject peoples. The building of new Christian churches was also discouraged and could only be undertaken, with permission, in purely Christian localities.[28]

'High' and 'Low' Cultures of Discourse

The hunt for evidence of the existence and character of Greek cultural activity in these first centuries of Ottoman rule remains a lively area of modern Greek scholarship. On the popular level this scholarship is often concerned with the so-called klephtic ballads, which do indeed represent a unique type in Greek literature and are important textual sources for the historian of the Tourkokratia. The klephts were literally 'bandits,' gangs of men led by a chief who preyed on Turks and Greeks alike. These ambiguities were largely forgiven however in the popular mythology that came later; now the klephts were freedom fighters and symbols of national resistance. Such accounts would no doubt baffle writers from the eighteenth century, Greek and European alike, who were prone to see the wild klephts as a telling exhibit of the barbarous degeneration of Balkan life.[29]

The notion of the klephts as irreconcilable 'freedom fighters' is also weakened by the fact that they often went to work as 'armatoloi'. Armotoloi were unofficial security forces in the pay of Turkish pashas or Greek primates[30], whose primary mission was to hunt down the troublesome bandits. The rather ambiguous code of loyalty implied by these arrangements is unabashedly celebrated in the folk ballads. In the song of Tziobaras, a klepht chief whose activities straddled the late seventeenth and early eighteenth centuries, we find a characteristic statement of the shifting allegiances of these men:

> Sing , swallow, sing...sing, poor dove,
> sing by the seaside where the boats sail.
> Ask there of Nikolo, the Captain Tziobara,
> Who was in Louro armatolos, in Karpenesi klephtes.
> He had a banner red, a banner red and blue,
> he had the Cross, he had the Christ, he had the Virgin too.[31]

It is also true that the klephtic ballads can effect at times a savagely anti-Turkish tone, wherein the author exalts his violent exploits and ethnic chauvinism.[32] An example is furnished by the ballad of Panos Zidros (1720-1770), who is visited by another one of those ubiquitous talking birds, this time on the eve of his death. The bird asks how such a wise and clever 'palikari'[33] should not have found some escape from death, to which the proud Zidrou responds: "What are you talking about, silly bird... forty years I lived as armotolos and klephtes, and if I lived another forty, again I could not escape death...." And yet the parting words of the unbowed Zidrou are void of any existential diffidence: "to all my relatives and all the pallikaria, I ask, keep up my house, slaughter the Turks and look after my child, the dark little Demetri, who is still young and unschooled in the ways of the klephte!"[34]

Admittedly, the klephtic ballads, for all their interest as historical artifacts, are a questionable source for making firm assertions about Greek popular 'consciousness' in the centuries preceding the revolution. The researcher is on much firmer ground when directing his enquiries to the character of the developing 'high' culture of these times. Here we note that the Greek world would enter a period after the fall of Constantinople considered to be the dark age of its intellectual history. Schools of higher learning in the City and other conquered lands were shuttered and no new generation of great scholars emerged to replace those lost to age or emigration. And yet the links between present and past are never so easily severed, as many important 'Greek' lands remained outside the pale of Ottoman conquest and were untouched by the events of 1453. In these lands the 'past' continued to function. To be sure, Byzantium had fallen. And now, in a surprising turn, the perpetuation of its high culture had come to rest on the beneficence of a former enemy, the Empire of the Venetians.

The Italian Era Begins

Venice had in earlier ages emerged as a center for East-West cultural exchange by virtue of the city's close contacts with the Byzantine Empire, its proximity to Padua University, and the possession of an empire itself composed of many Greek lands wrested from the Byzantines, most notably Crete, parts of the Peloponnesus and the Ionian Islands.[35] The city drew into its ranks a number of Greek mercenaries, the estradioti as they were called, in addition to finding itself the center of a prosperous Greek merchant community. In time Venice became a destination for numerous generations of Greek scholars and students.[36] In 1498 the authorities gave the Greeks permission to establish their own 'Adelphotetas,' or 'Confraternita,' in the city, furnishing them with a measure of autonomy including the rights to Orthodox worship. By this time the population of Greeks living in Venice had reached ten thousand, and it continued to rise throughout the century. Another important milestone occurred in 1514, when the petition of the Greek inhabitants to build an Orthodox church within the city, the future San Giorgio dei Greci, was officially approved. The church was ultimately completed in 1573.

The Greek community of Venice had turned its energies by this time to the establishment of its own schools. In 1593 the Hellenike Schole tes Adelphotetas, a Greek elementary school, had been established, followed much later by the creation of a high school.[37] This latter institution, the Flaggineio Schole (est. 1665), named after the tireless Thomas Flaggineis (1578-1648), would come to play a considerable role in the intellectual history of the early Neohellenic Enlightenment. A final milestone in the history of the Adelphotetas was the establishment in 1670 of Venice's first Greek printing press. It was from this press, founded by Nicholaos Glykydis, 'of Iannina,' as his title pages always read, that so many of the works cited in this study were produced.

The Flaggineio Schole served to prepare Greek students of Venice for higher study at the University of Padua. Of course, the enrollment of Greek students in Padua predates the Tourkokratia, however the events described above vastly promoted the University's importance to Greek higher education. Padua ultimately established two colleges for Greek students, the College of Saint John (1583) and Cottunian College (1653), and registered, according to one Greek scholar, four hundred and ninety five Greek medical students alone over the years 1634-1671.[38] These numbers, which do not include those Greeks enrolled in Padua's other main course of study, Law, are respectable when one considers that the average number of students at the University in any given year was around one thousand.[39] Medicine, nonetheless, proved to be one of the mediums of advancement in the Ottoman world, as will be discussed below, by virtue of the fact that high-ranking Turks took as personal physicians those Greeks, Armenians or Jews skilled in these arts (Turks being typically discouraged from such studies). Of course their own countrymen were no less impressed. In a letter to a medical graduate from Kerkyra, the seventeenth century Greek scholar Fragkiskos Skouphos expresses his admiration for the young man's achievement with language, as was Skouphos's custom, celebrating the Hellenic past. National regeneration depended on the efforts of young men such as this, he intimates, who symbolized the resurrection of an ancient tradition of learning, and perhaps also the return of the 'race' to respectability:

> I congratulate you, my noble one, in the science you have acquired and in the laurels with which your great virtue has been crowned by the famous School of Padua. And Kerkyra also congratulates you, your beloved fatherland (patrida), for it hopes to see in your noble face arisen Galen and Hippocrates and for the whole world to become a stage of your wondrous accomplishments. That the Heavenly Master raises you to all the honors that my heart wishes for you...[40]

Among the most notable Greeks to graduate from Padua during the early Tourkokratia was the cleric Theophile Korydalleus. Korydalleus, who was born in Athens in 1561, became known as the father of the Neo-Aristotelian revival in Greece, which was the school of thought much in vogue during his Padua years.[41] Korydalleus reflects in this case the pattern of encounter and appropriation that will be a fixture of the times to follow: returning to Greece, he vigorously attempted to introduce the 'new Aristotelianism' into the curriculum of Orthodox higher education at the ecclesiastical academies of Mount Athos and Constantinople—not, of course, without controversy and resistance.[42] Though ultimately successful, the new intellectual establishment that Korydalleus helped to create came under assault, nonetheless, by succeeding generations of logioi. Seventeenth and eighteenth century scholars, setting out on the same trek through the West, sought on their return to replace what they now viewed as Korydalleus's obsolete methods with newer forms of thought.

The educational developments in Venice were accompanied by similar ones in Rome, where in 1576 the Hellenic College of Saint Athanasios had been established. This Jesuit institution, created by the Catholic Church amid the ongoing turmoil of the Reformation, would issue from its doors graduates such as the important logioi Skouphos, whom we have met above, and Ioannes Patousas (1677-1712). Both would play important pedagogical roles in Greek culture. In addition to a significant emphasis on rhetoric,[43] Greek students in Rome were given a full course in philology based upon the great works of the Western heritage, both classical and Christian. Indeed what else was there? They studied Virgil and Cicero in Latin, Plutarch and Isocrates in Ancient Greek, the Christian Fathers in both languages. This was the standard curriculum of Padua and Flaggineio, as elsewhere, throughout the sixteenth and the seventeenth centuries; it would remain so until the succeeding years brought along something new, wholly new, that did not quite belong to either classical or Christian.[44] It should be noted finally that the experience of Greek students in Italy often served to realize the worst fears of their fellow co-religionists, in the sense that many did indeed convert to Catholicism.[45] This subject will be given much greater attention below.

Notwithstanding these developments in Rome, Venice would serve as the nucleus of Greek cultural activity in Italy. In fact it was to the larger and more numerous schools in Venice that the graduates of the Roman college often came to seek work, joining there Greeks from other lands, most notably those from the Venetian Empire. Of the 517 students, for example, who enrolled in the Flaggineio Schole (1665-1798)[46] the vast majority came from Venetian-ruled Greek lands. The Ionian Island Kefallonia contributed the highest single number of students at 119, followed by Crete and Kerkyra, at 76 and 61 respectively.[47]

The Greeks who passed through the Flaggineio Schole were among the most important logioi of the pre-Enlightenment period. These include Elias Meniates (1669-1714) of Kefallonia, who first came to the school as a student. Meniates would later develop into the most famous Greek rhetorician of his generation, and was greatly influenced by the writings of Skouphos, which he first encountered at Flaggineio. Ioannes Patousas was a director of the School and wrote texts for its curriculum, of which his *Philological Encyclopedia* (also used at Padua) is the most famous example. This four volume work, first published in Venice in 1710 and reprinted many times over the ensuing years, was required reading for students and teachers. It contains a collection of writings from the great figures of both antiquity and the Christian era, with Platonic dialogues set alongside the theological writings of Gregorios.[48] It was from such works that Patousas hoped to demonstrate to his students the proper use of grammar and rhetoric, which were essential parts of the Flaggeneio curriculum. Another cornerstone of the school's pedagogy were the rhetorical, grammatical and philosophical writings of Gerasimos Vlachos (1605-1685), a Cretan refugee, like Skouphos, and later Orthodox Metropolitan of Venice.

In addition to the works described above, the *Texne Rhetorike* or 'Art of

Rhetoric' (1681) of Fragkiskos Skouphos, a standard text at Flaggineio, merits special attention. The remarkable statement of cultural despair contained in this piece is ever more striking for the fact that it does not purport to be about history or politics, but is a manual on exposition. However one need not advance very far into the text to encounter important elements of the Neohellenic preoccupation with the national problem. The plight of the fallen nation, as Skouphos notes in the dedication to the reader, serves as his immediate source of inspiration:

> Thales the philosopher and one of the seven wise men admired through the centuries, for three blessings did he often thank the great gods. The first, because they created him as a reasoning man, and not some unthinking stone, a useless weight on the earth... the second, because they made him a man, and not a woman, knowing, as goes the common saying 'Fire, Sea, Woman, the three evils.' And the third, because he was a Hellene, or Romaios, in race... For the same blessings do I also thank God for making me, adding also the fourth, for giving me a little learning that I may benefit my race, formerly wealthy in every virtue and wisdom, and now for the pitilessness of fate naked and deprived. Therefore, with this intent I decided, O my reader, O friend of man, to compose this book.[49]

Such opening epistles, in which the logios presents his work as an instrument of progress and renewal for his beleaguered people, are a standard fixture of Greek publications from these times. In many ways, such earnest expressions of devotion to the improvement and happiness of the 'race' serve to illustrate most clearly the meaning of the term 'logios,' which has admittedly no simple definition. This is an ambiguity it shares with the term 'logos,' from which it derives: word, reason, spirit, argument, letter, cause, etc. A logios, as we see in the passage above, appears not simply to be a man of letters, but of learning, and one whose role in society concerns the diffusion and spread of learning. A teacher to the race, he is not just to produce 'letters' but beneficial and improving works.[50] That so many of the logioi came from the church may also be illuminating, for this was in many respects the natural role of the cleric in traditional society, variously referred to then, as now, as fathers, shepherds etc. We certainly have in the cleric-logios an excellent candidate for the 'cultural custodian' of Chickering's Imperial Germany, men especially conscious of their duties to the 'nation.'

The basic outline of Fragkiskos Skouphos's life is known, although there are gaps in the record. Born in 1644 in Crete, a subject of the Venetian Empire, Skouphos was educated as we have seen in Rome, although the timing and circumstances of his family's emigration from Crete are not clearly known.[51] Skouphos finished his studies in Rome in 1666 before moving on to Venice where he was apparently involved at some level with the Flaggineio school.[52] He then returned to the Hellenic College of Rome, now as a teacher, in 1672, and remained until 1678. It was apparently over these years that Skouphos wrote much of the *Rhetorike*, later published in Venice in 1681.[53] It was also during this time that Skouphos, an Orthodox priest, "completed his turn," as Tatakis writes, "toward papism."[54] He was subsequently appointed by the Catholic Church to the island of Kerkyra (Corfu) where he served the local Archbishop until shortly before his death in 1679. Skouphos's final days were spent on the island of Zakynthos, where, in ill health he could nonetheless be near to his brother Parthenios, who was himself an Orthodox cleric and vicar of the one of the island's churches (Saint Nicholas). Some of these intriguing elements of Skouphos's personal and professional life will be returned to below. It remains for now to consider some additional aspects of his one great work, the *Rhetorike*.

As the passage from the opening dedication indicates, Skouphos portrays the plight of the Greek nation in terms typical of the discourse we are considering: fallen from its former glory and languishing now "deprived and naked." However his task is not simply to dwell on these misfortunes but introduce methods for repairing them. From here he conducts a series of lessons on rhetorical style. Unlike the Jesuits in Rome who had trained him, Skouphos is not concerned with combating schismatics, but to provide the common reader with skills for improving his prospects in life. In a telling aside on the subject of 'invention,' apparently aimed at Greek merchants—an activity that the logioi of the these times will begin to see as an essential element of a nation's strength and prosperity[55]—he writes: "Invention finds the reasons, examples, and whatever else is appropriate to persuade the audience and compose the argument. This part, among the others, is the most difficult; for this also are the Hebrew men of business always praised and admired by the world for the acuity of their minds."[56]

In Chapter Eight, however, a lesson on the 'enumeration of the parts,' Skouphos presents us with more striking insights into his national consciousness. The stated intent of this chapter is to show how one may increase his rhetorical powers by dividing the narration of a particular event into its parts. He chooses to demonstrate this technique however through a curious choice of subject: a depiction of a Christian city overrun by barbarians. "If someone intended to bring directly before people's eyes a plundered city," he writes, "entirely laid waste from a barbarian enemy, and wanted to show a miserable and deplorable sight of human disorder, in order to move each listener to pity, one would separate the parts in the narration, and enumerate in similar manner one by one all the miseries of each."[57] Turning to the narration itself, Skouphos provides his students with a thorough illustration of rhetorical technique. He begins by setting the stage:

> The victorious and arrogant army had not yet entered the city, yet right away was the entire appearance of things altered, for before entering and spreading fire within the city to consume it with flames the enemy first burned the tormented people with fears; and before slaughtering them and drowning the city in blood, it was in the tears of the same people first submerged.

The subsequent 'enumeration' of the panic of the inhabitants is vividly drawn in the description of the young girl who "cries for her virginity, because she sees how a barbarian soldier intended to seize her and it would thus become for the enemy not a prize but a plaything." The young man girds himself for the coming struggle though grieving inside "for his youth, because he realizes that it wasn't yet fully sprouted, the flower of his tender years, and was about to see now the scythe at its roots." The terrorized mother grasped her children close against her breast, "suckling them not so much with milk as with tears, because she saw how this afflicted fruit, far from ripe, must fall soon at her feet mowed down at their roots by the cruel steel." And finally there are the old men who "condemn their inhuman fate, that it brought them to such age in order to make them suffer in the slaughter of their children and relatives."[58]

Entering the city, the victorious army spreads fire and destruction, leaving the streets littered with the dead and dying. "See the air blackened with smoke," Skouphos writes, and the sun "cloaked from its billows." Darkness and confusion prevails and "no light shines save from the flashes of the barbarian knives." The sufferings of the inhabitants are depicted with grim detail:

> ...you would see one, oh wretched sight, crying out for his hands, that the enemy has cut off; the other his feet; this one seeks the eyes that he has lost; another groaning from the wounds he has received; parts of heads in every street, intestines dashed out at every step, blood running like rivers and the entire city strewn with corpses and dead limbs....

Having sated their lust for violence on the helpless inhabitants of the city, the conquerors "gape open-mouthed now to sate their avarice." Soon they "fall upon the Churches" where inside each "struggles to surpass the other in disrespect." The altars are looted and hurled upon the ground, the crosses smashed. Once again in the streets, "trampling upon the dead bodies, on hands, and feet, and heads, all mixed up," the conquerors expend their remaining energies upon the marble statues, mutilating them too "in order not to remain in the city even the soulless forms of people." The narrative ends with a final scene of desolation:

> I leave here the groans of half-dead people, the agonies of women, the tears of the old, from the trauma of wounds that their spirits have not yet escaped; I leave the clamor of the barbarians, and the all consuming flame ....Only this do I add, that there didn't remain even a single stone, only a city entombed in its own ashes, and where once a people were nourished, is now a pastureland of animals.[59]

In Chapter Ten, a lesson in word choice and variation, becomes similarly a medium for vehement statements of a national nature. In this case Skouphos will use the art of rhetoric to support an argument for the influence Greek culture has exerted on European civilization. The premise of the ensuing diatribe, conducted against the opinions of an unidentified opponent, is that the praise of Greece, whose renown has been exalted for centuries, will never be quieted, even if it be a mantra that some find wearisome.[60]

"What are you laughing about, O envier of Hellenic glory," Skouphos angrily addresses his antagonist before submitting him to a sharp lecture on the civilizing role Greece had played in history:

> ...speak, if your envy doesn't drown the words in your throat, from where were perfected so many luminaries of wisdom, whose rays adorn the others, appearing like stars, where there would be darkness and charcoal? Didn't they light out from the East, from Greece, so many philosophers, and among them the Aristotles and Platos, whose words the world embraces and pays homage... these I say and myriad others are they not Greeks?

"Which race," Skouphos demands as the lecture continues, "can boast of a Homer... an Aristophanes, Euripedes, Hesiod and Demosthenes?" He appears to hold special regard as well for Pindar, "from whose mouth flows such lines, so many roses and flowers, that the honey bees were drawn to his language to suckle at its sweetness..."[61]

Skouphos does not identify his antagonist in these passages however when he pointedly remarks that it was 'from the East, from Greece,' that so many great figures came, it does suggest that his anger is directed at those of the 'West.' This alone is of great significance, as it reinforces the assumptions held here regarding the existence of a potentially delicate cultural self-consciousness among Greek intelligentsia, evident from Byzantine times. Skouphos labors mightily to restate Greece's case and worth to a Western world that had far surpassed it in material and intellectual wealth; indeed it appears his purpose to claim the dominion of the East over the creation of that European larger civilization, ancient and Christian, of which both are a part.[62] Although on the attack in this piece, the author's fierce Hellenism has a defensive quality, so especially visible in the revealing line,

"What are you laughing at?" In this way Skouphos gives voice perhaps to the suspicions of expatriate intellectuals who felt looked down upon by their hosts as men of a captive or degenerated nation.[63] The cultural self-consciousness of these scholars is exhibited in the repeated admissions of decline that appear throughout this piece and others of its time, as we will see again in the *Anthe Eulaveias*.

The nineteenth century Greek historian Konstantine Paparregopoulos described similar incidents of the cultural self-consciousness indicated above in his multi-volume history of the Tourkokratia. He cites at one point a letter of the Patriarch Kyrillos I, elected to this office in 1621, to a group of Protestant churchmen. Though a man of no small pride, even Kyrillos was forced to acknowledge that "many say and condemn the Eastern Church for its ignorance because the study of letters and philosophy has moved to other countries."[64] On another occasion from the seventeenth century, we have the angry response of an Athenian cleric to a company of French travelers. The latter had been mocking the awful manners of their Greek hosts, all the while interspersing their jibes with little lectures on the virtues of their ancestors. The old priest finally responds that "all the westerners who come to Athens and see the situation so different from ancient times despair because they see a glorious city occupied by barbarians..." For this however he blames the Christian kings of Europe, who "instead of warring among themselves, should unite and make war against the unbelievers and help us out of their own self interest." The Athenian concludes his remarks with a prideful recapitulation of Greek history that bears a startling resemblance to Skouphos:

> All those of your own who think themselves learned ridicule us, but do they, ask yourself, have the right? Hasn't it occurred to you that we gave you in antiquity the lights of civilization with Plato and Aristotle, Epicurus and so many others. And then later, during the fourteenth century, when you had lost everything, again we the Greeks enlightened you with Argyropoulos, Gazes, Trapezountis, Gemistos. You look at me now in astonishment with all that I say to you. So we wonder at the way you see us, we, the modern Athenians.[65]

Clearly these declarations of cultural worth were the expression of an impulse to strike back against the infamy of Greece's decadence. They may also be said to describe a general type of national discourse. Herder's prideful nativism in the face of French cultural 'boosterism' presents one such example of this tendency, but another more prescient one is offered by the writings of the Bulgarian monk known simply as Father Paiisi. More will be said about this figure in the next chapter, however for now it may be interesting to consider the subject of Paiisi's one great work, his 'Slavic-Bulgarian History of the Bulgarian People, Kings and Saints and of All Bulgarian Deeds and Events' (1762).

A monk at the Mount Athos monastery of Hilendar, Paiisi and his fellow Bulgarians were evidently subject to a certain amount of stigmatization by those of other nationalities. "Many times," Paiisi grumbled for example in the text, "have Serbs and Greeks reproached us for not having our own history." Like Skouphos, his response was to compile a record of the historical achievements of Bulgarians as a means to counter these affronts. Although, according to James Clark, this "first Bulgarian history by a Bulgarian" reflected the limitations of the writer, Paiisi did nonetheless succeed in "accomplishing his purpose—to produce a history for Bulgarians to outmatch that of their rivals and to furnish them with convenient arguments for refuting attacks from all sides and, thus to inspire or shame his readers into acknowledging their Bulgarian ancestry."[66]

It is highly doubtful that the *Rhetorike*, in which Skouphos waged his own struggle for cultural recognition, was read by many Westerners or that he expected it to be.[67] Like Paiisi's history, Skouphos's rhetoric was no doubt wholly intended for Greek readers. But what did he wish them to gain from it? Again, his rhetoric may have been aimed to furnish his readers with the inspiration and resources necessary to make a good account of themselves when exposed to the barbs and biases of their critics. Perhaps too Skouphos's arguments served as a defense against one's own internal doubts and demons. Here were words to fortify those who found themselves in the same predicament as he: the predicament of the Eastern logios in the great halls and cities of the West.

Continuing on with his tirade, Skouphos proceeds to the sciences, where he recalls the figures of Euclid, Hippocrates and Galen as "gods of medical art." The Hellenistic period is represented by Alexander, "who for his military prowess appears in the wars as another Ares, and... was worshiped by the world like the child of the great Zeus."[68] He ends his survey of the ancients with a final flourish:

> ...and finally Thucydides and Xenophon, and Plutarch, in these we see the wealth of each kind of learning, and wisdom, to say nothing of all the others in each science and virtue who were not simply exemplary men, but Heroes and Demigods, are not all of these offspring and children of the wise Hellas? Where did they flower the Academies of the divine Plato? Where the Promenades of the great Aristotle? Where the Areopagoi of the wise Athenians? Where the Stoa of the Stoics? From whence the Lycurguses, the Solons, and the other lawgivers of the world? From whence the laws which to the very present govern the world?[69]

"Why then," Skouphos concludes, "if you don't have eyes to see such light, do you have a tongue to bark like another Cerberus?" But of course his adversary is not quite subdued, holding yet one formidable objection to raise against Skouphos's Hellenes: they were pagans. Indeed, "I hear what you say," Skouphos concedes, "after the light of the Gospels banished the darkness of error, and lit the world in Faith, then was the glory of the Greeks extinguished." Not so. "You deceive yourself, clever one," he fires back, "for never did her glories shine more than with the rays of faith." It remains for Skouphos to recite the contributions made by Greece to the Christian civilization of Europe. He eagerly sets himself to work:

> How many teachers did Greece furnish, who, with their labors, exiles, and other hardships, fought for the Church? How many shepherds that with the milk of piety nourished the peoples, countries, kingdoms and drove away the satanic wolves? How many skilled pilots amidst the tempests of heresies, the cruel winds of persecution, the lightning flashes of swords, the thunder of tyrants, threatened thousands of times with death, yet steered the vessel of Peter that it never stray far from the harbor of Truth?

Skouphos's enumeration of the saints and martyrs "that Greece bore" includes so many St. Georges, who "rooted out from the hearts of man the thorns of error," and numberless brave and heroic martyrs who painted with their blood the "purple that adorns the Church." He asks finally of his antagonist:

> ...that scepter, that has, not in one or another country, but in all the world gained dominion, was it not acquired by the Athanasioses, the Gregorioses, the Basils, the Chrysostomoses, and so many other Fathers and champions of Truth, seizing the kingdoms from the tyranny of satanic world domination, and subjugating all under the sweet yoke of the Cross?[70]

A final example from the *Rhetorike* concerns the subject of "supplication" from Chapter Twenty Three. Here too Skouphos will choose an interesting topic for the demonstration of a rhetorical problem: "With the form of supplication," he writes, "I would like to call on the Liberator of the World, Christ, to free the Hellenic race from the slavery of the Hagarene, and from the hands of the Ottoman Briareo."[71] Supplication, he suggests at an earlier point in the chapter, is intended to move the listener to pity or extinguish anger. There will be room for the exercise of both these skills in Skouphos's ensuing appeal for national salvation.

"Enough, righteous Judge, enough," Skouphos boldly begins his supplication, before repeating those words that were a mainstay of Hellenic rhetoric from these times: "For how long (os pote) must the wretched Greeks have to find themselves in the bonds of slavery, and with the infamous foot of the Barbarian Turks stepping on their necks?" For how long, he repeats again, "must such an illustrious and noble race be forced to do obeisance to an atheist touloupani (?) atop the royal throne..?" Another fixture of the discourse surrounding Greece's fate appears in the lines that immediately follow, where Skouphos pins the manifold sufferings of Greece on her past 'sins':

> Ah, recall, I beseech you, that you are not only Judge, but father, and that you punish, but don't destroy your children. Undoubtedly the sins of the Greeks moved your righteous anger, undoubtedly also in the furnace of the same lawlessness they forged the lightning bolts that strike them from the face of the earth, You, who are entirely compassionate, absolve, and extinguish this rage in the ocean of your infinite mercy.[72]

The notion that God brought the Turks down upon the Greeks as punishment for their sins is a common theme from the Tourkokratia. But Skouphos does not name here the fateful sin, which may be significant. Greek Orthodox ecclesiastics who took a similar view of the destruction of Byzantium were often less ambiguous: the sin in question was the late Byzantine attempt at reconciliation with the Western Church. Of course, this would pose a problem for Skouphos, who at the time the *Rhetorike* was written was far along the path himself of renunciation.[73] It is at least interesting to speculate how these feelings may have played a role in his intense activism for the Greek cause, and his very bold intercession on behalf of the race to God himself.[74] In either case, Skouphos was confirmed in the view of history as 'revelation' as his writings illustrate. We note below the fragment of a letter written to his brother Parthenios, an Orthodox cleric on the island of Zakynthos, on the news of a recent earthquake:

> Your letter, esteemed one, filled my eyes with tears, for the fright suffered by the tortured island. Perhaps it is because man sleeps so deeply in sin, that to wake him the compassionate Master shakes the earth, or that the lawlessness of man is such now, the earth cannot bear any longer to endure its weight. Tormented sinners, and what would they do on that frightful day when a flaming sword comes to cut the chaff for hell, as surely now that as the earth shakes and dances a little all tremble and lose their senses. And certainly he who doesn't wake in these thunderings and clamors of heaven and earth isn't sleeping, but is already dead.[75]

The supplication, and the recitation of all the agonies of Greece enumerated in the *Rhetorike*, resembles in some fashion an act of self-flagellation, intended to demonstrate to God that man, or in this case the Greek Race, was indeed awake, regretful and deserving of a reprieve. Skouphos would seek to further this aim by recounting to God, as he had done previously to his human antagonist, the many services the Greeks had furnished to Christianity. As elsewhere in the text, Skouphos's words take on the character of a demand for cultural recognition and acknowledgment:

> Recall, Theanthropic Jesus, that the Hellenic Race was the first to embrace your divine Gospel; the first, that threw down the idols, and hanging on the Cross worshiped you as God; the first, that resisting the tyrants, who sought to uproot from the hearts of Christians your divine Name; with their labors the Greeks increased, O Christ, your Church in all the world; the Greeks enriched her with their treasures of wisdom, and with their language, and goodness, and with their very life championed her, running with infinite magnanimity into the prisons, and whippings, the racks, exiles, flames, tarrings, only to extinguish the error, to spread the Faith, to declare you Theanthropos, and to brighten, as the Sun brightens, the glory of the Cross...[76]

Skouphos's efforts to move God to mercy close with some final expressive and characteristic statements of the 'national problem.' Not only does he desire that God use his divine power to free the Greeks from the "yoke of Barbarian captivity," but that he "raise again to their former glory the Race, and from the dunghill in which it sits, give to it the scepter and the kingdom." One notes that Skouphos's geographical enumeration of the Greek world in the passage that follows, along with his appeal that the Race be given back "its kingdom," resembles the claims of the 'megale idea;' a notion of territoriality that will exert an enormous political influence on Greek history in the times to come. In this revealing part of the supplication, the author seeks to move God not only by his own tears, but by those of "your Saints, who call out to you from all the parts of wretched Greece":

> From Crete cries Andreas and asks that you exterminate the Hagarene wolves from that Kingdom; from the City cries out a Chrystotomos, and appeals to you that she not be ruled by the enemies of your Son; and Katerina showing you the rack on which she was martyred, asks that the wheel of fate turn again for Alexandria, the Ignations cry from Antioch, the Polycarpians from Smyrna, the Dionysians from Athens, the Spiridons from Cyprus, and showing to you the lions that ripped them apart, the flames that seared them, the irons that tortured them, hope from your high charity the Greek cities and all of Greece for deliverance.[77]

The "wretched" Greeks, "deprived and naked," squatting on a "dunghill," pleading to be raised again to their "former glory," are images that express with unusual vividness the elements of the national problem being studied here. And yet there are important things missing from the *Rhetorike* that serve to separate it from later works or mark it as an example of pre-Enlightenment Greek discourse.

The missing elements include the almost complete absence of any serious reference to modern Western authors in the piece, save Skouphos's hazy allusion to Bossuet (see below). Although Skouphos has made an impassioned statement of the 'national problem' and presents his works as an instrument of enlightenment, he deals exclusively with figures from the Greek tradition, indeed he expresses a fierce nativist attachment to this tradition.[78] Of course the *Texne Rhetorike*, printed eight years, as a matter of reference, before Locke's *Two Treatises on Government* (1689), comes at a time when the stirrings of the Enlightenment were yet to be deeply felt. In this sense the very absence of Western figures in the *Rhetorike* helps us to see the enormous excitement generated by the Enlightenment and its scale as an intellectual phenomenon when it did appear. Of course by this time too the circle of the 'learned' among the Greeks would have been wider and familiarity with Western figures more advanced. For now the classical and Christian traditions, the same traditions that served in late Byzantine times as an inspiration for the regeneration of the race, still reign supreme.

With these observations in mind, it is important to note that although the *Rhetorike* is not brimming with references to modern Western writers as later Greek works tend to be, it is yet an act of 'appropriation,' akin to those of the more prolific Korydalleus and Vlachos. All employ Western forms to address social, political or educational matters of an Eastern substance. The rhetorical works of Skouphos and Vlachos, as one scholar has noted, were the products of their Western cultural experience, particularly its ecclesiastical culture, which they hoped to see imported into the Greek world: "The new manner (of rhetoric) indicated by the introduction of these two analogous manuals that were written by Gerasimos Vlachos and Fragkiskos Skouphos existed as the starting base, from which set out Elias Meniates and the other ecclesiastical logioi, to perfect the homily, that is the religious sermon of the seventeenth century."[79] And of course from Meniates follows a line of Greek rhetoricians that include later luminaries such as Nikephoros Theotokes.[80]

Significantly, the sole European figure that appears in the *Rhetorike*, identified by Skouphos only as the 'Gallikos Heracles', is the bishop and historian Jacques Bossuet (1627-1704).[81] There certainly are elements of Skouphos's work that parallel the ideas of Bossuet, as presented in books such as *Discours sur l'Histoire Universelle* (1681). Like Bossuet, Skouphos appears to interpret history as a reflection of God's will and design, and thus it is to God that man must appeal for forgiveness and intervention, as he does in the passages above. This emphasis serves again to distinguish the *Rhetorike* from the polemics of later authors.[82]

One finally cannot escape the fixation on war and conquest in this text, as graphically depicted in the accounts of the taking of a Christian city in Chapter Eight. Events of this kind were of course a part of Skouphos's world. The Venetians, who had lost the battle for Skouphos's home island, Crete, found themselves hard-pressed to keep their remaining possessions in the Mediterranean as their struggles with the Turks continued. Such events helped to furnish Skouphos's work with images of a medieval quality that would be rarer in the succeeding century. And yet they are reminders of the continuation of the 'history' that did not end in 1453; the survival perhaps of the 'medieval,' in the context of Mediterranean history, to the very step of the modern age. Nor are such preoccupations unique to Skouphos. Visions of cities put to fire and sword, holy warfare, and the like appear in the texts of his contemporary expatriates in Italy. Indeed the verse collections authored by Greek students at Padua during these years, as Stergelles has shown, often display an even more polemical tone than found in Skouphos.[83]

The Orthodox Church saw its worst fears confirmed in the figures of men like Meletios Typaldos and Fragkiskos Skouphos, Orthodox Christians whose contact with the West proved fatal to the preservation of the 'faith of their fathers.' Nonetheless as converts and 'patriots,' their lives raise a number of interesting questions. On one hand the pronounced patriotism of these men presents a problem for modern historians who would tend to see instances of pre-modern nationalism as guided by religious values and identity alone. In this view the 'nationalism' of the seventeenth century Greek could not be of an ethnic variety but a religious one. Of course this is not so in Skouphos, a Greek Catholic, whose appeals for Greece's resurrection have thus a more ambiguous cultural character.

This fact raises the important question of how the national sentiments of the 'converts' may have been elevated by the renunciation of their faith.[84] Kairofelas has even suggested that the 'convert-patriot' was something of a universal type during the Tourkokratia. Included in this category would be famous men such as the late Byzantine scholar Bessarion, later elevated to the rank of Cardinal, who used their new powers within the Western Church to aid Greece.[85] A radical extension of this view was once offered by Konstantine Demaras. Demaras suggested in the case of the controversial Metropolitan of Venice, Meletios Typaldos (1648-1713), that conversion to Catholicism was part of a strategy to increase his influence on European policymakers, an influence he hoped to use to engineer a final reckoning with the Ottomans. Meletios was thus a self-sacrificing patriot singularly devoted to the liberation of Greece. Being an Orthodox in a Catholic empire, Demaras reasoned, Meletios's advocacies of Venetian intervention would always be looked upon with scepticism. Converting to Catholicism enabled him to make his appeals for the liberation of Greece with greater legitimacy; perhaps they would be less prone to draw resistance now for being motivated by Orthodox zeal.[86] A speculative argument to be sure, but so must they all be that attempt to illuminate the deeper motivations of these individuals.

Of course 'national' rhetoric of the kind found in Skouphos will resurface in the texts of the unconverted as well, as the following chapters will show, with Orthodox clerics often leading the way.[87] It should be noted finally that the works of the 'converts' were not necessarily subject to immediate or universal censure. Skouphos's renunciation of Orthodoxy for example proved no barrier to his influence on the great Orthodox cleric and rhetorician who succeeded him, Elias Meniates. Meniates, as noted above, studied the *Rhetorike* at Flaggineio and probably later taught from it. It is in fact no exaggeration to say that Skouphos's influence on Meniates was immense. The most extraordinary example of this influence is exhibited in the latter's Panagyri of 1688, an early piece from the author's oeuvre which ends with an impassioned plea for the liberation of Greece borrowed virtually word for word from Skouphos. Meniates's one significant innovation was his substitution of the Panagia (Virgin Mary) for God.[88]

At times a melancholy note appears in Skouphos that recalls the Hellenistic nostalgia of Argyropoulos from the beginning of this chapter. It is tempting to view these misty reveries over an exalted and faded past as a kind of salve for the battered soul of the diaspora logios. If so, another distinctive example of this condition is presented in the form of the *Anthe Eulaveias* (1708) or 'Flower of Piety.' This anthology of verse written for the most part by Flaggineio students, presents a rare and valuable insight into the thoughts and preoccupations of the young scholars of the Italian era and the influences acting upon them.

The *Anthe* was published as a mixed volume of epigrams, sonnets and odes written variously in Latin and Italian, as well as both ancient and demotic Greek. To whom this 'flower of piety' is offered is readily apparent, the Virgin Mary, a point that demonstrates again the Catholic influences that permeated the Orthodox theologians and culture of the city. Anthologies of this kind were evidently part of Venetian social and cultural life. They were the printed records of poems or addresses that had first been performed at public ceremonies, usually on the occasion of a great event, such as a victory of Venetian arms, or the commemoration of the life and virtues of a city father.

The occasion for the *Anthe Eulaveias* was the celebration in 1708 of the 'metastasin' or Assumption of the Virgin Mary, to whom the volume was dedicated.[89] It is not certain whether the works recited on this occasion were delivered at the Flaggineio Schole or at the Orthodox Church of St. George, which was a common venue. One notes finally that many of the pieces in the small anthology include salutations to the local Orthodox Metropolitan Meletios Typaldo, no doubt an expression of the poets' admiration but perhaps too a recognition of the bishop's probable role in subsidizing the ensuing publication.[90]

The anthology begins with an opening address by one of the teachers of the school, Georgios Patousas, brother of the author and School Director Ioannes, followed by the works of various students, although according to tradition at least one outside scholar was included.[91] As noted above the poetical works are a mixture of sonnets, odes and also several epigrams, showing again the Italian influence on the literary development of Greek culture in the City.[92] We also find figures from ancient and Christian times blending together or collaborating in these brief works, as they do in Skouphos's or Patousas's pedagogical texts, to offer instruction and guidance to the young student of letters. However when expressed in the form of a sonnet or epigram the mingled fragments of ancient and modern in the *Anthe* exhibit a Hellenic nostalgia that recalls again the melancholy of Gennadios or Argyropoulos as they watched the Byzantine world dissolve into the past. An epigram devoted to the school director Ioannes Patousas is characteristic:

> He found her spread out near a cave the Attic muse her boy Lytous and get up, O aunt, he said to her.
> And she sighing deeply said: I find myself far from the Hellenic earth and contemplating on its awful plight.
> Then the golden-haired Apollo answered striking the chests of the gods with a silver arrow.
> Get up, Isocrates and the divine Homer you will find in the immortal wisdom of Patousa.[93]

The ode 'To Greece,' composed in modern Greek, expresses the same notes of despair over a tradition fallen into decay. Thoughts of Greece's luminous past, and, inescapably, her less luminous present, produce in the slumbering narrator a fit of discomfort:

> In the shade of a tree at sleep
> breathing deeply, but with a heart
> so melancholy, because the happiness
> and spirit of Greece I had in my mind.

At this point the dreamer is suddenly roused by an insistent voice. "What manner of sleep is this?" it asks him, "What is this misfortune you have and lie there so distressed." Stirred from sleep the narrator is greeted with a remarkable sight:

> I wake and see directly above me
> the very same forthright Athena
> and so coming upon me from above she speaks to me.
> Of the great glory of Greece
> such glory time can never wither
> for wisdom is an amarynth.[94]

We have a final example, in this case a sonnet that combines rumination over Greece's glorious past and decline with a triumphant vision of her future revival:

> Greece, glorious mother, printed with the famous footprints
> luminous of the great heroes, for from her artless dwellings
> the love of virtue she had chosen for a guide.
>
> This that guides the wise virtue to the acme of glory, her
> children were later benumbed from the difficult years. But now
> we see (this virtue) to light still in her present
> children.
>
> Now that they follow the impulses of their inborn courage and
> deep knowledge, to what great height do I see her now to rise!
>
> And it is so magnificent that gazing at it I become dizzy.
> And if it should become grander still her greatness, it will become the grandest of all
> and the envy of the world.[95]

The circumstances of this sonnet devoted to Greece, written originally in Italian by a twenty year old scholar from the island of Kerkyra, brings into view the tension between assimilation and tradition of which the entire Neohellenic history of Venice is a part. The energetic efforts of the Venetian Greeks to preserve their heritage, to build churches and schools, recalls again the pronouncement of Acton that "exile is the nursery of nationalism." These impulses, the vague reflex to protect or preserve an identity, are quite visible but so too are the influences of the surrounding culture, its language and religion, upon the consciousness of these Greek writers. It is apparent in the 'form' of their art, whether a manual of rhetoric or a sonnet. The outcome of this strange calculus is manifested best of all in those hybrid creations that inhabit the *Anthe* itself, where fixtures of the Eastern tradition are expressed through literary devices of a foreign origin: melancholy odes to Hellas written by Greeks in Latin, patriotic oaths composed in the Italian vernacular or set into sonnets, and drifting all around the noble, airy forms of gods, muses and the Panagia herself.[96]

The Ionian element in the Diaphotismos, like the clerical element, would remain prominent, however by the close of the seventeenth century we start to see the influence of important changes that had been taking shape within and without Greek society. Padua would continue to be the institution of choice for later generations of Greek students, but the Venetian element had started to fade; these new students were increasingly likely to come from the Phanar or the emerging trading capitals of the Greek world. Political, social and economic developments such as these would collaborate in the reconfiguration of the geography of Greek learning and culture over the next century.

The Greek dialogue or preoccupation with the past that has featured so prominently in this chapter, was also destined to continue and by its presence to serve as the basis for the intense acts of cultural appropriation that animate later times. But in the ensuing years the predicament of modern Hellenism would become the subject of an ever more thorough critique, one more pointed, more pervasive and ever more indelicate in its diagnoses until we arrive finally, at the end of the century, with works that appear to take an almost perverse delight in their relentless inventory of Greece's inadequacies; a discourse that trips alongside the path taken by the Enlightenment in its ever bolder examination of the sources of human progress and decay.

Notes

1. Ioannou Argyropoulou, 'Monodia eis ton Autokratora Ioannen Palaeologon,' in *Palaiologeia kai Peloponnesiaka*, Edited by Spyridon Lampros, (Athens: Bas. N. Grigoriades, 1926), 314.

2. 'To Parsimo tes Polis' in Demetrios Petropoulos (ed.), *Hellenika Demotika Tragoudia*, (Athens: Vasike Vivliotheke, 1958), 152.

3. The Russo-Turkish war of 1768, aroused widespread hopes that the prophecies which spoke vaguely of the

'blond race' and the liberation of the city were about to be fulfilled. One of the more interesting sources testifying to these hopes comes from Ioannes Pringos a Greek merchant of Amsterdam. His diary entry from July 22nd, 1771: "Now should be fulfilled the prophecies of Leo the Wise, where he says 'Two eagles shall eat the snake,' these are the two insignia or flags of the Russian Empire the double-headed eagle, the flag of the Roman, and the snake is the Turk, who has wrapped himself around a dead body, in other words the Kingdom of the Romans, where he (Leo) says, as they have been explained, 320 years they will remain the Turks in the City and now it is from 1453 when they took her until now 1771, 317 years. He has made it possible the Lord in these three years for the Russians to cast the Turk out of Greece and Europe." 'To Chroniko tou Amsterdam,' *Nea Estia*, 10, (1931): 914.

4. C.M. Woodhouse, *George Gemistos Plethon The Last of the Hellenes*, (Oxford: Clarendon Press, 1986), 71. This view is also advanced by Basil Tatakis in his classic work, *Byzantine Philosophy*, Translated and introduced by Nicholas J. Moutafakis, (Indianapolis: Hackett, 2003), 234. "By the fifteenth century," wrote Steven Runciman, "most Byzantine intellectuals alluded to themselves as Hellenes." *The Great Church in Captivity*, (Cambridge: Cambridge University Press, 1968), 119-120.

5. Quoted from Woodhouse, *George Gemistos Plethon, The Last of the Hellenes*, 102-3. Parts of the Address can also be found in Tatakis, *Byzantine Philosophy*, 235, and Steven Runciman, *The Great Church in Captivity*, 120-122.

6. Runciman, *The Great Church in Captivity*, 120. Plethon, who was one of the most colorful and controversial intellectuals of his time, has been the subject of much debate over the existence and character of Medieval Greek national consciousness. His famous struggle with Scholarios is discussed below.

7. Deno Geanakoplos, *Greek Scholars in Venice*, (Cambridge, Massachusetts: Harvard University Press, 1962), 77.

8. Deno Geanakoplos, *Interaction of the "Sibling" Byzantine and Western Cultures in the Middle Ages and Italian Renaissance (330-1600)*, (New Haven: Yale University Press, 1976).

9. E.g.: it had not suffered the serious disruptions and upheavals experienced in the West following the fall of Rome and the subsequent 'Dark Ages.'

10. We must add here the disastrous consequences of the Fourth Crusade (1201-04) in which the imperial capital was occupied by the 'Franks' until 1261.

11. Geanakoplos, *Interaction of the "Sibling" Byzantine and Western Cultures in the Middle Ages and Italian Renaissance (330-1600)*, 6.

12. This subject described by Geanakoplos in *The Interaction of the "Sibling" Byzantine and Western Cultures*, 13-24. The author concludes that "the Greeks, now in a defensive position, fearing not only Turkish attack but subversion from the Latin West as well, had come to equate their Orthodoxy with what was unique to them alone, the ancient Greek cultural heritage. And it was the conjunction of these two factors, cultural "nationalism" and religious "nationalism," that produced the ideological origins of the later, modern Greek sense of national consciousness." Ibid, 48. These are ambitious arguments, nonetheless it may be possible that Plethon for one, a man of ambiguous Orthodox beliefs, was motivated in his anti-unionism by a quality of national or cultural resistance, in contrast to Scholarios whose forceful objections to the Councils rose from his determination to keep the Orthodox Church safe from the taint of the Latin heresy. This position against the Councils provided the two great Byzantine figures with a rare, albeit superficial and short-lived, occasion for unity.

13. The 'sins' of the Byzantines appears repeatedly in the correspondence between the German classicist Martin Crusius (1526-1607) and the Constantinople scholar Theodosios Zygomalas in the sixteenth century. See Martino Crusio, *Turcograecia,* (reprint, Modena: Editrice Memor, 1972), 74-98. These desperate gestures to avert destruction will figure greatly in later 'official' views of the Church on the causes of the fall of the Empire, and in a most surprising way. Reunification, the grand heresy, brought God's wrath upon the City in the form of the Turkish conquest. This conquest also served to protect the Orthodox faithful from new indiscretions, placing in the powerful Ottomans, a great bulwark against any further incursions into the East by the corrupt Latins. Such views were the centerpiece of the famous 'Fatherly Teachings' of 1798 (discussed below).

14. 'Millet' literally 'nation' in the Turkish language, but in the context of Ottoman times a conception of nation defined by religious faith. Thus the Serbs, Vlachs, Bulgarians and other Orthodox peoples of the Balkans were lumped with the Greeks into the Orthodox millet, within which of course the Greek influence was dominant. The other three raya/non-Muslim millets within the Ottoman Empire were the Jewish, Catholic and Armenian Gregorian.

15. The religious foundation and nature of the Ottoman state stands out sharply in every history of the Empire. And yet, unlike the great empire built by Spain over the same years, the centralizing element was more remote, for the Ottoman Muslims put no great emphasis on conversion and certainly made no attempt at the kind of undertaking that is so distinctive a feature of Spanish rule in the Americas. These two factors, a vision of the inseparability of identity and faith, but one absent of any consistent universalizing zeal, largely determined the heterogeneous, ethno-cultural division of the Empire from its beginnings to its fall. In some ways such 'zeal' was more manifest in the Hellenizing activities of Greek elements within the Empire, an activity that was encouraged by the rise of the Phanariots and the revived power of the Patriarchate.

16. This brief description does not of course serve to represent the weighty position held by Scholarios in the ecclesiastical and intellectual circles of Byzantium. He was and is considered by many, including Tatakis, to be the "last great representative of Byzantine erudition." (Tatakis, *Byzantine Philosophy*, 247) Extremely well versed in the schools of both Aristotle and Plato, over whose respective merits he conducted a famous and vigorous public debate with Plethon, Gennadios was surely a force to be reckoned with in late Byzantine thought. His elevation in fact to Patriarch afforded him an opportunity to strike a blow in the continuing culture wars within the Greek world. Certainly the most famous incident here concerns Gennadios's public burning of Plethon's manuscript, The Laws, teeming with the paganistic reveries that mark his later works, and which of course Gennadios found horrific, in the streets of Constantinople in 1460. Despite the destruction of this, the only complete version of the manuscript, Plethon's drafts of the Laws survive and have occasionally been reprinted over the years. A survey of one of the more recent publications, printed both in its original ancient Greek and in French translation, depicts a work of peculiar character, one that draws both on pagan and Zoroastrian traditions to elaborate a new system of political and moral ethics. George Plethon, *Nomon Syggrafes, Ta Sozomena (Traite des Lois, Recueil Des Fragments)*, introduced and edited by C. Alexandre, with French translation by A. Pellissier, (Amsterdam: Adolf M. Hakkert, 1966).

17. See Apostoles Vacalopoulos, *The Greek Nation 1453-1669*, Translated by Ian and Phania Moles, (New Brunswick: Rutgers University Press, 1976), 101.

18. Cited in Vacalopoulos, *The Greek Nation 1453-1669*, 115.

19. Cited in Tatakis, *Byzantine Philosophy*, 242. The works of Gennadios, Plethon, Argyropoulos and other Byzantine figures are assembled in the *Patrologiai cursus completus*, series graecolatina, 161 volumes, Edited by J.P. Migne, (Paris: 1857-66).

20. Vacalopoulos, *The Greek Nation 1453-1669*, 115.

21. There was a considerable variety of experience at the local level. In some cases large numbers of Greeks converted to Islam and there were too parts of mainland Greece most notably the mountainous regions of the Peloponnesus, the Mani, where Turkish control was never completely established. This was also true of the Ionian Islands which remained in the hands of the Venetians up to the French Revolution, after which they were traded about by the Great Powers, as discussed below.

22 .It is nevertheless startling to consider the extent to which separate identities can linger and persist despite centuries of shared history. The peculiar arithmetic of tradition and assimilation was especially manifested in the case of the 'karamanlides,' a group of Anatolian Greeks who came to Greece as part of the massive population exchange of 1923. Orthodox in religion, they nonetheless spoke Turkish, which they wrote using the Greek alphabet.

23. Konstantas and Philippides, *Geographia Neoterike*, 100.

24. McGrew, 'The Land Issue in the Greek War of Independence,' 114. It is difficult to speculate on the nature of the relations between the Turks and the Greeks in these lands, although it appears that the Turkish communities were concentrated in areas where the land was arable (perhaps only twenty percent of the total land in question). The fertile lands of Thessalia, for example, birthplace of Regas Velestinlis, drew a Turkish population of some two hundred and fifty families that probably outnumbered the Greek 'raya' population of the village. Most evidence points, in summary, to a general tendency toward population segregation. See Leandros Vranousis (ed.), *Regas - erevna, synagogi kai meleti* (Athens: Vasike Vivliotheke, 1953), 7, for a demographic description of pre-revolutionary Thessaly. See also the invaluable descriptions of eighteenth century village communities in Northern Greece contained in Athansios Psalidas and Kosmas Thesprotos, *Geographia Alvanias kai Epeirou*, (Iannina: Society for Epiriot Studies, 1964). Note finally Noel Malcolm's observations regarding the rise of ethnic tensions in Ottoman Bosnia: "The main basis of hostility was not ethnic or religious but economic: the resentment felt by the members of a mainly (but not exclusively) Christian peasantry towards their Muslim landowners." Noel Malcolm, *Bosnia*, (New York: New York University Press, 1996), xxi.

25. Runciman, *The Great Church in Captivity*, 179.

26. The practice may have continued in some areas of the Balkans until the first decade of the eighteenth century. See Vacalopoulos, *The Greek Nation, 1453-1669*, 41. Vacalopoulos estimates that during the high point of this practice, which he regards as occurring from the middle of the 15th to the middle of the 17th centuries, the numbers of children taken ranges from five hundred thousand to one million. Ibid, 41.

27. See Vrygonis, 'The Greeks Under Turkish Rule', 51.

28. Runciman, *The Great Church in Captivity*, 179.

29. Konstantas and Philippides for example, showed no romantic attraction for the klephts, whose activities did much to reinforce the prevailing discourse of Balkan torpor and lawlessness. However, as men of enlightenment, they considered these evils to be only the most notorious result of the tyrannical and irrational rule of the Sultan: "Ah! What a kingdom would Turkey be!" they lament in their geography, "how feared from without, how well off inside if it was well governed." These deficiencies were responsible for the exodus of commercial talent from Greece and its resulting impoverishment. Konstantas and Philippides, *Geographia Neoterike*, 46.

30. 'Primate' refers to a class of Greek landed gentry, sometimes referred to as 'kodjabashis' in the sources. The rise of the armatoliks was increasingly apparent in the eighteenth century as a method of dealing with internal lawlessness. This worsening brigandage may in turn have found its origins in the changing patterns of

landownership and in particular the appearance of great estates, ciftliks, that reduced the Balkan peasantry to sharecroppers. See Trajan Stoianovich, 'Factors in the Decline of Ottoman Society in the Balkans,' *Slavic Review*, XXI (1962): 623-32.

31. 'Tou Tziobara' in *Hellenika Demotika Tragoudia*, 178.

32. Perhaps the most colorful depiction of klepht life before the revolution is to be found in the memoirs of Theodore Kolokotronis, who came later to play a central role in the Greek Revolution. Kolokotronis has in fact furnished historians with one of the most oft-quoted statements of the entire period: "Our rising was totally different from any which had taken place in Europe before our day. The revolutions of Europe had always been against their rulers—they were civil wars. Our war was more just than any of them—it was a nation rising up against another nation—it was a war with a people whom it never desired to acknowledge as ruling them; to whom it had never taken oaths of fealty, except when made to do so by force; neither had a sultan at any time any inclination to regard the Greek people as his people, but only as slaves." Theodore Kolokotronis, *Memoirs from the Greek War of Independence 1821-1833*, Translated by E.M. Edmonds, (Chicago: Argonaut Publishers, 1969), 252.

33. 'Palikari: typically used to describe a stout and gallant young man.

34. 'O Thanatos tou Zidrou' in *Hellenika Demotika Tragoudia*, 179-180. The age of these ballads is difficult to date although there is evidence for some to suggest they may go as far back as the sixteenth century. It should be noted that the character and significance of the ballads remains a lively subject of debate. George Dizikirikes remarks in *Ho Neoellenikos diaphotismos kai to Europaiko Pnevma, 1750-1821*, (Athens: Strates G. Filippotes, 1984), 84, that the 'klephtic song of the Greek people, as ideology and aesthetic, is an immediate reflection of its life, an artistic revelation that among others has as its basic target chiefly the war against the Turkish conquest and the conscious collaboration with it, as the Phanariots aspire." Dizirikes makes a case here against the characterization of the klephts as something more than the 'wild men' on the fringes of civilization as they were apparently viewed by Gellner (*Nationalism*, 41). We see them here endowed with a definite political role. Note also the author's characterization of the Phanariots—they too remain a subject of debate within Greek historiography, as discussed below.

35. The latter were never made part of the Ottoman Empire, being held by the Venetians until the Napoleonic Wars during which they fell into and out of the hands of a succession of European powers. These islands were given to the Kingdom of Greece by England in 1878. Crete was held by the Venetians until 1660 and the Peloponnesus passed in and out of their hands, with the final Turkish takeover occurring in 1715.

36. It was through Venice and Padua that even El Greco passed before settling finally in Spain. Greco's life and work are themselves interesting studies in cultural identity. Indeed his identity and apparent self-consciousness have continued to intrigue to the very present, as one reviewer wrote of a recent exhibition of the painter's work: "That he continued to sign his name in Greek may be insignificant, or maybe not. It implies that he remained, in his mind a painter of mixed artistic heritage, someone from elsewhere, distinguished by his difference from those around him. Call him an early outsider artist, a kind of modern credential." 'El Greco, Bearer of Many Gifts,' *New York Times*, October 3, 2003, B31, 35.

37. These developments should indicate the considerable wealth of the Venetian Greeks. The Church of St. George, designed by leading Venetian architects and built no doubt at great expense, and later the schools that were also funded through the community's resources, were undertakings of a kind that were beyond the reach of any contemporary Greek community in European Turkey. The rise of these educational institutions is also indicative of the concentration of Greek scholars in Venice, some of course refugees from the ongoing conflicts, but also of the relative intellectual vitality of the Venetian held provinces from which they typically came; this is most especially true of Crete.

38. E. G. Vallianatos, *From Graikos to Hellene: Adamantios Koraes and the Greek Revolution*, (Athens: Academy of Athens, 1987), 13. Note: it is not clear how closely Vallianatos has scrutinized these figures as Padua had two basic schools: Law (Nomike) and Arts (Iatrophilosophon), which turned out theology students in addition to medical ones. For an introduction to the question of why Padua became such an important center of Greek education throughout the middle ages and early modern period see Paschalis Kitromilides, *The Enlightenment as Social Criticism: Iosopis Moisiodax and Greek Culture in the Eighteenth Century*, (Princeton: Princeton University Press, 1992.). As Kitromilides notes, Padua, established in 1405, became by virtue of the Venetian Empire the "main center of university education for Greeks from those Greek lands occupied by Venice." See *The Enlightenment as Social Criticism*, 39-40.

39. Aristeidis P. Stergelles, *Ta demosieumata ton Hellenon spoudaston tou Panepistimiou tes Padouas ton 17o kai 18o aiones*, (Athens: Parnassas, 1970), 46.

40. Fragkiskos Skouphos, *Patriotica kai Ethica*, edited by Kostas Kairofelas, (Athens: Syllogos pros diadosin Ofelimon Vivlion, 1940), 185-6.

41. George Patrick Henderson, *The Revival of Greek Thought 1620-1830*, 16. It may strike some as ironic that a Greek cleric-intellectual, Korydalleus, should learn his Neo-Aristotelianism by way of Padua, and yet this is another interesting example of the cultural encounters and groupings of this era.

42. Although the reforms championed by Korydalleus were ultimately adopted, they were to become for him the source of no small personal and professional hardship. The eighteenth century reformer Eugenios Voulgaris (1716-1806) would come to experience similar hardships. See Henderson, *The Revival of Greek Thought 1620-1830*, Chs 1 and 2. See also Runciman, *The Great Church in Captivity*, 220.

43. The College was evidently created with a 'prosletyzing intent,' a goal which its heavy curricular emphasis on rhetoric was an instrumental part. The intensive courses on rhetoric were designed to serve the Jesuit goal of training new ecclesiastics in the art of persuasion—necessary skills for defeating the arguments of the schismatics. It is not perhaps surprising that the great Greek rhetorician Skouphos was himself a graduate of the College (and later a convert to Catholicism). Patousas also laid a heavy stress on rhetoric in his Egkyklopedia; he also exhibited considerable Catholic affinities and it may be that his premature death prevented a formal renunciation of Orthodoxy. Athanasias Audale, *He Egkyklopaideia Philologike tou Ioanne Patousa*, (Athens: Library of Historical Studies, 1984), 55-56, 62.

44. Audale, *He Egkyklopaideia Philologike tou Ioanne Patousa*, Chapter 1.

45. Note that the earliest Greek college in Rome had been established in 1513, a collaboration of the Greek scholar Ioannes Lascaris (1445-1535) and Pope Leo X. This short-lived institution disappeared in 1520 though not on account of the efforts of the tireless Lascaris who tried on at least two other occasions to revive it, first in Milan in 1522 and then again in Paris in 1526. A confidant of Popes and Kings, Lascaris represents one of the last of the late generation of Byzantine scholars. In addition to his efforts to establish Greek schools of higher learning in Europe, Lascaris conducted several manuscript collection expeditions to the East in search of works for Western libraries. He is also credited, finally, with the primary editorial role in the 1494 edition of the 'Palatine Anthology,' a work that will have enormous influence on Greek pedagogy and letters over the succeeding centuries, of which the *Anthe Eulaveias* is a ready example. See James Hutton, *The Greek Anthology in Italy to the Year 1800*, (Ithaca: Cornel University Press, 1935), 114-121.

46. Athanasios E. Karathanases, *He Phlangineias Schole tes Venetias*, (Thessalonike: 1975), 174.

47. Ibid, 183. The students of 'unknown origin,' 79 in total, could also be assumed to derive from Venetian parts. The contribution of students from eastern Greece was negligible. From Constantinople came only 15

students over this period and from Smyrna and Chios only one apiece. Of course by the middle of the eighteenth century new schools had begun to appear throughout these eastern lands and cities.

48. The original edition of this work appeared in 1710. My own acquaintance is with the 1819 edition: Ioannes Patousas, *Enkyklopaideia philologike, eis tessaras tomous dieremene*, 4 Volumes, edited by Spyridon Vlantes, (Venice: Nicholas Glykei, 1819). Notes above refer to the contents of the first volume.

49. Fragkiskos Skouphos, 'Texne Rhetorike,' in Tatakis, *Skouphos, Meniates, Voulgaris, Theotokes*, 50. One is tempted to look with humor on some of Skouphos's most outlandish statements such as his characterization above of the female sex as one of the 'three evils.' And yet he was apparently confirmed in this opinion, if the tirades against women and marriage found in his letters are any proof. Here is one addressed to a young acquaintance in Rome: "A man doesn't seem very wise to me who though born free would like to bind his feet with chains and become a slave. Marriage is a kind of slavery of such severe harshness that it only ends with life itself. I hear that you want to marry and as your friend I remind you not to let the comeliness of a woman deceive you, that charm is only in appearance for all that comes later is false. The roses that you now wonder at in that face, once you turn away from them, they will be changed for you into thorns and the pleasure of the bridal chamber that now rules you has in its sweetness something bitter, as sweet as it is in the beginning so much more in the end does it pour out bile and poison. Oh what a wonderful thing it is to man his freedom. To not have his feet bound with chains that nothing can sever save death. That God will enlighten you not to lose such a valuable and divine gift I remain ..." 'Pros ton timiotaton kai prosfilestaton veon Georgion Melissenon,' in Skouphos, *Patriotica kai Ethica*, 193-4.

50. The highly-admired modern Greek poet Solomos for example is rarely included in the company of the logioi. This definition is further reinforced by the facts, again visible through practice not objective definition, that the logioi, the learned, were typically holders of advanced degrees, such as Skouphos (who was by virtue of his education in Rome a Doctor of Theology). These criteria precluded most school teachers, a class that emerged in the eighteenth century, from the ranks of the logioi as well. In summary, advanced studies along with some publishing activity intended to improve the race were required credentials.

51. Tatakis, editor's introduction, *Skouphos, Meniates, Voulgaris, Theotokes*, 35. Crete was at the time of Skouphos's birth about to experience a final, protracted period of war between the Venetians and the Turks. His family may well have been refugees from this conflict.

52. Again, the sources here are divided regarding whether or not Skouphos ever formally served as a teacher at the School. See Kairofelas, editor's introduction, *Patriotika kai Ethika*, 14-16.

53. Tatakis, editor's introduction, *Skouphos, Meniates, Voulgaris, Theotokes*, 36.

54. Ibid, 36.

55. This will be especially evident in the work of one of Skouphos's contemporaries, the later Metropolitan of Athens Meletios Metros and his *Geographia palaia kai nea*, published posthumously by Glykeis in 1728.

56. Skouphos, 'Texne Rhetorike,' 57.

57. Ibid, 60.

58. Ibid, 60.

59. Ibid, 60-61.

60. Ibid, 65.

61. Ibid, 65.

62. In a way the author expresses a dilemma that is present in Greek culture to the present; one notes the competing Greek impulses to rank themselves as Europeans and yet to hold firmly to a culture of 'apartness.' The issue takes on an interesting form in Skouphos for reasons stated below. Perhaps because Europe is viewed as 'the West,' assimilation has come to acquire the aspect of capitulation. As Skouphos also indicates above, some Greeks held and perhaps still hold tight to what they might articulate as an 'Eastern' component of the European tradition (but one must also consider decisive events in the history of the independent Greek state as influential in the perpetuation of this attitude). In the case of Skouphos the existence of an Eastern and Western European tradition appears rather pronounced and quite so without deriving its energy purely from a Catholic versus Orthodox conflict. Interesting and valuable discussions of this issue can be found in George Seferis, 'Dialogue on Poetry: What is meant by Hellenism?' in *On the Greek Style*, Translated by Rex Warner and T.D. Frangopoulos, (Boston: Little Brown & Company, 1966), 86-97; Nikos Kazantzakis, 'Ta Problemata tou Neoellenikou Politismou', in *Taxideuontas*, (Athens: Eleni Kazantzakis, 1969), 324-330.

63. These terms and expressions used specifically by Greek writers such as Moisiodax and Katartzes in the following century.

64. Cited in Konstantinos Paparregopoulos, *Historia tou Hellenikou Ethnous*, Volume 15, (Athens: Kaktos, 1993), 61. Kyrillos could at least take heart in noting that "these ignorant easterners are at least fortunate, for they don't know how catastrophic are the issues and disputes of these times."

65. Cited in Paparregopoulos, 126.

66. Dennis P. Hupchick, ed., *The Pen and the Sword, Studies in Bulgarian History by James F. Clark*, (Boulder: East European Monographs, 1988), 98.

67. Although it is true that non-Orthodox Venetians were permitted to attend the Flagginieo School, where Skouphos's text was taught. In this sense the later directors violated one of Thomas Flaggineis's original principles. (See Karathanases, *He Phlagineios schole tes Venetias*, 46-7) Unfortunately the records relating to the 'forestieri' as the Catholic students were called, do not provide a clear picture of the numbers enrolled. See Karathases, introduction to *Anthe Eulaveias*, k.

68. Skouphos, 'Texne Rhetorike,' 66.

69. Ibid, 65-66

70. Ibid, 66. Skouphos appears to suggest that it was the innate wisdom of the early Hellenic peoples that enabled them, first among others, to discern the truths of the Gospels and champion their dispersion.

71. Ibid, 118.

72. Ibid, 118.

73. Skouphos's intense patriotism might appear as a means to compensate emotionally and psychologically for the renunciation of his faith, the turn to Rome, which some Greeks held as the principle cause of their conquest by the Ottoman Turks. Accordingly, Catholic converts such as Skouphos would find themselves subject to the perception that their betrayal of the 'true faith' had brought the Empire to ruin; they were the guilty party, the ones most responsible for the sufferings of the Greek people. It is at least significant that

Skouphos does not identify the sins for which he concedes God had punished the Greeks, as Orthodox prelates were likely to do. Was the ardent national position taken by Skouphos an unconscious attempt to assuage such guilt or simply an act of social preservation, necessary to maintain his relationships to family and kin? These and other possible psychological motives for his actions will be discussed below.

74. Skouphos, if more were known about his life, would be an interesting subject for a Freudian study in 'sublimated' guilt. A guilt derived from his internalization of the at large assumption of 'union as destruction.' His psychological escape, as a convert to Catholicism, from the responsibility and thus the guilt for this catastrophe might be reflected in his personal and vehement appeal to God for the salvation of the race.

75. Skouphos, 'Pros ton logiotaton Parthenion ton Skouphon,' in *Patriotika kai Ethika*, 201-2.

76. Skouphos, 'Texne Rhetorike,' 118. These remarks are consonant with works from the early Christian period written by the 'Apologists' and 'Church Fathers' who first attempted to join the new faith with the Greco-Roman tradition. The Apologist Justin for example spoke of the Platonists and Stoics, as 'Christians before Christ.' See Nels M. Bailkey (ed.), *Readings in Ancient History*, (Lexington: D.C. Heath and Company, 1976), 430-31. See also Justin's comments on the 'Logos' in J.N.D. Kelly, *Early Christian Doctrines*, (London: Continuum, 2000), 96-98. It was perhaps on the basis of this tradition that Skouphos was emboldened to make the claim that the 'Hellenic Race,' singular in wisdom, was first to recognize the truths of the Christian faith.

77. Skouphos, 'Texne Rhetorike,' 119.

78. Nonetheless, the *Rhetorike*, like the texts of philosophy written by Korydalleus, does express the influence of a Western method and form, one that Skouphos had studied to emulate over the course of his Jesuit-led education in Rome. And yet he does not enumerate the modern European authors who may have influenced his thought, as later Greek scholars were prone to do (perhaps as a means to reinforce their work's legitimacy or prestige). This evolving pattern may serve to suggest the widening circle of Greek intellectual life over the ensuing century, its growing familiarity with the figures of the Enlightenment, and perhaps too an increasingly ardent desire to see themselves as a part of it.

79. Audale, *He Egkyklopaideia tou Ioannes Patousas*, 166. The 'homily' was itself a direct Western export to the East.

80. Theotokes's *Stoicheia tes Geographias* (1804) will be discussed in depth in later chapters.

81. This is at least the assumption of Tatakis. Editor's note, *Skouphos, Meniates, Voulgaris, Theotokes*, 52.

82. The hope for divine intervention will not disappear completely from Greek letters with the arrival of the Enlightenment as discussed in Chapter 4 below.

83. Stergelles, *Ta demosieumata ton Hellenon Spouaston tes Panepistimiou Padauas*, Ch 1. As the author notes the majority of the Greek students during the seventeenth century at the University were, as at the Flaggineio Schole, Cretans and Ionians. Ibid, 46. The writings of the Cretan Gerasimos Vlachos also belong in this category. For an excellent introduction to the life and work of this important figure see Basil Tatakis, *Gerasimos Vlachos, ho Kres*, (Venice: Library of the Hellenic Institute of Venice of Byzantine and post-Byzantine Studies, 1973).

84. Earlier Greek historians tend to reverse the emphasis, asking why the change in faith did not *diminish* the ethnic consciousness of the individuals involved. This is true of both Tatakis and Kairofelas.

85. Kairofelas, *Patriotika kai Ethika*, 12. Bessarion was from the same generation of late Byzantines that included Lascaris and Argyropoulos.

86. Konstantine Demaras, 'Eisagogika ste melete tes sylloges Anthe Eulaveias,'in *Mnemosynon Sophias Antoniade*, (Venice: Library of the Hellenic Institute of Venice of Byzantine and post-Byzantine Studies, 1974), 347-8.

87. See for example Voulgaris's 1771 translation and publication of Voltaire's appeal to Catherine II for Greece's liberation. Voulgaris, 'Ouoltairou Epistole pros ten Autokratorissan ton Rosson,' in Philippos E. Eliou (ed.), *Prosthekes sten Hellenike Vivliographia*, (Athens: Neohellenikes Erevnes, 1973), 303-308.

88. Elias Meniates, *Didachai*, 2 Volumes, edited by Anthimios Mazarakes, (Athens: Prometheus, 1925), II: 151-2. The Skouphos and Meniates texts are reproduced and discussed in Ch 4 below, along with another piece from the eighteenth century. For Skouphos's general influence on Meniates see also the following key works: K.G. Kasines, *He Rhetorike ton Didachon tou Meniate*, (Athens: Syllogos Pros Diadosin Ofelimon Vivlion, 1998) and Athanasios Papodopoulos, *Epidraseis tes Texne Rhetorikes tou R. Skouphos epi ton Didachon tou Elia Meniates*, (Athens: Keimena kai Meletai Neohellenikes Philologias, 1965).

89. Skouphos's *Rhetorike* was also dedicated to the Virgin, the greatest rhetorician of all, who, "with your virginal compassion (splagxna) composed the LOGON incarnate..." 'Texne Rhetorike,' 49. Note: 'splagxna' could also be translated literally as 'insides.'

90. Karathanases, editor's introduction, *Anthe Eulaveias*, le.

91. This was Demetrios Notaras, nephew of the Bishop of Jerusalem Chrysanthos Notaras. Notaras's *Eisagoge eis ta geographika kai sphairika* (1716) is analyzed in Chapter 5.

92. These latter show the direct influence of the 'Palatine Anthologia' of Lascaris that was taught at both Flagginieio and Padua. Karathanases, editor's introduction, *Anthe Eulaveias*, ls.

93. Demetrios Georgoulis, 'To the ever pious and brilliant holy teacher Ioannes Patousa, Headmaster of the Flaggineion Hellenomouseiou,' *Anthe Eulaveias*, 43

94. Fragkiskos Gerardos, 'To Greece,' *Anthe Eulaveias*, 30.

95. Ioannes Voulgaris, 'In Praise of Greece,' *Anthe Eulaveias*, 44.

96. See 'Eis ten metastasin tes Panagnou,' by Fragkiskos Kolombes for a typical image: the departing Virgin, sailing victoriously up to heaven, to the consternation and grief of the faithful below. *Anthe Eulaveias*, 21.

III. The Mature Enlightenment

> *Seeing that you selected me and judged me worthy and esteemed me (as you are men of experience) as a member of your company; this was incentive enough to move a young man who seeks to honor himself and his race (genos) ... These fine preludes gave me such hopes that I imagined I would do a business here as never a Greek (romios) before.*[1]

Adamantios Koraes wrote the words above in 1774 during a brief and not very successful interlude in his life as a Greek merchant in Amsterdam. In the long letter that follows, the twenty six year old Koraes tells his superiors of the many hardships he had suffered in his quest for fame and fortune and his final decision to leave their company. In this case his path to honor and recognition would have to take another course and fortunately for him, a young man of no small ambition, another existed. But had he succeeded from the first, Koraes might well have entered the ranks of those Greek merchants known to history not so much for their commercial exploits as for their collective acts of philanthropy, acts directed of course to the improvement of 'genos' and 'patrida.'

The part played by the merchants in the cultural revival of Greece was considerable, as it was these men, those who succeeded at least, who provided the financial resources for the creation of schools, the publication of books and all the other foundation-building tasks that the Neohellenic Enlightenment was to be raised upon. The merchant as benefactor, or as one logios proclaimed, 'father of the race,' was a common motif in eighteenth century Greek letters. He was a man of respect almost universally lauded by the logioi for the example of industry and competence he presented to the world, a counter to the image of Balkan torpor and degeneracy that was all too familiar. Here finally was something to be proud of. Perhaps ironically, few of the later logioi were more impressed by these figures than Koraes himself.[2]

The celebration of commerce held a pedigree of some vintage in the Neohellenic discourse. An early example was provided by Meletios Metros's *Geographia Palaia kai Nea* (1728), in which the author tended to associate the vitality of the West with the increase of its commerce and trades. The much later

Geographia Neoterike (1791) carried this assumption even farther.[3] As we will see below, it was not uncommon for the geographers Konstantas and Philippides to single out the great merchants of a particular locale, much as they would a Church father or man of letters, when digressing on the merits of its famous sons. Such works raise up before the reader the image of the merchant-hero, one who honored the race by his industry and devotion to its needs. Of course such highly celebrated men, founders of schools and patrons of learning, could be hard acts to follow.

And yet the mold had been cast in the figure of men like Ioannes Pringos (1725-1789) a famous Greek emboros (merchant) in Amsterdam. Here was the ideal model of the prosperous man of commerce turned benefactor, there for all to admire and emulate. As Koraes intimated above, he too sought through business to "honor himself and his race," and to acquire a share of the renown enjoyed by the great emboroi of these times. Of course, for every success there were bound to be a great many failures, and unlike Koraes, not all could atone for their defeats through a life in letters. The failure to meet the ideal of the merchant-benefactor that their society exalted added a special force of its own to the grievances of men already humbled by adversity. From the ranks of these discontents came a new generation of crusaders, even if it was not so clearly the fallen nation they sought principally to redeem. Such ambiguities are visible in the membership rituals of the Society of Friends, the secret organization that led the 1821 revolution. The devotional letters and oaths of the Society, in which the new members made fictional contributions to schools or printers, present the somewhat pathetic spectacle of men who could mimic only in words the great deeds of the merchant heroes they had aspired to become.

The public discourse over the national problem, as depicted in the image of the deprived and wretched 'ethnos,' acquired a greater figure in Greek society as the eighteenth century progressed. In its mature stage, located here in the middle and late decades of the eighteenth century, the Diaphotismos vaulted well beyond the confines of the logios's study. The widening social absorption and appreciation of the 'national problem' was one outcome of a general improvement in the spread of learning and commerce in Greece. The present and succeeding chapters will give special attention to those groups within Greek society that played significant roles in this process. One of these groups, as introduced above, was the rising merchant class. Another concerns a peculiar group of Balkan logioi, distinguished best of all by the figure of Iosepos Moisiodax, but including also men like Daniel of Moschopolis, Demetrios Darvares, and Kosmas ho

Aitolos. Intense advocates of Hellenic learning and enlightenment, these noteworthy men were yet unique for another intriguing quality: they were not Hellenes.

Before moving on to the writings of these latter scholars, we should consider some developments that were also serving to erode the influence of Venice in Greek intellectual history as the eighteenth century progressed. The commercial revival of Greece, as we will see, was one of the main factors behind this development. The other source of change in the geographical reorientation of Greek culture was the Phanariots, the great Greek families of Constantinople that succeeded in winning high places for themselves in the Ottoman state.

The Phanariots and Their World

A career in the Orthodox Church was the primary vehicle for obtaining a higher education for young Greeks over much of the Turkish era. These cleric-scholars, often the children of peasants who displayed from an early age an exceptional aptitude for learning are among the most fascinating figures in the history of modern Greek intellectual history. The Orthodox Church was largely composed of men from this class up to and including very often the Patriarch himself. However by the late decades of the seventeenth century and continuing through the eighteenth, the social backgrounds of Greek students and logioi became more diverse. These changes were reflected in the rise of the Phanariots.

In one of his autobiographical writings, the celebrated demotic poet Kaisarios Dapontes (1714-1784) described the new opportunities for learning and distinction presented to young Greeks of intellectual promise during the heyday of the Phanariots. He recalls below his coming to the 'City' as a secretary for one of these grandees:

> At sixteen or seventeen years of age,
> my father took me out of the schools.
> To the dragoman of the fleet he sent me to Constantine
> Ventoura, of Pariano that very famous one.
> And in January I arrived in the City,
> the thirtieth day of the month, receiving the honor,
> of seeing her for the first time and greeting her
> the Queen City, and to walk her streets...[4]

The rise of the Phanariots provided a new career path for bright and aspiring youth, who like Dapontes, were also increasingly more likely to come from lands outside the Venetian orbit.[5] From here it was on to the noble houses of Constantinople where the young scholar took a position as secretary or private teacher to an important family. The final step was a period of service in the Danubian Principalities where the Phanariots had established themselves as princes or Hospodars. This was the course followed by numerous young men, including Regas Velestinlis, over the century or so of Phanariot ascendance in Constantinople and the Principalities.

The Phanariots hold a controversial place in the historiography of the Greek Enlightenment and the rise of the nationalist movement. A wealthy elite who inhabited the 'lighthouse'[6] neighborhood of Constantinople, they have been judged as 'anti-national' or even reactionary figures by some prominent historians, and were among the groups condemned by the anonymous author of the *Hellenike Nomarchia.*[7] Though not the descendants of Byzantine nobles they were prone to portray themselves as, the Phanariots nonetheless very self-consciously played the role of 'cultural custodians' in Greek society, and are thus an intriguing subject for study within the Neohellenic Enlightenment.

The Phanariots had managed to rise to the highest rungs of power in Constantinople by means of their wealth and educations. Like other ethnic groups within the Empire, such as the Jews or Armenians, the Greeks ventured into fields such as trade or finance which Muslims were discouraged from practicing. This appears to have been the route taken by the early founders of the great Phanariot families. In time this rising 'moneyed nobility' as Runciman calls them, migrated to the lighthouse district of Constantinople, the Phanar, in order to be closer to that major center of influence in the Ottoman world: the Orthodox Church. Having infiltrated the Patriarchate, the Phanariots looked ultimately to new conquests within the Ottoman state itself. Medical studies in the West served as the typical agency here, and it is no coincidence that the first Grand Dragoman or official interpreter of the Porte, Panayioti Nikosios (1613-1673), was formerly the Sultan's personal physician.[8] Nikousios was succeeded by Alexander Mavrocordatos (1641-1709), another Padua educated doctor, who served the Sultanate for nearly forty years.[9] Beyond medicine, the Phanariots offered other services which the Sultans found increasingly valuable. Their knowledge of European mores and languages was enormously influential, as the Porte had entered a new era in its dealings with the West. By the close of the seventeenth century Ottoman expansion in Europe had come to an end; on the defensive from this point forward, the Empire found itself increasingly dependent on negotiation and diplomacy.[10]

The final milestone in the Phanariot conquest of power in the Ottoman state occurred in 1711, when the first Phanariot was appointed Hospodar or prince of the Danubian Principalites of Wallachia and Moldavia.[11] These parts of the Empire had been ruled in the preceding centuries by local Danubian princes. The Principalities had already become an object of Phanariot attention in these earlier times because of their distance from Constantinople; here the prospering Phanariots could acquire land and otherwise conceal their wealth from the scrutiny of Ottoman overlords. In time they established themselves among the elite houses of these provinces. It was thus to the Phanariots that the Sultans ultimately turned after suffering a series of separatist revolts from the local nobility.[12]

Like the Church, the Phanariots occupied a unique position in the Greek world.[13] As holders of wealth, education, and even state power, it is not surprising that from their ranks should come important logioi such as Alexander Mavrokordatos (1754-1819) and Demetrios Katartzes (1720-1807). The determined efforts of the Phanariots to 'Hellenize' Wallachia and Moldovia, revealed as well their aggressive chauvinism. It was on account of these activities, and the often rapacious efforts to enrich themselves at the expense of the inhabitants of the Principalities, that the revolutionary designs of the Philike Etairia met with little support among the local peoples.[14]

Their excesses notwithstanding, the Phanariot courts did furnish the resources and setting for a major surge in Greek intellectual activity. The pronounced westward looking posture of this activity, as amply demonstrated by the figure of Demetrios Katartzes, is quite significant.[15] In a typical passage from his 'Logos protreptikos' (Word of Exhortation) which includes another of those ubiquitous confessions of cultural decline, Katartzes hails the benefits to be won from Western learning: "There is no need here to say again any more about our ills, and in what ocean of absurdity we sail," Katartzes urged his compatriots, "but to consider well how to undo them and how to bring about to our Greek nation (ethnos) the education and learning of Europe."[16] And yet Katartzes's writings also contain many revealing glimpses of the Phanariot predicament: his conflicting loyalties to nation, class, and empire. "I confess," he once wrote, "that at this time, we are not a nation that in truth forms a state, but we are subject to a greater one. For this, and taking the definition of politics given by Aristotle, some Franks scorn us that we don't have a fatherland (patrida); but this is not the way it is..."[17] In any case, he countered, through Orthodox belief the Greeks were joined in a community that was far superior to any mere political union. Nor had they to submit to that obscene logic which demanded loyalty to the state over church and family. He also hastened to add that some Greeks did fill political roles within the Empire and many had even acquired the honor of going about in the dress and medals of Ottoman elites.[18]

Over the course of the eighteenth century Bucharest and Jassy became centers of Enlightenment that attracted the most significant intellectuals of the Greek world. Both cities became the home of important academies.[19] From Constantinople it was to the Principalities where Dapontes continued his career and where his life proceeded to take some interesting turns.[20] Regas Velestinlis would follow a similar path, from village school to Constantinople, and on to Bucharest. However, unlike Dapontes, Regas was drawn into the even wider world of intellectual experience offered by Vienna. As a final mark of the new geographical orientation of Greek learning, Vienna would ultimately become the 'school of the West' for later generations of logioi, supplanting Venice in this role. It was in Vienna that the Bucharest intellectuals found access to the latest developments in European culture and published many of their own works. It was here too that the first Neohellenic literary journals, *Hellenikos Telegraphos* and *Hermes ho Logios*, made their appearance.

Moisiodax and the National Problem

The list of men who came through the new academies of Bucharest and Jassy would include virtually all the chief luminaries of the later Neohellenic Enlightenment. Certainly one of the most influential and intriguing of these was Iosepos Moisiodax (1725 -?1800).[21] An enigmatic and even sympathetic figure, Moisiodax authored few works but ones which very often contain subtle examinations of the myriad social, political and intellectual dilemmas of contemporary Greek life. These dilemmas included most notably the highly contested language debate or 'zetema.' Moisiodax's intellectual indepen-dence and his ability to take bold positions on such issues, are further elements of his novel standing among the logioi of his times. These features of his work and personality are considered below within the context of his unique position as a non-Hellene in the Neohellenic Enlightenment. Moisiodax's own 'predicament', in this case, can offer special insights into the origin and character of Greek nationalism over these years.

The place of Moisiodax's birth, like his death, is not precisely known. However his name indicates that he was from Southeast Romania and that he was a 'Moesiodacian,' or, from the Greek, a 'lower Dacian.'[22] Moisiodax's name and ethnic origin introduces the most remarkable and yet least understood element of his story: this fiery and determined advocate of the Hellenic renaissance was not himself a member of the 'race' he tirelessly championed.[23] Moisiodax's self-conscious effort to represent himself as a Greek, self-conscious in no small part for the skepticism that his re-invention evinced from his critics, appears as another case of the interplay of identity and status that we have been dealing with throughout. In Skouphos we encountered an extreme cultural self-consciousness consistent with an older discourse of a nation fallen from glory. This uncomfortable awareness of the national problem, exacerbated by life in 'foreign parts,' could be the source, alternatively, of melancholy ruminations or stormy calls to action, the experience of this discomfort driving each according to his temperament to intense patriotism, or, like the merchants and students vilified in the *Nomarchia,* the impulse to shed one's 'dog collar' and merge into the surrounding culture. When playing the part of the Greek logios, it was the former of these impulses that Moisiodax followed in his writings—but this, of course, only after he had first made a rather thorough identity reorientation of his own.

Although Moisiodax's early years are not well documented, his *Apologia* does present a summary of his later life and educational background. It is here where we learn of his studies in Thessalonike, Smyrna and ultimately the Athonian Academy, where in 1753 he first encountered the 'great man' of Greek letters Eugenios Voulgaris (1716-1806).[24] By the time of his first visit to Venice in 1759 Moisiodax had been made a deacon in the Orthodox Church. His first book *Ethike Philosophia* or 'Moral Philosophy,' a translation of a work by the Italian historian and philosopher Ludovico Muratori,[25] was published two years later. The preface to this work, which Kitromilides tells us was sold through a subscription drive mainly supported by Greek diaspora merchants,[26] contains one of Moisiodax's earliest and most explicit accounts of the 'national problem.' Indeed the choice of subject matter is our first indication of the translator's perspective on the condition and needs of Greek society. The preface to the *Philosophia* also indicates the growing taste for empiricism that contemporary Greek logioi often exhibited. The works of Bacon, Newton, or Harvey, whether studied abroad, or in the case of Locke's famous *Essay Concerning Human Understanding* in Greece itself, represented the prime texts in this discourse.[27] Nonetheless, the growth of empirical philosophy had the effect of introducing new divisions within the Greek intelligentsia, most of whom of course, belonged to the Orthodox Church. The official Church tended to look with disapproval upon these trends and by the eighteenth century had engaged itself in the work of policing them. This was conducted through the establishment of ecclesiastical printing presses and ensuing publications of high ranking officials. Of the latter, the pamphlet 'Fatherly Teachings' of 1798 is one well known example, wherein the narrator uttered the famous retort that "God raised up out of nothing this mighty empire of the Ottomans" to guard the Orthodox faithful from the western heretics.[28] Another famous example of this genre of literature was Gregory's Patriarchal Encyclical of 1819.[29]

Beginning with his *Ethike Philosophia*, Moisiodax carried the discourse of the 'fallen nation' to an extreme of candor that may well have unsettled logioi of earlier generations. Indeed Moisiodax's writings contain some of the boldest statements of this theme in all of Neohellenic Enlightenment literature. We see this in the preface of the *Philosophia* where Moisiodax established himself at once as a champion of the race and its struggle for rejuvenation and respect. Like other logioi past and present, he begins his tale of Greece's fall from grace with a glowing account of the intellectual and cultural vitality of classical times. Moisiodax's references to 'freedom' and 'captivity' in the prologue strike a political note that are also worthy of special notice:

> When Greece lived with freedom and autonomy, when nourished by the love of political virtue... then did flourish not only the public arts, which strengthen states, not only the few, as established by laymen, but moreover all, or virtually all the kinds of learning.

Like Skouphos before him, Moisiodax rattles off the litany of "skilled statesmen, the glorious generals, the ingenious architects, dextrous sculptors, inspired artists, then also the physiologists, mathematicians, philosophers, orators, historians and simply all the remaining classifications of genius." Greece then resembled a "fertile earth," he continues in a rush of metaphors, "bursting with all kinds and noble fruits or like a flowing spring that with waters of golden ethics and education nourished, I say, not only her own plants but all the others that had vital sap..." And yet this dazzling civilization was poisoned by one great flaw. Like those before and after him, Moisiodax associates Greece's fall from grace with her tendency toward divisiveness, and thus "forged with envy," and weakened by "civil wars" Greece was ultimately "compelled to put her neck into the yoke of the Romans."[30]

What Moisiodax calls 'zelofthonia,' acute envy—variously termed by other authors such as Koraes and Philippides as 'stasis' or 'dixonoia'—is frequently cited as the telltale flaw that rendered the Hellenes vulnerable to the depredations of other peoples. It was to 'discord' too that much earlier logioi such as Meniates and Meletios Metros were drawn when speaking of the fall of classical civilization. Nonetheless, out of the Roman conquest a new empire emerged, the Byzantine, to restore Greece's status in the world. Unfortunately it too was destined to fall, an event that ushered in the dark ages of her recent history. Whether, Moisiodax writes, "for the many sins of its people, or the poor administration of the kings of Constantinople," the "barbarous nations," whom he defines variously as "Huns, Goths, Bulgarians, Scythians, Saracens and Turks," grew in strength. Upon contact with such "deadly marauders" the last vestiges of Greek civilization were smothered out of existence, replaced by "oppression" and "malignance" until "nothing else remained for the poor Muses but a den of thieves." Moisiodax summarizes the ensuing desolation in terms that appear to offer little hope for a reprieve:

> And behold the entire scene in disorder! Behold the stage upset, the state swept away, nobility extinguished, genius banished, and ignorance now instead to reign, crudeness, misery, in brief, everywhere misfortune. And behold the results this deplorable wretchedness has brought about. Deprived are the descendants of those remarkable Hellenes of autonomy and burdened to provide not only for the means of life, but similarly the tax of captivity, nothing could they take care for, other than to satisfy these two needs, causing them to neglect their Church, overlook the Gospels, teachers, lessons, books, schools, all scorned and so much so that in a little time they found themselves, priests, citizens, nobles, all reduced, all fallen into primitiveness.[31]

The prologue therefore to the *Ethike Philosophia* provides a revealing glimpse of the logios-benefactor at work. Here as in most other 'improving texts' the author begins with a short recantation of the nation's decline and present misery before moving on to its remedy. Moisiodax takes up this task with a characteristic spirit, but this is not all. More directly than almost any of his predecessors, contemporaries or successors, Moisiodax acknowledges the national self-consciousness that lay just below the surface of this discourse. "Europe deplores Greece ...." he declares at one point later in the prologue, a fact that the logioi were well acquainted with though often unable to put down so explicitly in print. Nor was it for Mosiodax to retreat from the distress created by this awareness. His manner is always defiant, seeking nothing less than to regenerate the race and restore its position on the world stage. "Alas," he writes in a typically revealing passage from the preface of his *Ethike Philosophia*, "Greece must awaken and welcome again its fervent zeal, its vigorous striving for perfection, she must bear in mind the renown of antiquity, in a word she must represent to the world, and this at least if nothing else, that it is inhabited yet by a

Greek."[32]

The *Ethike Philosophia* presents itself as an instrument of improvement very much in the spirit of Skouphos's *Texne Rhetorike*. Both books, though separated in time by almost one hundred years, reflect an urgent desire to rehabilitate the 'race' and the image that it projected in the world. We see also that Moisiodax's work contains some important new elements that mark it off as a true example of the Diaphotismos. Like other works of its kind from the eighteenth century, Moisiodax's *Ethike Philosphia* is a translation of a European text, a fact that demonstrates the power of that larger phenomenon, the Enlightenment itself, and the influence it had come to exert on intellectual life in the Balkans. But even more than this, it is Moisiodax's willingness to go *outside* the Greek tradition of letters, ancient and Christian, to seek inspiration for the improvement of the race that distinguishes his writing from Skouphos.

As discussed above, Skouphos manifested a cultural self-consciousness, despair and defensiveness in the *Rhetorike* that took refuge in the formidable redoubt of the Hellenic past. His lessons would seek to renew and disseminate not only the rhetorical tradition but even the vitality of spirit that had distinguished earlier generations of the race; and he certainly did not waste any opportunities this subject afforded him to wax dreamily on the hallowed luminaries of the golden age. In the *Philosophia* of Moisiodax, the statement and mediation of the national problem does not lead the author down a similar path. True, Moisiodax would ask his readers to "bear in mind the renown of antiquity," but ultimately he introduces a mandate for cultural renewal that looks beyond the Hellenic tradition, fixes on the modern, and even assumes, most radically of all, that modern learning had surpassed the ancient.[33] It is worth asking, as we consider the novelty of some of Moisiodax's positions, whether the 'outsider' element of his personality contributed to the candor with which he was able to challenge traditional views, and the solutions that he, without the cost to conscience another might suffer, was able to advocate.

In this regard there were three ideological principles of Moisiodax's work that were most revealing of his intellectual independence. The first is that he was a tireless advocate of the modern. One important manifestation of this principle is the audacity with which he challenged, of all things, the supremacy of antiquity. In this way Moisiodax represents one of the first and most direct critics of what has sometimes been called 'progonoplexeia' by modern observers of Greek life: the unique malaise of 'ancestor-fixation,' as clearly witnessed in the bombast of Skouphos.[34] Moisiodax's critique of this 'defect' is set down quite plainly and memorably in the Prologue to his *Philosophia*:

> Today Greece nourishes and nurses two defects the most improper to her glory. She is conquered like a country by the esteem and by the negligence of antiquity. Her first generated that thriving prejudice that all that the ancients produced or cultivated was great and perfect, and the second brought about the scarcity, or veritably the absence of most of the ancient writers. It doesn't suffice. The prejudice later raised an implacable hatred against everything that is modern, and the scarcity stripped her of nearly all the most capital works of the ancients.[35]

In the passage above Moisiodax begins by condemning the prejudice that prevented the Greeks from both taking adequate stock of their problems and enjoying the benefits of European learning. But this is only the prelude to a more radical proposition. As we see below, Moisiodax proceeds to rank the modern *over* the ancient. The author's judgment in this case was heavily influenced by his admiration of the scientific breakthroughs of recent times, as the following passage indicates:

> The Europe of today, through its sound administration and the knowledge loving inclination of the noblemen of its lands, exceeds in wisdom ancient Greece. She is inundated with writings and texts, such that neither the Academy, the Lyceum, the Stoa, could similarly boast of. She has facilitated and discovered more sciences, a thing that the Ancient, with all its incomparable intelligence, and for various circumstances that for the moment I won't mention, she neither managed to accomplish. She, in short, is flooded with distinguished Academies, every one of which could be judged as the most dignified Elikon of the Muses.

According to Moisiodax, the modern Greek must reconcile himself to these developments, realizing that "prudence demands that advantage should always and from everywhere be sought and gathered." The miserable plight of the nation required that "good examples" not be scorned "on account of various dishonorable feelings that are raised up from a mean small-mindedness.[36]

Moisiodax certainly held the ancients in high regard, however his insistence that Europe had exceeded the classical world in wisdom and that the Greeks must free themselves of their psychic dependence on the past, distinguishes him as a unique voice.

Moisiodax was also clearly aware, as the numerous expressions of conciliation throughout the text demonstrate, that such bold positions as these had the power to offend. As we have noted above, the perspective of the Greek world on the West contained the assumption or acknowledgment of its power and superiority. This tradition extended back to the days of Byzantium. Nonetheless it was another step entirely to reduce the stature of the ancients, this final refuge for a fallen people and a steadying element in their national ethos. Indeed, the shame and wounded 'philotimia' (self-respect) of the modern Greek as he imagined himself under the reproachful gaze of his illustrious ancestors, was one of the rallying fixtures of pre-revolutionary literature. This acute sense of intimidation and inadequacy—and consequently, the call to duty—is expressed in the melancholy lines of the 'Passage to Thermopylae' by the poet and physician Giorgios Sakellarios (1767-1838). There, on the final resting place of Leonidas and his gallant Spartan 'equals,' the poet finds himself suddenly stricken by a voice from the past:

> "You there, man!" I hear it say completely subconsciously.
> "You don't realize the ground, the earth you are walking on?"
> "And yet you are, you say, a Hellene, and with words glorify us,
> "But with your actions, how much you scorn us!"[37]

In the most severe forms of progonoplexeia, as above, the modern Greek experienced the nation's torpor, ignorance and ill repute as an act of defamation against his mighty ancestors. In its milder forms, as we have seen in the *Anthe Eulaveias*, the ancient heritage offered a mystical and unvarnished refuge from reality. Certainly both of these reactions take their inspiration from a highly romanticized imagination of a faultless and ideal world. It was characteristically the glorious, larger than life heroes of ancient Hellas and the Church that Skouphos had marshaled onto the page to bludgeon into silence the imaginary critics of contemporary Greek society. He, like the other Greek logioi, was acutely aware of Greece's decline and Europe's ascendance. And even if the latter's greatness could be heralded, as it increasingly was as the eighteenth century progressed, it was another thing entirely to deprive an already depleted race of its one great possession. Certainly Moisiodax emphasized the glory of the ancients in his works, however it is true that he does not express the kind of intense relation to this heritage that we find in men like Skouphos, Sakellarios or even Koraes, who was also given to rhetoric of this kind.[38] Moisiodax's distance from the ancients, in relation to his contemporaries, is a key and distinctive aspect of his teaching and as a consequence a very sensitive one. One gains an insight to the forces confronting him from the fine balancing act that he attempts to perform in the *Philosophia*, as he seeks to wean his audience from its old dependencies without harming too badly the ego or provoking an outright rejection. "Finally I say to all, small and large," Moisiodax reminds his audience, "to recall the love of learning of the ancients." Emulating the inquisitive spirit of their ancestors, modern Greeks "must become accepting and open to the gifts of Europe." Europe after all seeks to do good by the Greeks for "she is grateful." Nor does she "hide at all the lights she received from Greece, nor the duty she has to her." Note finally the author's comments on the peculiar effect Europe's beneficence is deemed to have on the alleviation of Greece's sufferings:

> She (Europe) is ready to bring her up to date with all the kinds of learning. Rhetoricians, historians, dialecticians, naturalists, metaphysicians, moralists, all, all desire to lend their efforts. These are sufficient to welcome again the ancient brightness, and certainly also to lighten the weight of tyranny. For consider, isn't the roughness of a master lightened (even the most severe and savage) more by the educated than the ignorant slave?

This section of the prologue closes with another call to action, climaxing with Moisiodax's bold statement that "all of Europe deplores Greece and deems it miserable not so much for its captivity as for its ignorance..." Such infamy, Moisiodax grumbles, is not only an unbearable stigma, but a bitterly ironic twist of history. Imagine such a state of affairs, he glumly observes, in which:

> All the European nations have become enlightened and wise and civilized, many of which, or certainly all, the Hellenes as much as the Romans called barbarians... And imagine, should it be that we, the descendants of the remarkable Hellenes, who were the first teachers of decency and wisdom, alone consent to the poverty of learning, alone endure the fog of ignorance over the clarity of knowledge?[39]

Moisiodax encourages the Greeks to adopt European methods and free themselves from the scholastic 'punctiliousness' and slavish worship of the ancients that had carried them to the point of profitless idolatry. To imitate Europe means to think freely and borrow freely, emulating here the example of the "good honeybee"—a popular symbol in Greek culture of diligence and civic duty—that "harvests the beneficial honey"wherever it is found.[40] He describes how in Europe all learn from each other without inhibition or prejudice, "Britons borrow from Gauls (French), Gauls from Italians, Italians from Batavians, Batavians from Germans, Germans from Russians, etc." Finally, Moisiodax concludes this section with a dramatic declaration that he will reprise in later publications: "Greece needs, it needs Europe. Since today the one is inundated and the other is deprived of the significant lights of learning."[41]

Moisiodax has placed before himself a formidable task. He is not simply a disseminator of improving works, or even another Skouphos, who through force of rhetoric would rally the race off the 'dung-hill' of poverty and despair. Moisiodax performs instead an act of social psychology on his subject. A Greece "deprived" and "deemed wretched" he shows, falls that much more easily into its old dependencies and addictions. Alongside her, meanwhile, strides Europe, unencumbered by such burdens, and ever gathering to her new honors and accolades.

Finally, though a man of the Church, Moisiodax gives only lip service to the old mantra that Greece's troubles were owing to her sins, most of all her late Byzantine flirtation with unification. This theme had tremendous staying power in Greek history. Nonetheless there is cause to argue that there had long existed the assumption that certain national problems such as illiteracy, ignorance, infamy, etc, could be ameliorated by human effort. Skouphos's *Rhetorike* contains for example a strenuous statement of sin and supplication, however the intent of his work was to teach skills conducive to self-improvement. In Moisiodax the emphasis on enlightenment as a means to social progress is not intimated but quite explicit; meanwhile the role of 'sin' in the destitution and destruction of the race is noted with a few obligatory and superfluous words.[42]

A second aspect of Moisiodax's modernism or even 'Westernism' is his eager acceptance of the scientific revolution. As we have seen above, it was this area of thought that Moisiodax judged to be the great contribution of modern times. His excitement with the prospects for even greater advances influenced his ideas for educational reform, and it is here where Moisiodax's views clashed with those of his former teacher Voulgaris.[43] Moisiodax's openness to scientific enquiry is readily manifest in his advocation of positions that were resisted by most of his peers in the East. The most obvious of these was his view on Newtonian astronomy. These views, which were subtly endorsed by Moisiodax in his *Theoria tes Geographias* (1781), form a major departure from the Greek tradition, represented by men like Notaras, whose geographical works rejected the 'modern' positions.[44]

A final distinction of Moisiodax's work was his promotion of the demotic as the language 'instrument.' This too may have been a consequence of his modernism, as he never tired of remarking how Europe was moving in this direction.[45] Of course, this view of language was probably another outcome of his more moderate position on antiquity; the language debate for Moisiodax resembled another case of a culture afflicted by progonoplexeia. In this and other issues confronting Greek society he could see things and write about them in ways that were often beyond the grasp of 'native' Greeks; an outcome which leads one to speculate whether he experienced this society in a different manner, perhaps with a different consciousness. Moisiodax's works therefore have a character of objective scrutiny and candor that are closer to the critique one would encounter from a European observer.

Moisiodax made his language principles clear in his prologue to the *Ethike Philosophia*, and again in both the *Apologia* and *Geographia*. He confessed in the earliest work that there were some deficiencies in the modern language but that these were a product of its "neglect or defamation."[46] He preferred to emphasize the connections between the two idioms. If the modern lacked the richness of the ancient, then this could be repaired by incorporating older words into the common dialect.[47] In this way Moisiodax foresaw a kind of steady rehabilitation of the language, one he intended to encourage by advising "Greek preachers when they teach" and the "learned when they discourse," to employ a high form of the common speech, "something higher than the banal." He makes furthermore the revealing observation that "this is what the Europeans do without the higher-ups suffering any harm to their status. In this manner little by little the Hellenic words will be synthesized, and in addition be facilitated the comprehension of the entire Hellenic language."[48]

The Language 'Zetema' and the Discourse of Self-Contempt

Moisiodax's view of the language question was not unique to himself. There were other champions of the demotic, of whom Skouphos and Meniates were important forerunners, in addition to contemporary writers such as Demetrios Katartzes, Athanasios Xristopoulos (1772-1847), and of course the geographers Konstantas and Philippides. The existence of a high and low method of Greek literary discourse also had a very old vintage and was early recognizable in the debate over the publication of the New Testament.[49] The logioi of succeeding centuries had the option of using either the ancient or the modern idiom in their works and there are many examples where a writer set down his work in the 'aplos' or simple dialect in order to broaden its diffusion.[50] We have seen examples above in the case of the *Anthe Eulaveias*, which featured both older and contemporary Hellenic forms in addition to Latin and Italian.[51] Skouphos's *Texne Rhetorike*, also discussed in detail above, was written in a kind of high demotic as a means to extend its circulation and utility, in the same manner that Notaras and Meletios produced their early geographies.[52]

The discussion of Moisiodax's views on language and the criticism they engendered broaches one of the most important subjects of the Neohellenic Enlightenment, the language 'zetema' or question. Opponents of Moisiodax tended to employ a characteristic and revealing term when dismissing the demotic tongue. We find it throughout one of the most significant and influential texts of the pre-revolutionary era, the *Melete tes Koines Hellenikes Dialektou* (1818) of Panayiotes Kodrikas (1762-1827).[53] In the *Melete*, a polemical work of considerable length, Kodrikas often refers to the common language as the 'xydaika.' It is in the employment of this term, and the imagery surrounding it, that the language debate reveals itself as one of the most spectacular examples of the often fierce Neohellenic self-critique.

'Xydaika' is a difficult term to precisely define. Its closest Western counterpart might be the French 'vulgare.' However in the Greek, xydaika, the language spoken by xydaioi, has a much more negative connotation. It describes something 'common,' but very likely also 'contemptible' or 'detestable.' In its social context it refers to the 'mob,' and this in its basest meaning. On the other end of the language spectrum of course was the 'archaica,' the classical idiom, or the language associated with Greece's ancient greatness.[54] And thus the language 'zetema,' which was concerned with picking the 'language instrument' through which the work of enlightenment should be conducted, came to be clouded with many other sociological and psychological factors. These included the not inconsiderable question, given the national self-consciousness that many of the antagonists felt, of which language would not only best reform the race, but represent it.

Some logioi such as Kodrikas and Doukas experienced a hyper-sensitivity to the xydaica as witnessed in their polemics against its elevation to the status of the national language. It is noteworthy that Moisiodax however did not. Nor was this aversion felt by the other non-Hellenic figures considered in this section, such as Kosmas ho Aitolos or Demetrios Darvares. However for those seeking a 'pure' language to build the Hellenic revival upon, the demotic idiom, also called the 'romaica,' could not suffice. The common language as spoken in the villages of Greece was an indifferent entity, a hybrid idiom cobbled together from various other tongues. Kodrikas describes how this situation came about, articulating a rather dim view of the 'romaica' shared by many purists. The author's discussion of European opinion in this passage is quite noteworthy as well, and exhibits another indication of the national self-consciousness of the writer. Kodrikas may not see the issue solely through the eyes of world opinion, however it is a factor that exerts some influence on his consciousness and positions:

> The successive contacts with the barbarians and the invasions of the Hagarenes (Turks) served to transform the shape of the common speech of the people, and so was developed a new Demotic Dialect, which formed differently by place, and with foreign words and xydaika phrases mixed together differently in every place, and by every order spoken and written. This newer Demotic Dialect we on the one hand call the simple Romaic, and the Western European Hellenists **grec moderne**, or later **grec vulgare**, or indifferently they call it Xydaian Greek. However this duality of name is not for us a matter of indifference.[55]

And yet it was to Moisiodax. For him it was the speech of the 'laos' (people) and thus the instrument best placed to carry out a program of enlightenment.[56] Moisiodax's emphasis on utility, the same position taken though for somewhat different purposes later by Kosmas and Darvares, contrasts with Kodrikas, or what has been called the conservative faction.[57] For Moisiodax it was the common language, for Kodrikas the language of the mob, a tangible symbol of the decline of the race and therefore a chief cause of the contempt engendered by Greece's decay, a contempt felt especially by the ex-patriot logioi who circulated within these societies.[58] One can imagine the prideful Kodrikas cringing at the words of the English traveler William Martin-Leake as he described the condition and mores of the demotic speech: "The modern dialect of the Greeks," wrote Leake, who would certainly characterize himself as a philhellene, "bears the same comparison with its parent language, as the poverty and debasement of the present generation to the refinement and opulence of their ancestors."[59] Or again, later in the book, when he notes: "In the corrupted dialect of an ancient language, written in the same character, but deprived of its refinements of sound and flexion, and spoken by an ignorant people, it is natural to expect a great uncertainty in the rules of orthography."[60] It may not have been much consolation to the Greeks that their Balkan neighbors were prone to be the recipients of even more dismissive rhetoric, if they were spoken of at all.[61]

Moisiodax could articulate the existence of this contempt more directly than most; similarly, his responses to the problem were typically less defensive. These observations lead one to ask whether he therefore felt this 'contempt' as deeply as others, realizing that there were matters, of course, that he too was hesitant to speak of. This was most true in the case of his ethnic background, a subject on which Moisiodax remained studiously and frustratingly silent throughout his life, despite the questions his identity aroused from contemporaries.[62]

If mostly silent about his own deeper doubts and insecurities, Moisiodax spoke plainly nonetheless of how Greece was perceived in the world and what could be done about it. His approach was straightforward and utilitarian, shorn of the bitterness and discomfort that weighted down some of his contemporaries or influenced them into positions that had not always strictly to do with enlightenment. He made a simple arithmetic of people, language, and education when addressing the problem. However simple arithmetic could not suffice for everyone. In this regard Kodrikas, who refused to see the language question in purely utilitarian terms, presents us with another revealing and sharp contrast: "Everybody has their prejudice in this world," Kodrikas asserted, "and I have my own too. I believe that a national polity is made happy when, according to the Divine Plato, the Archons philosophize, and the Philosophers are Archons; and perfectly unhappy the Nation where the Philosophers are xydaioi, or the xydaioi philosophize."[63]

As these examples attest, language held a special place in the preoccupation with worth and status that was such a pervasive fixture of Greek Enlightenment intellectual culture. Certainly it is the language question, of all the subjects that emerged to attract the attention of eighteenth and nineteenth century Greek thinkers, that takes special precedence. It is also one that will have considerable bearing on the future of Greek culture. The language question reflects too, and reflects it in a dimension more visible than most, the self-conscious preoccupation with national status we have noted throughout, without which the Neohellenic Enlightenment would be lacking one of its great motivations.

"Our language is melodic and poetic, so all the foreign peoples confess," wrote the authors of the *Geographia Neoterike* in defense of the demotic, "we however don't know it." Endorsing a position much in line with Moisiodax, they indicate how the zetema had become entangled in issues of cultural inadequacy and progonoplexeia, or the sharp reaction felt by some logioi to the poor figure that modern Greek (and the Greeks themselves) cut in the world. "It appears that as a nation," they observed, "we are like an aged man and suffer from things that age brings, afflictions of the eyes wherein we don't see things nearby and recognize the treasure we have..." Instead, embarrassed by the awful condition and infamy of the race, the Greeks "gaze off in the distance to the verses of the ancient Greeks, the Italians and the Franks, not realizing that the Italian and Frankish verse is not comparable to ours..." The geographers close their critique with expressive lines that tie together so many salient themes of Neohellenic discourse:

> When will we free ourselves from this geriatric anesthesia, when will we throw off these old wings and become young again. The administration doesn't impede us at all in this, we ourselves with our ignorance and our ancestral inheritance, discord, are the cause of our misfortunes. Someday learning will enable us to escape our ruinous decline, showing us many examples from our ancestors of whom wickedness rendered all into dissension, however as long as we despise our language, so do we wish to remain ignorant and wretched and a prey and pastureland for others.[64]

The fact that there were a number of forms of Greek in existence served unfortunately to complicate the disputes that Konstantas and Philippides allude to above. In addition to the vernacular and the ancient language there was yet another language, the 'koine' or New Testament Greek, which was preserved as the language of the Church. A new species of Greek was added in the eighteenth century with the emergence of 'katharevousa' or purified Greek. This latest innovation was the work of intellectuals, Koraes foremost, who wished to purge the vernacular of 'barbarisms': words and foreign elements that had been acquired from Turkish, Slavic or Italian. Moisiodax bears a certain relation to the katharevousists, though these later men carried the idea much farther than he appeared to advocate in his writings.[65]

Nonetheless, the purifiers attempted to reform the modern language by continuing down the path of using the ancient language as a template. Thus the modern word for fish, 'psari,' became 'psarion,' a new ending based on forms of syntax used by ancient writers. The method was succinctly explained by Anthimios Gazes in the first edition of the katharevousist journal *Hermes ho Logios* (the Learned Hermes). The intent of the journal, he wrote, was to "provide news of philology, relating chiefly to the knowledge of science and learning; to the study of the Greek language; to the similarity of phrasings and idioms of the modern with the ancient language; and in the purifying of the modern."[66] Of course, *Hermes ho Logios* was not the final word on the purifying of the language, as this was a highly subjective kind of work. Once the innovation was introduced, divergent methods emerged, as Kodrikas bitterly observed, and so there was no single form of Katharevousa in currency.

As the zetema matured, all of the disputes above increased in magnitude. Factions appeared, complete with their own organs or journals.[67] The rhetoric of the debate intensified as well. Proponents of katharevousa and archaica became especially hostile and there were even incidents of violence. Neophytos Doukas (1760-1845), a prominent cleric and archaist, was brutally attacked one Sunday morning on his way to church and nearly killed. As it was, the fifty-five year old Doukas required almost three years to recover from his injuries.[68] The incident occurred in Bucharest which had become at that time a center of the katharevousist camp. A measure of revenge was exacted by the archaists in the form of the satire '*Korakistika, or the correction of the Romaic Tongue; a play in three acts*,' by the archaist intellectual Iakovos Rizos Neroulos (1778-1850).[69] In the play, written in 1814, it is the language innovator Sotiros ('saviour') who is this time on the receiving end of a severe beating, administered by a rude mob of his former acolytes.[70]

The modern Greek philologist Konstantine Demaras argued once that the language question grew out of the classical revival of the eighteenth century. Western classicism, Demaras suggests, had an important influence on "the young (Greek) national consciousness of these years .... closely bound with the view of the greatness of ancient Greece, as well as the French revolutionary excitement."[71] The latter event was replete with exuberant expressions of neo-classicism including the revival of ancient names and even religious practices. All of this "had its correlative," Demaras continues, "in the classical instruction of the time, which taught that it was possible to approach the classical original through the path of imitation. From such a view to the conviction that with the imitation of the ancient language we can approach the glory of ancient letters, the distance, isn't great..."[72]

True enough, however Demaras could have more fully emphasized the socio-psychological significance of these cultural developments. The turn to classicism within Neohellenic culture itself reveals especially well the sense of inadequacy felt by modern Greeks. It expresses furthermore the remarkable degree to which the modern Greeks judged themselves through the eyes of their Western beholders, and the degree to which they may have sought, by adopting the ancient tongue, to approach nearer to those wonderful images of Hellas and Hellenes embraced by the West. Peter Bien illuminates some important implications of classicism on the language debate when writing of the 'predicament' of Koraes. Bien speaks below of an episode surrounding the preparation, in Paris, of one of Koraes's Greek publications:

> Korais was caught, so to speak, between his progressivism and his professional milieu. We see his predicament all too blatantly in the following confession placed directly in the midst of a plea for the common language: 'My notes, written in our common tongue, were ready for the printers when some friends of mine—philhellenes expert in our ancient but not our modern language—eventually persuaded me to Hellenize (my notes) so that they might be understood... by the scholars of Europe, who are ignorant of Modern Greek.'

Bien concludes that "despite all of Korais' protestations about the dignity of the spoken tongue," he wrote for philhellenes as well as Greeks and even shared with the former "a romantic (and sometimes preposterous) vision of the moral, cultural, and intellectual effect that a revival of the past would have upon the Ottomanized modern Greeks."[73]

Koraes's 'predicament' could be more directly stated as that of a modern Greek living in a society that preferred the older vintage (he preferred the same himself) and exerted a certain pressure on him to conform to that model. That the philhellenes embraced a romantic fantasy of the glories of the ancient past is obvious. Koraes embraced the same fantasy, although his attachment sprung from deeper or more personal sources. Indeed, a foreigner, a Greek man of letters, his actions were conditioned very clearly by the desire to be the Greek that this society wished him to be; this was a work that was equal parts romance and self-preservation.

If the language question had been based solely on the exigencies of spreading education, then the choice of language would have been simple: the demotic. This was after all the language spoken by the overwhelming majority of the Greek people and especially those who were most in need of enlightenment, as the intellectuals of the era constantly testified. However this apparently was not the first consideration given the vehemence of the debate and its outcome. In fact the 'archaizers' eventually won the battle, a victory that had, most have argued, negative results for the long term development of Greek culture.[74]

Most observers of the pre and post revolutionary language question have tended to conclude that the parties to this dispute were locked in a struggle that had a much larger meaning than language. Ioannes Kordatos, the most famous Marxist historian of modern Greece, wrote in a typical passage:

> If the question was only about words, using 'υδωϱ' or 'νεϱο,' 'πατηϱη' or 'πατερας' it would have long since ceased to matter....Into the middle of the language question entered however other questions...Underneath the various arguments are concealed general cultural positions that indirectly benefit or harm certain social groups and classes.[75]

For the Marxist historian Kordatos, archaists like Neroulos were the "representatives of feudalism,"[76] who, along with the Patriarchate, served as the "intellectual leaders of the old classes." Alternatively, "the newer classes" who advocated the "simple katharevousa or the common language were the representatives of neohellenic urbanism."[77] Kordatos took a provocative approach to the interpretation of the language question but his categories were drawn much too broadly and simply. Demoticists and katharevousists represent two very different positions and should not be lumped together. Additionally, the members of the different factions do not conveniently separate themselves on the basis of age or occupation. Clerics, for example, which as a 'class' represent an immense force in the Greek Enlightenment, do not neatly align themselves on one side or the other in this key area of ideology. Gazes and Doukas for example were both clerics and yet great opponents on the language question. The linkage of ideology and identity can perhaps one day provide a new contribution to our understanding of the language zetema over the course of the Diaphotismos, however it will require a more finely drawn sociological analysis than the kind performed by Kordatos and his disciples. Nor can such an analysis omit to consider the social origins of this most obvious element of the language zetema, the perception of cultural inadequacy and delinquence.

Moisiodax and his Predicament

If Koraes had the special predicament of being a Greek man of letters in a western capital of Enlightenment, then so too did Moisiodax have a predicament of his own. His of course was to circulate in both these worlds, East and West, as a Vlach logios. Despite Moisiodax's tireless advocacy of the cause of Hellenism, it is clear that his status as an ethnic outsider was an issue of some influence in his life and career. The language problem in fact became the occasion for revealing comments regarding the peculiar position Moisiodax occupied in the Neohellenic Enlightenment and the degree to which he was truly accepted by the 'race' he had adopted.

As the language issue became more intense and divisive with the passage of the eighteenth century it appears that Moisiodax's ethnic background came into play. More specifically, Moisiodax's ethnicity provided his detractors with a unique opportunity to discredit his position; one which they did not fail to exploit. The criticisms directed at him were acknowledged by Moisiodax himself in the first paragraph of the prologue to his *Apologia* of 1780. He lists the charges made against him in short order:

> firstly, that my lessons are for grocery clerks, secondly, for how I write, that I teach through the simple form because I don't know Hellenic (ancient Greek), and thirdly, that I don't teach the Logic of the illustrious Eugenios (Voulgaris), similarly because I don't understand it ...however I am not so miserable as to not know the Logic of the illustrious Eugenios, or not to be able to write in Hellenic.[78]

Moisiodax did not identify his critics in the *Apologia* but in time one would come forward to bring into open view the cultural self-consciousness that must have been part of Moisiodax's experience as a Hellenized Vlach. The critic in question, Panayiotes Kodrikas published his views of Moisiodax and the language question in a work we have already encountered above, the *Melete tes Koines Ellenikes Dialektou* of 1818. The *Melete* features a remarkable passage on Moisiodax, which the author prefaces by first appealing to his readers to accept his words as innocent of any intent to slander the deceased logios. "Permit me to speak of him officially," Kodrikas asks, "since I knew the man personally, and as to a Teacher I often spoke with him, and finally as a Writer, by duty I protected him. I don't speak of him therefore out of prejudice or out of hearsay."[79] Kodrikas then proceeds to present his view of the 'true' causes of Moisiodax's demoticism:

> The man was truly erudite. In many kinds of foreign Dialects and all the sciences was he excellently educated in the Academies of Western Europe. However a foreigner by birth to the Race of the Hellenes he was accordingly untasted of the milk of a Hellenic upbringing. For him the Hellenic Language was by study and haste learned and so not by usage from infancy Natural. His Vision, and his mind were exercised in the study of the ancient Writers. His hearing however was not accustomed to the melody of the Dialect of the Modern Greeks. Consequently it wasn't easy for him to imitate the skillful phrasing nor in the simple Demotic Dialect to legitimately express himself.

Like those of a similarly deficient familiarity with the language, Moisiodax "sought shelter therefore in the banal refuge of the half-learned pedagogue, to wit, that the Common Language of the Modern Greeks is corrupted, and requires correcting." Such a course resembled an act of hubris wherein the guilty party "attempts himself to render, by his own lights, the imagined correction. And thus in an arbitrary Language did he (Moisiodax) write."[80]

Moisiodax acknowledged the negative values often associated with the terms 'mixo-barbarous' and 'koinon efos' when describing the language of his *Philosophia*. He also was aware that such epithets as "rude" or "contemptible," revealed the prevailing compulsion to have a language deemed respectable by the world. Nonetheless his attitude was to interpret this problem as a matter of rational rehabilitation. There could be no enlightenment of the race without the agency of the common speech, which though neglected had yet the potential to develop into an idiom of learning and respect. "This is how it appears to me," he wrote, "that if corrected, it can become (the common tongue) a complete language, sufficient for every purpose, and worthy of being compared with the most eloquent dialects of Europe."[81]

Moisiodax of course was long gone from the scene by the time Kodrikas's critique appeared, however his legacy was defended by the editors of the journal *Hermes ho Logios*, who published an extended review of the *Melete* and its arguments.[82] In this case his defenders spoke in the spirit of the Moisiodax of the *Ethike Philosophia* or the *Apologia*, not however, the Mosiodax of the later works. For it does appear that over time Moisiodax was influenced by the pressure of his critics to change the manner in which he wrote. This is visible in the gradual evolution of his style over the course of his publishing history. Readers of the demotic will find the way increasingly difficult in his final works, which were progressively 'archaized' and not apparently with success. This outcome has led one of Moisiodax's biographers to consider whether the critiques of his antagonists contained a measure of truth.[83]

The material above reminds us that Moisiodax's participation in the Neohellenic Enlightenment was conditioned, according to some of his peers, by the fact that he was a 'Lower Dach.' Clearly, it was not so simple for him to submerge himself within Greek culture. The motivations behind his identity orientation and the relentless ministrations which he made on behalf of the revival of Greek culture can only be subject for speculation. However if one source of motivation was environmental, as it was for the Greeks undergoing similar experiences in Europe or upon exposure to European attitudes, then there is some evidence to consider this factor too in the case of the Vlach Hellenizers.

An example of the superior or at least highly condescending attitude of educated Greeks toward the Vlachs appears in the Jaunuary 1, 1811 edition of *Hermes ho Logios*. In addition to its customary surveys and reviews of noteworthy trends in literature and learning, the edition included a description of a meeting of the newly established Philological Society of Bucharest. The meeting was closed with an especially rousing address by the local Orthodox Metropolitan, Ignatios, one of the founders of the Society, praising the efforts made by the Greeks and Dachs to enlighten themselves.[84] However Ignatios's words reveal important Greek assumptions regarding the Dachs and their historical relationship to the larger, guiding force of Hellenism:

> The present luminous celebration brings double joy to the Greeks and Dachs, for it is the epoch of their regeneration... I see the Greeks and Dachs, united for so long by religion, to be joined now by another tie, divine philosophy. The Greeks very conscious of and grateful for the asylum that Dacia gave her, yearn to give back as a holy duty the lights of learning and philosophy. The Dachs, so honorable, not wanting to remain lower than them, the two parts from here now joined with the new Society, giving themselves the duty to transmit Enlightenment in Dacia and Greece. This is not new to the Greeks, since their ancestors were to such depth beneficial and generous... For the Dachs however this is entirely new and certainly it does them great honor.

"Let enlightened Europe look on them with admiration," Ignatios declares, "a people so few, as are these of Dacia, to honor themselves by giving back to Greece that which it received from her." Such lines sufficiently express Ignatios's chauvinism, so much so that one almost overlooks the author's admission of his frustration over the infamy suffered by both peoples in the next sentence. "Let Europe see," Ignatios demands, "that it isn't sloth which makes the Greco-Dachs ignorant, but other external causes. See that when they have the time they don't lose a moment to enlighten themselves and others." It is true, he concedes, that the Bucharest Society cannot "equal those of the enlightened nations," but from such origins do all great undertakings begin. "Let the foreign peoples not scorn the Society for its smallness," Ignatios cautions, "for this is not just..."[85]

The Metropolitan's remarks on the Dachs exhibit nonetheless a measure of the attitude found in the texts of Western philhellenes seeking to rescue Greece from its ruin and decay. The Dachs, in this case, lagging somewhere below on the yardstick of civilization, were to be raised up by the more advanced Greeks. The hope of enlightenment in the East was thus bound to the consolidation of its peoples behind the guiding force of Greek language and learning. Proponents of this view were inclined to rest their case on the test of rationality, in the sense that the adoption of a common language was necessary to advance the work of enlightenment.[86] It was through such means that the rather meager resources of Balkan society could best be concentrated, organized and mobilized.[87]

To a degree Balkan culture was already somewhat organized around Hellenism by virtue of the presence of the Greek Orthodox Church. One could not advance very far in the Church without acquiring the Greek language, and of course the path to education often led through the higher academies of the Church. As school-building accelerated over the later period of the Tourkokratia, Greek continued to dominate as the medium of instruction, even in places like Moschopolis that were ethnically quite diverse. To remain a Vlach therefore was, if only on the level of language, incompatible with any ambition to acquire a decent education or move up the ranks of educated society. Of course this experience may have come at the cost of the student's esteem as "Greek education" one historian has recently written, was likely to instill a "feeling of inferiority into young Bulgarians." The same author remarks that this "feeling of self-contempt" was "transmitted by spouses to each other and by parents to their children."[88] These not inconsiderable factors certainly had an influence on Moisiodax's youth and career.[89]

Moisiodax's intense crusade nonetheless in the service of the Hellenic 'race,' which he designated himself a member of, remains intriguing for its very thoroughness. As Peter Mackridge comments, Moisiodax "while proudly indicating his geographical origins in his surname, seems to have had no regrets that he was in the mainstream of Greek culture; when he writes of 'our forefathers' and 'our race' there is no doubt that he sees himself as a Greek." Mackridge adds that "it is not only later Romanian and Bulgarian scholars who consider him as Romanian or Bulgarian, for some of his contemporaries were also conscious of his non-Greek origins."[90] In fact, Moisiodax's attempts to perpetuate this 'identity,' against the objections of those equally intent to insist the contrary, are among the most arresting mementos of his writing life.

The obvious energy that Moisiodax put into the subject of his own identity parallels what we often find among the Greek logioi of his times, men who similarly came to feel themselves as burdened or reduced by the specter of national delinquency. Unfortunately for Moisiodax, the Vlach past may not have offered the type of redeeming refuge enjoyed by his Greek peers, at least it was not prone to be presented that way. The 'superiority' of Hellenic culture was also validated to some extent by the general opinions held and circulating in the West regarding Greece's Balkan neighbors. It may not be as Micholopoulos asserts that Westerners were "unaware" of the existence of the surrounding ethnic groups,[91] nonetheless the attitudes of men like Leake indicate how the peoples of the region were typically ranked. In a passage from his discourse on the linguistic history of the Balkans, Leake observed, for example, that the Greek language had managed to retain some of its ancient stature on account of its "refinement, perfection, long-established fame, extensive use, and the superior civilization of the people, who, however debased, have always been superior in this respect to the surrounding nations in the North and East."[92]

Like all emigres Moisiodax faced the problem of being 'identified' among the foreign nations and cultures of the East and West in which he circulated. The experience of 'xeniteia' would have confronted him with the issue of identity (even if he had put little thought to it himself) with special urgency, posing before all else and innumerable times the fundamental question of 'what are you?' And truly what should he call himself, which appellation would carry more weight? A Vlach, a lower Dach? The turn to Hellenism may have afforded him a means of escape from the ignominy of an indifferent national origin, for one more recognized, perhaps more 'credible,' and one, of course, that had the simple virtue of being close at hand.

The fact that Moisiodax did not refer to his ethnic origins in his writings is a tendency that he shared with other Vlach logioi and clerics who also functioned in these environments.[93] Some of the figures we might include in this context are the Vlach Daniil Mihali Adami Hagi (1754?-1822/5), better known as Daniel of Moschopolis, the intensely reform-minded monk Kosmas ho Aitolos (1714-1779), and finally another Vlach man of letters, Demetrios Darvares (1757-1823). The experience and writings of these men add further depth and insight to the issues encountered above.

Daniel and Darvares

As a cultural convert to Hellenism Moisiodax's experience was not unique. The writings of Daniel and Demetrios Darvares provide further examples of Vlachs who were intense advocates of Greek culture. By such acts of negation or reorientation they present themselves too as potential examples of the interplay of self-worth and identity as it has been treated throughout this study. The ministrations of both men were especially concerned with the subject of the Greek language, which they sought to disseminate among their fellow Vlachs. The language instrument favored most by both men in this case, perhaps significantly, was the simple dialect. Through the Greek language one gained greater access to the sacred works of the Orthodox faith as well as a world of secular learning, both ancient and modern due to the vigorous translating activities of the logioi. Greek's role as a language of trade in the Balkans also figured heavily into the arguments of the cultural evangelists.[94]

Of course such activities point in contrast to the correspondingly low or expendable value accorded by these men to their own native language or culture. To a degree the efforts of Darvares and Moisiodax to submerge themselves in Hellenism recall the rhetoric fired at the Greek merchants of Europe by the author of the *Hellenike Nomarchia*, Greeks, he complained bitterly, who had tried to disappear within the culture of their adopted countries; an exchange of identities intended to advance one's standing and prospects in the world by escaping the stigmas attached to the old country. It is in fact worth comparing the accusations from this piece with those of a 'founder' of Bulgarian nationalism, the eighteenth century monk, Father Paisii. The reader may recognize this quote from the first chapter where the author of the *Nomarchia* had leveled his charges:

> So many there are that don't bother themselves about our fatherland and with every effort attempt to mimic the ill manners of the other races in order that none recognize that they are Greeks. And if there was a way to change fatherlands they would buy for themselves a foreign one though it cost them one of their own eyes. O true enemy and worse tyrant than the very Ottomans of Greece! O shame of our race and mortal wound of the fatherland! ... [95]

Father Paisii similarly vilifies the actions of Bulgarians who had abandoned the customs of their homeland out of shame for its status and ill repute:

> Read and know so that you will not be ridiculed and abused by other peoples and nationalities... There are those who do not care to know about their own Bulgarian nation and turn to foreign ways and foreign tongue; they do not care for their own Bulgarian language but try to read and speak Greek and are ashamed to call themselves Bulgarians... O, you senseless and stupid people! Why are you ashamed to call yourselves Bulgarians and do not read and speak your own language?[96]

Clearly the experiences and reactions of these contemporary Hellenized and Hellenizing Vlach logioi have much to teach us about the forces acting on Moisiodax. And as we can see above, they have a great deal to teach us too about the forces acting on the Greeks themselves. Of course the latter, fortunately or not as Moisiodax might grouse, had the classical past to retreat to. This past furnished the logioi with a clear direction in which to channel their energies or discomfort and fight back against the sting of contempt. For the Vlach logios the answer was not so simple.

A unique and revealing text from these years is the *Eisagogike Didaskalia* or 'Introductory Teaching' (1802), of the Vlach cleric and Moschopolis Academy teacher Daniel. This work must surely stand as one of the most memorable documents of the 'Balkan Enlightenment.'[97] Although not a great deal is known about Daniel himself, the dictionary he authored is a well known source to scholars.[98] There are four languages contained in the lexicon, including of course Greek (romaikes), 'lower Vlach,' Bulgarian and Albanian, these latter three being rendered phonetically in Greek letters.

Daniel's approach to vocabulary building in the lexicon is nearly as affecting as anything else about this unique souvenir of Balkan history. The vocabulary lessons are incorporated into a succession of small portraits of village life and customs, mementos of a pastoral world that finds its rhythm in the unhurried comings and goings of the seasons. But these little cameos also have an instructive intent, with special emphasis placed on the reinforcement of spiritual and social conventions. The very first vocabulary lesson thus begins: "God made heaven, the earth, the sun, the moon, the stars..."[99] One learns when to feast, when to fast, the foods best taken when ill, how to respect the dead, etc along with firm reminders on matters of piety and Orthodox practice: "Whoever likes to frequent the Church better have the fear of God and not go empty-handed but take a candle and light it in front of the saint and bring a little offering for the priest that he entreat the Lord for his sins."[100] The youth are taught to mind their elders, be diligent, honorable and never disgrace themselves or their parents.[101] The lexicon is finally brought to a close with another call to prayer: "Come now and lets hold the kombologia (prayer beads) and kneel to God and receive from him forgiveness for our sins so that we may acquire paradise amen."[102]

And yet so lulled, the reader is roughly shaken back into reality by the bold social critiques that Daniel occasionally levels throughout the volume. At one point he abruptly observes that "The judges (kretai) and the pashas strip the people naked. And the leaders (archontes) with great art drink their blood. For this God becomes angry and burdens us with weakness, plague, pestilence, death..."[103] These lines are followed by another strange passage where the author describes a peculiar nightmare: "This evening I had a dream where I was tied up with a rope and strap and two Turks were pulling me from the front and behind in order to cast me into a deep well (or possibly tomb 'lakkos'). And with great force I freed myself. However now that I rise from sleep I shiver all over and am taken with fever."[104] No doubt an unusual approach to vocabulary building, yet no more so than the rhetorical exercises of Skouphos which featured pillaged cities and supplications for divine liberation.[105]

The *Eisagogike Didaskalia* is equally if not more remarkable for some lines of demotic verse that appear at its beginning. These lines embody a quality of cultural prejudice that is striking even within the context of the present study. The disarmingly straightforward message of the piece is that Hellenization offered the Albanians, Vlachs and Bulgars a means of escape from ethnic purgatory. A sample has been translated below:

> Albanians, Vlachs, Bulgarians, speakers of other languages, rejoice,
> and prepare yourselves all of you to become Greeks (romaioi),
> leaving the barbarian language, voice and customs,
> that to your descendants will appear like myths.
> To your race (genos) do honor, and also your fatherlands.
> Make the Albano-Boulgarian (fatherlands) into Greek ones.
> It is no longer difficult, to learn Greek,
> And not to speak as a barbarian with five or ten words.
> Have it in your hands, and study it often,
> This newly printed book wherever you go....
> Acquire ideas of diverse things,
> Your mind to be established as fertile and bountiful
> Glory to bring to yourselves all this,
> Among the other nations, and among those of your own race.
> Peoples before of other tongues, however pious in divine things,
> The Greek language acquire and speak.
> A great benefit to your occupations,
> and to all your commercial endeavors.
> Young Bulgarians rejoice, Albanians, and Vlachs,
> Deacons, priests and monks,
> Awake from the deep sleep of ignorance.
> Learn the Greek (romaika) language, the mother of wisdom...[106]

This remarkable exhibition of cultural proselytization has not escaped the notice of historians. Unfortunately, Western scholars have tended to mistakenly attribute these lines to Daniel. This however is not the case. The verse is in fact the work of the Greek writer Michael Sxenas.[107] This information may serve to ameliorate the radical act of Vlach self-contempt otherwise implied by the verse.[108] However it remains as a vivid testimony of the cultural assumptions of these times, for it is only a more explicit statement of the attitudes expressed by Ignatios in his address to the Philological Society of Bucharest.[109]

At least one Greek historian has judged the acute 'chauvinism' manifested in the Sxenas piece as evidence of the practices that ultimately stimulated the growth of national movements among the Vlachs.[110] The very important issue of resistance enters into Kostantakoplos's recent discussion of this problem as well, although she is the first to admit that a sociological analysis of the motivations behind these 'language revolts' suffers from the small sample of authors involved.[111] There is too the fact that important questions exist regarding the ethnic backgrounds of some of the actors in the dispute.[112]

The Lexicon remains an intriguing document and even with the exclusion of the Sxenas verse demonstrates the active participation of its Vlach author, Daniel, in the dissemination of Hellenic culture; an effort intended to upgrade the manners, mores and even the business acumen of the local peoples through the civilizing agency of Greek language and culture. It is also necessary to emphasize the ecclesiastical motivations behind the book. This is apparent in the dedication, written in ancient Greek, that Daniel addressed to the local Metropolitan, Nektarios. Nektarios had in fact originally encouraged Daniel to produce the book out of concern for the spiritual welfare of his ethnically diverse flock. In a rationalizing spirit very consistent with that of Kosmas ho Aitolos, the Greek language became here another instrument in the crusade for Orthodox rehabilitation.[113]

The fact that Daniel used the ancient dialect in the dedication of the *Eisagogike* is revealing of the pressures he faced, like Koraes, to comply with the standards of his social and 'professional milieu.' As we have seen above with Moisiodax, these pressures were not insignificant, and perhaps Konstantakoplos is justified in ranking this issue as most influential in explaining both Daniel's predicament and perhaps its resolution in his flight to the haven of Hellenism.[114]

When Peter Mackridge spoke of Moisiodax as one who "had no regrets that he was in the mainstream of Greek culture," or who, when writing "of 'our forefathers' and 'our race' there is no doubt that he sees himself as a Greek," he may well have been speaking of another Vlach logios, Demetrios Nikolaos Darvares (1757-1823).

Like Mosiodax, Darvares made virtually no indication of his ethnic origins in his writings, devoting himself instead to the realization of the Greek enlightenment project, with a special emphasis on its dissemination among the Balkan peoples. He also spent a much greater portion of his life outside of the Balkans than Moisiodax, and eventually settled in Vienna, where all of his many books, perhaps thirty three in total, were published.[115] Darvares was also a frequent contributor to *Hermes ho Logios,*[116] and was even a member of the Bucharest Philological Society described above, as was Koraes.[117] In summary, Darvares, though a Vlach by descent, was no small figure in the intellectual circles of the Neohellenic Enlightenment.

Such credentials aside, Darvares wrote for an audience much closer to the one addressed by Daniel than Moisiodax, with the result that the mainstay of his works were overtly concerned with matters of pedagogy and upbringing. In some cases the books are to be read by the pupils, in some cases by their parents.[118] Many of his writings actually take the form of 'cheiragogia,' or works that seek literally to lead the youth 'by the hand' in matters of language, manners, religion, and vocation, much like the *Eisagoge Didaskalia* of Daniel. The *Sophias Apanthisma* for example contains a series of short lessons on life and ethics gleaned from the works of various wise men, both ancient and contemporary.[119] There are even occasions throughout the book where the two traditions collaborate, as when Darvares quotes from 'Casimir Perrier' on statecraft: "'however free the administration of the state, so strict and respected must be the laws, so severe must be the upbringing of youth.' This sentiment was supported throughout his very own life by the divine Socrates."[120]

Works of religious instruction, in some cases translated from Russian, feature prominently in the Darvares bibliography as well.[121] Here again Darvares's method parallels that of Daniel in both subject matter and style; that is, the tendency toward works of 'cheiragogia' rendered in the 'aplos' or simple dialect. Moisiodax on the other hand more fully conceived himself as the logios who worked in the higher realm of theory and thought, territory charted by Voulgaris and Photiades. His choice consequently to circulate in this higher atmosphere by means of the demotic represented a significant rupture of the tradition, and one for which he suffered no small trouble.[122]

An expatriate logios not unlike many of the other men considered in this study, Darvares was no doubt highly conscious of the images of Balkan degeneracy circulating among Europeans. His writings reflect the discomfort caused by this awareness and even, to some degree, the way in which the very Enlightenment itself struck the logioi of the East with the force of an indictment, pressing upon them the personal duty to arrest the cycle of decline and draw their world back within the pale of civilization.[123] "In all times the enlightened races were those who took care for the common education," he wrote in *Alethes hodos*. "Such as in our own times the most educated races of Europe have raised diverse schools." And yet acting with "malevolent pretense," we fail to "imitate them" and do what is necessary "to enlighten our Race and not consequently be so much held in contempt by the other races as ignorant and barbaric."[124]

Undaunted, it was to the dissemination of Hellenic culture that Darvares turned to solve the problems of both Greek and non-Greek Balkan Christians alike. He set down his grand design in the introduction to the *Eklogarion Graikikon*:

> I was ruminating a great deal in my mind of how necessary is the simple dialect of the Greeks to all the common races (omogeneis) not only for the study of the holy dogmas of our Orthodox faith, but also for the carrying out of business matters, by which most live and manage their lives. I thought that if immediately from the beginning such a book was placed in the hands of the children of our common race in the simple form composed it would be for them highly beneficial; for we are deprived of such books as with many other kinds for those beginning study...

"I worked in the collection of this book," Darvares tells us, not only to move the curiosity of children, but also "to sharpen their mind" in order to "prepare them for higher and greater lessons, that is to say namely Greek lessons." From these, as from "some strong flowing spring" they would draw "every kind of learning divine and human toward the enlightenment of the mind, the correction of the heart, and the perfection of their morals."[125]

Although Darvares's attitude toward the native culture of the Vlachs does not take the extreme of Sxenas, he nonetheless exhibits a clear conception in passages such as these of the necessity of learning Greek as a precursor to cultural rehabilitation, and thus a first step toward the eradication of the 'contempt' heaped upon the 'race' by foreign nations.

This section on Darvares closes with the consideration of one final passage from his *Sophia Apanthisma*, a chapter entitled "What is patriotism (philopatria) and what duties does it impose upon the citizen.' In addition to its interest as a primary source in the history of nationalism, this chapter provides us with another example of how closely Darvares associated himself with the Greek past, and how he intended his readers to do the same:

> Every man loves his place (topos) not because it is the most excellent place on earth, but because it is the place of his birth. And if he is acquainted with the advantages of foreign countries, he still doesn't stop to love his own place, however meager it may be. And if he were born and raised in a desert and later moved to another more pleasant country, again he would feel yearning for the place of his birth. This passion is innate in the human being...

This innate passion, coincides with the "patriotism" or "love and sympathy toward the peoples that one belongs to," which the author defines as the "peoples that speak the same language as he and practice the same religion and have a common past and future, common problems and hopes." Such "divine feeling or love toward the fatherland," Darvares says, "when it exists warm and vital in all the citizens, makes the nation happy and great." Of such truths, he claims, "the history of all the nations provides many examples and certainly the history of our glorious ancestors."[126]

The casual way that Darvares associates himself with "our glorious ancestors," which can only mean the Platos, Plutarchs and Aristotles featured so prominently in his writings, recalls passages cited above from Moisiodax, who spoke in a similarly casual way of "hoi progonoi mas." The assumed manner of this association tends to mute what is otherwise a not inconsiderable act of negation and cultural reorientation, given that Darvares was, like Moisiodax, first a Vlach, and thus, given the attitudes we have seen above, not so casually accepted by the Greeks as an equal. In many ways Darvares appears to exemplify the 'new man' that Sxenas sought to conjure into being from the 'indifferent' nations of the Balkans, one who had come to take flight from his "barbarian language, voice and customs" and to his "race (genos) and fatherland do honor" by making them into "Greek ones." No doubt a certain extra element of irony is added here by the immediate subject matter of the chapter, patriotism, described by Darvares as the innate and indestructible love and sympathy one feels for his homeland, his language, and his past, no matter "how meager."

Kitromilides and Konstantakopoulos are quite right to emphasize the environmental pressures that Daniel, Darvares and Moisiodax faced as they attempted to make their way within an intellectual society structured around Greek culture. The exigencies of their vocational milieu, whether as clerics or teachers or men of commerce, imposed upon them the necessity of learning Greek and adopting it as the instrument of discourse in their work. But is this enough to explain the enthusiastic manner in which they took on the mission of Hellenization? One can learn Greek to function in his vocation, but need not 'become' Greek, claim Aristotle as his ancestor or proselytize on behalf of Greek universalism. These men went well beyond the goal of simply 'fitting in.' Certainly the Vlachs may have been conditioned to see Greek culture as superior to their own, or simply as a more identifiable entity both within the Balkans and without. Greek culture was finally close at hand, a simple but not inconsiderable virtue. But beneath all this was the underlying awareness, which their intense activities as 'fathers of enlightenment' demonstrate, and which they felt as dearly as the Greeks, of the spectacle of ignorance and barbarism that they furnished to the world. And this with all its uncomfortable consequences, not the least of which was the general contempt that this spectacle elicited. This contempt attached itself to them, all the logioi of the Balkans, as reflexively as the 'people' whom they sought to raise up. They clung to the Hellenic past of course for the natural reason that it was an entity that inspired admiration and was thus a source of pride for all who could find a way to associate themselves with it. But few doubted that they circulated among 'the enlightened' as a truant race; and so it would always be until the people or genos to whom they belonged could somehow be made to appear more presentable to the world.[127]

Culture, Contempt and Evangelism - Kosmas ho Aitolos

Demetrios Darvares presented us with the example of a Vlach who stressed emphatically the employment of Greek language and culture as a kind of handmaiden of Balkan enlightenment. Certainly the Greeks were little better off themselves in any measure of civilization, as their own logioi constantly testified. Nonetheless by joining their energies to the efforts of the Hellenists, all, Vlach, Bulgar, Albanian and Greek, contributed to the great project of establishing themselves among the ranks of the civilized peoples of the world.

A study of the sources from this period reveals however another motivation behind the push for Hellenic language and cultural rationalization among the Balkan peoples. The logioi, Greek and non-Greek alike, had recoiled in disgust from the spectacle of the nation's delinquency and ignorance. These were the evils that left the race mired in poverty and defenseless against the contempt of the world. But this was not all. For many of the logioi, and especially those who were also Orthodox clerics, the poverty, ignorance and illiteracy of the nation had wreaked havoc as well on the practice of the Orthodox faith. Again and again do we find in the sources from these years bitter statements of what these men saw as a widening spiritual catastrophe; of peasants and priests degenerated together into apathy or superstition; of rural clerics as ignorant in matters of Orthodoxy as the villagers themselves and barred by virtue of their own illiteracy from access to the works upon which their very faith rested. Darvares himself when explaining the duties of the different classes to society insisted that the clergy "must always be educated."[128] Many would have agreed with his claim that education was the handmaiden of Orthodox reawakening. And the handmaiden of education, it appeared to Greeks and some non-Greeks alike, was the Greek language.

This critique, both social and spiritual and the motivation for enlightenment that it inspired, serves to remind us of the ecclesiastical backgrounds of a large number of the logioi of these times. Many of the great 'enlighteners,' such as Voulgaris devoted the mainstay of their publishing activities to holy works and pursuits. Indeed one of Voulgaris's first publishing efforts was the polemical 'Prophetike epistole pros tous orthodoxous christianous' (1756) in which he strenuously attacked what he claimed to be the proselytizing offensive of the 'papists' in the Balkans.[129] It was in this spirit that the stormy Moschopolis cleric and teacher Nektarios Terpos (1675-?) published his popular *Pistis* (Venice 1732), declaring that it had not been "composed for the wise and educated people, but for the uneducated and villagers, since in these parts of Turkey are found Christians, who deny Christ and put themselves in the hands of the devil."[130]

Moisiodax was equally concerned with the fate of Orthodoxy in the Balkans. We have already encountered a few expressions of this in the *Ethike Philosophia*, in which he had written spiritedly of the "neglect of the propriety of the Church and the Gospels." He continued on this theme later in the same piece when he asked "what spiritual good can a priest do, when he doesn't know dogma, maxims, writings, the mysteries or even the number of the articles of the Holy Covenant?"[131] Psalidas's student and collaborator Kosma Thesprotos had a similar view of the villagers and priests he surveyed in his geography of Epiros noting that "the Mohammedians and Christians have a dim idea of their religion, since works in their language they don't have, nor books, schools and teachers."[132] His impression of the monks living in the numerous monasteries of the region was little better, as when he remarks that Epiros

> doesn't enjoy any benefit from these, their income they uselessly squander, the spendthrift, superstitious, illiterate and contemptible monks wastefully spending it. If these monasteries made a contribution (to society) in proportion to their abilities, it would at least be possible to establish in Epiros schools of Greek learning, and in many parts the young men of Epiros would be enlightened and plucked out from the darkness and the labyrinth of illiteracy and barbarism.[133]

It was in the spirit of critiques such as these that we find another intense push for enlightenment from Hellenic and non-Hellenic Orthodox writers alike. Of the latter, the Orthodox monk and martyr Kosmas ho Aitolos (of Aitolos) merits special attention.

Kosmas was probably born around 1714 in the village of Mega Dendro, in the region of Greece or European Turkey then known as Rumely.[134] Like Moisiodax and Daniel, Kosmas was not Greek although there exists no information to make a positive identification of his ethnic background.[135] Kosmas himself, from one of his teachings (didachai), provides us with only the slimmest of autobiographical sketches:

> My patrida, the false, earthly and vain, is of Apokouro. My father, my mother, my race (genos) were pious orthodox Christians. I am myself, my brothers, a sinful man, worse than any other in the world. I am however the slave of my Master Jesus Christ, of the cross and of God...

Departing from his patrida, Kosmas tells us, he "walked among many places, castles, towns and villages and even to Constantinople, but even more I resided on Agio Oros (Mount Athos) seventeen years and cried over my sins." Eventually he was to find comfort and his calling: "close to the infinite grace my

Master blessed me, he claimed even me the sinner and I learned a few letters of Greek, and became a monk." Such learning enabled him to read the "divine and holy Gospels" where he found "many and diverse meanings, all of which are pearls, diamonds, treasures, riches, joy, faith and life everlasting."[136]

Kosmas's rather brief but vigorous career as a country preacher, in which he insistently pressed upon the villagers of northern Greece his wish that they build schools and learn Greek, has caused him to be cast (perhaps miscast) in some histories as a kind of proto-nationalist in the manner of Regas—an affinity in fact that Kosmas's martyrdom in 1779 at the hands of the Turks served to reinforce.[137] The result is that the intent of Kosmas's admittedly pronounced Greek evangelism is frequently taken out of context. Certainly his own autobiographical silence on these matters of identity and background is the greatest source of trouble. The passage above for example omits to mention that while at Mount Athos Kosmas was a student of the ubiquitous Voulgaris, who was then acting as the school's director.[138] Kosmas was thus more than the itinerant preacher that he tended to portray himself as.

Setting aside the question of his ethnic origin, it is apparent that to a significant degree Kosmas's avid Hellenism served as a means to a much larger end: the revival of Orthodoxy. This point is brought out quite clearly in another one of his teachings:

> Forty years did the prophet Moses study to learn reading and writing in order to understand where he walked... If you fathers didn't learn then see that your children learn Greek, because our Church is in Greek and if you don't study Greek, you can't understand that which our Church testifies... It is better my brother for you to have a Greek school in your village than springs and rivers. And if you teach your child reading and writing, then he may rightfully be called a human being, but if you don't teach him letters, he is no more than a little pig. The school opens the church, the school opens the monasteries.[139]

Kosmas's resolute emphasis on education serves to connect him to the reformers identified earlier who had similarly interpreted the crisis of Orthodoxy as an outcome of the national problem. Certainly in the explicit nature of his social critique Kosmas stands apart and in this sense his testimony of degeneracy endures as one of the most severe encountered in the entire period under review. His taste for the particularly pungent term 'gourounopoula', piggish-children, was no doubt encouraged by his view of its effectiveness, given that it appears many times throughout his teachings.[140] Clearly the punishing tone of his social critique was an important part of his method, the words and images used to inflict a certain amount of shame on the villagers of his circuit and move them to action.[141] Depictions of 'piggish-children' are matched with passages such as this:

> forty years did Moses study letters. So must we study to know where we walk. And if the parents didn't learn reading and writing then they have to make it that their children learn. You don't see how our race has turned wild (pos agriepse) from illiteracy and that we have become like savage beasts? For this do I urge you to make possible by whatever means to have schools in your towns that you will understand the holy Gospels, and not walk about in darkness.[142]

It was assumed by Kosmas that the educational demands of the people and the faith could only be served by the dissemination of the Greek language. Nowhere for example does Kosmas advocate translating the Gospels into the local dialects. On the surface, simple expedience, e.g. that "our Church is in Greek," seems to play a not inconsiderable role in this choice. Nonetheless, these pragmatic considerations were surely advanced by a measure of his own personal bias toward the 'superiority' of Greek culture, given the role that Greek education had played in his own life. One recalls that Kosmas had studied under Voulgaris at Mount Athos—an experience that brought him into direct contact with the wider world of the Neohellenic Diaphotismos.

Nonetheless the dominating influence of Orthodox revival on Kosmas's Hellenism has been somewhat distorted by the legends surrounding him. When Leake for example passed through the domains of Kosmas's former ministry in 1809, thirty years after Kosmas's martyrdom, it was only the 'secular' element of the monk's preaching that attracted notice:

> It is said that one of the most efficient instruments in persuading the Greeks to establish schools as the best mode of improving the nation, was a monk of Apokouro named Kosma, who during eight years traveled over the country as a preacher, and made this subject a principal means of his discourses... He fell a martyr to his zeal, having been put to death in 1780 by Kurt Pasha.[143]

The intense theological character of Kosmas's Hellenism serves nonetheless to separate him from Darvares or Moisiodax, non-Greek logioi whose cultural reorientations introduce more complex questions regarding the interplay of status, self worth and identity. Kosmas was a social reformer and Hellenist as these passages show. However his distress over the people's ignorance and thus his Hellenism was closely tied to the deterioration of Orthodoxy in the East, against which he devoted himself with a single-minded zeal. And yet in this alone he demonstrates the remarkable extent and uses to which the discourse of self-contempt was put. Certainly this discourse found in him a voice that few would ever match, inhabited as his teachings are with children that are like so many 'little pigs' and human beings who have degenerated into wild beasts on account of ignorance and illiteracy.

Summary

The eighteenth century witnessed a development in the scale and spread of Greek learning on the level of an upheaval. Centers of enlightenment appeared amid the courts of the Phanariot Hospodars that drew to them the new generations of students and logioi, developments that are discussed further in the following chapter. The discourse of the national problem spread in consequence and found new voices, powerful ones, in the figures of men like Moisiodax and Voulgaris, the immediate precursors to Koraes and Regas. In Moisiodax too we find that the diffusion of learning and enlightenment throughout the Balkans produced a new type of logios, the non-Hellene drawn nonetheless into the orbit of Hellenism, and often too a Hellenizer himself, as a condition or means of entry into the wider world of letters and learning.

The issue of 'identity' remains the immediately intriguing aspect of these 'Greek enlighteners.' The material above has attempted to explore the factors that would lead someone to undergo such a reorientation. In its most elemental form this act expresses a rejection or negation of the former identity borne by an awareness or sense of its inadequacy. It is abandoned for another that carries more weight. And it is here where we find the circumstances of the Vlachs to shed light on the experience of the Greeks.

The Greeks undertook a similar act when attempting to unite themselves with a culture that was equally as 'foreign': the classical past of Aristotle or Pericles. Confronted with the spectacle of decline that hung from them like a millstone, the logioi had always looked fondly on and sought to connect themselves to an imaginary and long deceased world which, in so many ways, they had only a fictional relation to. This fixation on ancient glory, this 'progonoplexeia' often served of course to simply reinforce the dilemma and predicament of the modern Greek, to heighten or bring into even sharper relief the 'wretchedness' and inadequacy of the present.[144] But apparently this was a price that was worth bearing. For in ancient Hellas they found an object that inspired admiration, that carried some weight in the world. How well these impulses were described in Koraes's famous 'Memoir' when he spoke of the diaspora emboroi who "frequent European theaters" that they may bask for a moment in the celebration of "our ancestors'" prodigious contributions to civilizaton. And yet "gaining honor from the Greek name," Koraes would remind such men, "it is in turn your duty to bring it honor, by calling forth once again in the midst of degraded Greece, its ancient exaltation and splendor."[145]

Melancholy ruminations or longings for the past had featured prominently in the Hellenic discourse since the beginnings of the Tourkokratia, but the social scope and diffusion of the discourse was growing wider, the message becoming shriller and some elements shriller still: the emphasis on shame, duty and mission that would come to prove such potent fixtures of the revolutionary catechism. Certainly no one would question the progonoplexeia of Skouphos or Meniates nor their flamboyant sense of duty, even to the point of pleading the case of their forlorn race to God himself.[146] Whether a sign of social diffusion or secularization, a waning of faith in prophecy, the decline of the Ottoman Empire, Western advances and the heightening sense of expectation that these events engendered, all matters to be discussed below, the space given by these earlier writers to punishment and supplication was yielding to an emphasis on human action, agency and responsibility. Of course the Enlightenment too supplied an influence of no small force in this transition, if alternately through the dispersion or the sting of its precepts.

Whether the Enlightenment was a revolution-inducing force in history remains a remarkably vital subject of debate. It did at least voice a wish to perfect society often expressed by its luminaries in terms of a personal duty to bring happiness to humanity. As Diderot concluded in his Foreword to Volume VIII of the *Encyclopedia* "the reward to which we aspire will be ours if one day our contemporaries and our nephews will say that our life was not entirely useless."[147] This mission required a certain devotion characterized by the *Encyclopedia* itself, a work that swallowed thirty years of labor and reached finally thirty eight volumes. And yet the authors had put themselves in the service of an idea, so they said, that justified in the end all sacrifices: "we have brought our fellow men to love and tolerate each other and to recognize at last the superiority of universal morality over the many separate moralities that foment hate and strife and break or loosen the bond of virtue that links us all."[148] There is no less civilizing spirit or ardor in the words of men like Moisoidax or Katartzes, but D'Alembert's cosmopolitan mission had become for them a purely national one, as if the gaze of the Enlightenment were fixed upon them, as if 'they' were the ones implicated in its urgent appeals to banish ignorance, darkness and superstition from the world. One senses the force of this indictment in the declaration of Gazes: "Don't suffer any longer for us to be in the darkness of ignorance (amatheia)," he demanded of his readers in the introduction to his republication of Meletios, "and from this by the other nations to be held in contempt, we the descendants of those who were the very Fathers of science and learning!"[149]

Many a logios felt the same way and looked urgently for a way out of the 'labyrinth of illiteracy and barbarism' that enclosed them. And to a degree they too were engaged in a work of negation and invention. We noted above the curious dimensions of the 'conversion' of the Vlachs; it was not simply their ambition to learn or speak Greek, but to become Greek, even to adopt Greek ancestors as their own. In truth the modern Greeks attempted the same thing, being as distantly separated as they were in time and culture from antiquity and yet carrying on in the delusion that they were descended "in direct line" of "Miltiades or Themistocles."[150] Some pressed this delusion much farther than others of course, seeking to negate the rude image of the Greek from modern consciousness and morph themselves into the noble forms of the figures from Herodotus, to take their language, to change their names.[151] These too were acts of negation that would have delighted at nothing less than to banish the odious figure of the modern Greek from existence; a radical step, but perhaps radical actions were necessary if one hoped to escape the 'hideous spectacle,' in the words of Koraes, of ignorance, illiteracy, and ill fame.

Notes

1. Stamates Petrou, Adamantios Koraes, *Grammata apo ton Amsterdam*, edited and with an introduction by Philippos Eliou, (Athens: Hermes, 1976), 59.

2. The best example of this is to be found in his 'Memoire sur l'etat actuel de la civilisation dans la Grece,' (1803), and also his later political works which anticipated a Greek state led by the merchant classes. For him these men represented the 'modern' and modernizing element in Greek life. See Chaconas, *Adamantios Koraes: A Study in Greek Nationalism*, 115-118.

3. Discussed in detail in Chapter 5.

4. Kaisarios Dapontes, 'Kipos Xariton,' in *Hoi Prodromoi*, edited by Leandros Vranousis, (Athens: Vasike Vivliotheke, 1955), 4-5.

5. Dapontes was born on the Aegean island of Skopelos.

6. From 'phanari' or 'lamp'. The Patriarchate, not coincidentally, was also located in the Phanar.

7. The author refers to them throughout the text as the "rich ignoramuses of the Phanar," and, again, using one of the more pungent idioms in the modern Greek lexicon for a prefix, the "Fetid/befouled-archons (vromoarchon) of the Phanar." Note the glib candor of the Hospodar in another satire from those years: "The freedom of Greece means poverty for me." Konstantine Demaras, (ed), *Ho Rossanglogallos*, (Athens: Poreia, 1990), 17. This short, anonymously written piece circulated in manuscript form within Greece. Both Byron and Leake came into contact with it during their pre-revolutionary travels. Ibid, 34.

8. Nikousios attained this office, which was much more than its title suggests, in 1669. The Dragoman functioned as the Sultan's chief diplomatic advisor to the West. Mango, 'The Phanariots and the Byzantine Tradition,' in *The Greek Struggle for Independence*, 42.

9. Medical science was an especially prevalent field of study for these early diaspora scholars. Mavrocordatos's own doctoral dissertation, written on the subject of blood circulation (heavily influenced by Harvey), earned him some notice in the West. And it was in the pursuit of medical studies that Koraes ultimately persuaded his parents to permit him to settle in Europe. Koraes acquired his doctorate in medicine at Montpellier in 1788. See Vallianatos, *From Graikos to Hellene: Adamantios Koraes and the Greek Revolution*, (Athens: Academy of Athens), 38.

10. The Treaty of Karlowitz of 1699 serves as the typical milestone for most historians. These events are covered in Leften S. Stavrianos's *The Balkans since 1453*, (New York: New York University Press, 2000), a standard text of Balkan historiography. See pages 175-176.

11. This honor was awarded to Nikolaos Mavrokordatos (1680-1730), the son of the 'Grand Interpreter' Alexander.

12. The occasion for the final 'treachery' presented itself with the outbreak of Peter the Great's 1711 war against the Ottomans. As his armies moved forward the Tsar issued a proclamation to the Balkan peoples to rise up and join him to fight "for faith and fatherland, for your honor and glory, for the freedom and liberty of yourself and your descendants." Cited in L. S. Stavrianos, *The Balkans since 1453*, 179. The effort ended in complete failure as the Greeks, like many other Balkan peoples, viewed the Russian appeal with skepticism. The revolutionary activity was mainly limited to Moldavia which was located in a more agreeable position, but this too was doomed to failure given that Peter's army was stretched far too thin to become a conquering force. Undaunted, the Russians attempted to inspire yet another uprising in Greece in conjunction with the Russo-Turkish War of 1768-1774, an event that led to the disastrous Orlov revolt.

13. As noted above, the Phanariots found themselves masters of the Principalities for the fact that they appeared more obedient to the Turks than the native rulers of these lands. They appeared equally so to the occasional western observer of Turkish affairs. Richard Clogg cites a few remarks from the English traveler William Eton taken from his *A Survey of the Turkish Empire*, published in 1799. Eton writes: "Though styling themselves noble, and affecting a superiority over the other Greeks, they are the only part of their nation who have totally relinquished the ancient Grecian spirit; they seem not anxious, as the islanders are for liberty, but delight in the false magnificence, and the petty intrigues of the seraglio; and their pride is to appear in their dress like Turks..." Clogg, *The Movement for Greek Independence 1770-1821: a collection of documents*, 47. The attainment of such power and influence was sure to put the Phanariots in a unique position with the rise of the independence movement in the time to come. A brief but valuable 'historical sketch' of the Phanariots is rendered by Cyril Mango in 'The Phanariots and the Byzantine Tradition' which appears in the essay collection *The Greek Struggle for Independence*, 41-66.

14. However as Athanasios Karathanses shows the movement toward the introduction of Greek learning in the Principalities had been initiated by the 'boyar' rulers before the advent of the Phanariots. See *Hoi Hellenes logoi ste Vlaxia (1670-1714)*, (Thessaloniki: Institute for Balkan Studies, 1982), Chapter 1.

15. According to Demaras, such orientations toward Western culture were partly influenced by the exigencies of Phanariot political life, noting that "the French language, which had been imposed and recognized as the official diplomatic language, was studied systematically by the Phanariots; their children learned French and absorbed French culture. This period marks the most important stage in modern Greek culture." Konstantine Demaras, *A History of Modern Greek Literature*, translated by Mary P. Gianos, (Albany: State University of New York Press, 1972), 113.

16. Demetrios Katartzes, 'Logos Protreptikos' in *Ho Koraes kai he Epoche Tou*, 64. Because the majority of Katartzes's works were not published in his lifetime and have come down to scholars in fragments, they are notoriously hard to date.

17. The 'Frank' in question appears to be Voltaire, whom the author speaks critically of throughout the text. Demetrios Katartzes, 'Symboule stous Neous,' in *Ta Evriskomena*, (Athens: Hermes, 1970), 44. The date of this text has been judged to be 1785.

18. It is on the basis of such statements that the Phanariots were harshly judged as Ottoman apologists by more nationalistically minded intellectuals. On the other hand Katartzes's insistent advocacy of Western learning and enthusiasm for the Enlightenment inspired contempt from men like Michael Peridikaris (1766-1828) who saw him as "Gallicized" and a symbol of how a high born soul can 'in absurdity fall.'" See Konstantine Demaras, *Neohellenikos Diaphotismos*, (Athens: Philippos Iliou, 1977), 180. Peridikaris's essay on another 'false philhellene' (Regas) is discussed below.

19. The establishment of the Bucharest Academy was advanced by the efforts of the high cleric-logios Chrysanthos Notaras. Notaras's works will be featured prominently in Chapter 5. See Karathanases, *Hoi Hellenes logioi ste Vlaxia (1670-1714)*, 114-127.

20. He found himself the object of a legal dispute, was jailed and ultimately retreated into monastic life. Vranousis, editor's note, *Hoi Prodromoi*, 2.

21. Moisiodax's birthplace was indicated by Regas on his famous 'Map of Greece;' he was the only contemporary Greek figure to enjoy this distinction. The two men apparently met in Bucharest although no records or sources exist to furnish the details. See Regas Velestinlis, 'He Charta tes Ellados,'(1797) in *Regas*, 359-369.

22. Paschalis Kitromilides, *The Enlightenment as Social Criticism: Iosepos Moisiodax and Greek Culture in the Eighteenth Century*, (Princeton: Princeton University Press, 1992), 18. Note: this text is largely the translation of an earlier work by Kitromilides written in Greek entitled, *Iosepos Moisiodax, Hoi syntetagmenes tes Balkanekes skepses ton 18o aiona*, (Athens: Morfotiko Idroma Ethnikes Trapezes, 1985). The Greeks often used the term 'Dakia' to identify the lands which today constitute Romania. For example, Meletios titles his chapter on this region, "On Dakia, that is, Moldavia, Vlachia and Transylvania." Meletios, *Geographia Palaia kai Nea*, (Venice, Nikolaos Glykeis, 1728), 227.

23. Kitromilides's studies of Moisiodax cannot be said to add much dimension to this intriguing aspect of his personality or development. The sources are few and virtually nothing is known of Moisiodax's first twenty seven years of life. Readers of *Enlightenment as Social Criticism* will find that Moisiodax's own *Apologia* serves as the basic source for Kitromilides's biographical information; an interesting work to be sure but one that deals only obliquely with the themes mentioned above. As described in this chapter this seems to be consistent with Moisiodax's intent to minimize these elements of his identity.

24. This represents one of the great milestones in Moisiodax's intellectual development. Voulgaris will appear from this point forward in his works as a subject of both praise,(*Ethike Philosophia*) and criticism (*Apologia*),

subjects to be discussed below.

25. Antonio Lodovico Muratori (1672-1750) was a prolific author. His *La filosofia morale* was first published in 1736.

26. Kitromilides, *Enlightenment as Social Criticism*, 49.

27. Locke's Essay had been translated and introduced to the Athonian curriculum by Voulgaris (Greek title: 'Peri tou kata anthropoton nou'). See Kitromilides, *Enlightenment as Social Criticism*, 31. See also Alkhes Aggelou, 'Pos e noellenike skepse egnorise to 'Dokimio' tou John Locke,' *Angloellenike epitheorese*, 7, (1954): 128-149.

28. This work, which was especially inspired by the French Revolution, is believed to have been written by the Patriarch of Constantinople, Gregory V, during his first term at this post. For a translation and commentary see Richard Clogg, "The 'Didaskhalia Patriki' (1798): an Orthodox Reaction to French Revolutionary Propaganda," *Middle Eastern Studies*, V (1969): 87-115.

29. Gregory's Encyclical of 1819, written during his third and final term as Patriarch, illustrates the internal conflict described above rather well:

> "What benefit does it serve the young in the teachings of this kind, the study of numbers, and algebra, and cubes and the roots of cubes and triangles, and trianglulated tetragons, and logarithms and symbolic logic and elliptical projections, and atoms, and vacuums, and power and attraction, and gravity, and peculiarities of light, and northern lights and matters of optics and sound and myriad other such things and monstrosities, as if to count the sand of the sea and the drops of rain....if in speech they are barbarians, in writing ungrammatical, ignorant in religion, in morality hasty and corrupt, harmful to their states, obscure patriots and unworthy of their ancestral calling?"

Gregory V, 'Patriarchal Encyclical of 1819' in *Ho Koraes kai he Epoche Tou*, 293-294. Gregory was later executed on the outbreak of the 1821 revolution despite his efforts to appease the Turks by excommunicating the rebels.

30. Moisiodax, 'Prologue, Ethike Philosophia,' in Appendix I of Kitromilides, *Iosepos Moisiodax, Hoi syntetagmenes tes Balkanekes skepses ton 18o aiona*, 323. Moisiodax's observations of life under Ottoman rule represent another intriguing aspect of his thought. Although he has been identified as a representative of Enlightenment 'cosmopolitanism' by authors such as Peter Mackridge, ['The Greek Intelligentsia 1780-1830: A Balkan Perspective,' in *Balkan Society in the Age of Greek Independence*, edited by Richard Clogg, (Totowa: Barnes & Noble Books, 1981), 72], the passages considered here portray a writer with a far from ambivalent perspective on the virtues of 'freedom' and 'captivity.'

31. Moisiodax, 'Prologue, Ethike Philosophia,' 324-325.

32. Ibid, 340.

33. This was difficult even for Koraes, who lived much of his life in Paris and came to look with great admiration upon French culture. Confronted with the advances and dominance of the west, Koraes, like the logioi Konstantas and Philippides, was apt to see the French as the "Athenians of today," a conclusion that takes a somewhat diplomatic position on the issue of 'ancient versus modern.' See Demaras, *Neohellenikos Diaphotismos*, 19.

34. This might be most colloquially expressed as 'living in the past.'

35. Moisiodax, 'Prologue, Ethike Philosphia,' 327.

36. Ibid, 330-331.

37. Giorgios Sakellarios, 'Diodos ton Thermopolon,' in *Hoi Prodromoi*, 161. This poem was part of a collection originally published in 1817. Sakellarios will merit attention again later in this study on account of his relationship with Regas with whom he worked on translating and publishing the famous text of Enlightenment historical geography, 'Voyage de jeune Anarcharsis' (1788) by the abbe Barthelemy. Sakellarios is an excellent example of the Neo-Hellenic Enlightenment generation that comes of age, like Regas, in Vienna, where he pursued his medical studies. Sakellarios later worked as a physician in the court of the infamous Ali Pasha of Yannina, spending his final years in the town of his birth, Kozani, where he continued to work on translations of western writings until his death in 1838. He is also one of the few Greek intellectuals that the English traveler Leake spoke of with genuine respect and admiration. Leake, *Travels in Northern Greece*, 4Volumes, (Amsterdam: Adolf M. Hakkert, 1967), I, 354-55, 380. Sakellarios's participation in the effort to recover the past is well represented in his concise (but rather dull) *Archaiologia Synoptike ton Hellenon*, (Vienna: L. Polyzoe, 1796).

38. Koraes's great publishing project, The Hellenic Library, is stuffed with examples of the 'shame' and 'duty' complex found in Sakellarios. The following passage is taken from Koraes's introduction to an edition of Plutarch's 'Parallel Lives' (1814): "Why are they naked, your mother cities, of the books of your ancestors in whose language you are versed and of whose glory you are not ashamed to usurp? You dare call yourselves GREEKS when you tolerate the disgrace of Greece?" Koraes, 'Akolouthia kai telos ton autossxedion stoxasmon peri tes Hellenikes paideias kai glosses' in *Ho Koraes kai he Epoche Tou*, 155.

39. Moisiodax, 'Prologue, Ethike Philosophia,' 339. In this context Moisiodax describes the recent experience of the Russians who "before the reign of Peter the Great, as all of our historians say, were in such a primitive, such an ignorant condition that they called wisdom heresy and nobility sin (such is the power of ignorance)." And yet thanks to the heroic efforts of Peter "so much did they refine themselves, so much did they regenerate themselves, that today by their wisdom and nobility they are regarded among the first nations of Europe." Ibid, 339. These words herald the dramatic appearance of Russia in the eighteenth century Neo-Hellenic dialogue. Moisiodax's praises demonstrate the respect and admiration for the Russians in no small part for the role they played as enemies of the Ottomans and their successes in the ongoing conflicts between the two empires; a most immediate and persuasive demonstration of Russia's growing power. Even more lavish are the statements made by Theotokes in his *Stoicheia tes Geographias* (discussed below). Theotokes of course like Voulgaris later came to accept important ecclesiastical posts in Russia from Catherine the Great. Voulgaris's publishing activities included a 1771 Greek translation of Voltaire's famous 'Epitre a l'Imperatrice de Russie, Catherine II' of the year before (noted above). See also Stephen K. Batalden, *Catherine II's Greek Prelate, Eugenios Voulgaris in Russia, 1771-1806,* (New York: Columbia University Press, 1982). This reconfiguration of power in Europe and the Balkans represented by the rise of Russia had an immense effect as well on people like Pringos, as we will see, who found new cause in these events to embrace the old prophecy of the 'xanthon genos.'

40. The diligent honeybee was the symbol adopted by the Greek printer Glykeis and appears on the frontispiece of many of his publications. It was also the title of a short-lived but influential Neo-Hellenic journal, 'Melissa' (honeybee) published in Paris from 1819-1821. It was characteristic therefore that Demetrios Darvares would remind his readers not to be disconcerted when encountering elements of paganism in the study of the ancient authors, but to "imitate the honeybee which we see to fly to all the flowers but takes only that which is useful." *Alethes hodos eis ten eudaimonian*, (Vienna: Georgio Vendote, 1796), xvii.

41. Moisiodax, 'Prologue, Ethike Philosophia,' 331. Furthermore the statement was reprised with an even more telling addition: "*I am not a bit shy to say* that Greece has a need for Europe..." See Moisiodax, *Apologia*, 153.

42. Even those who expressed this view in the most emotional terms were given to doubt and scepticism in more reflective moments. This will be especially apparent in the melancholy notes and diary entries of the Amsterdam merchant Ioannes Pringos, as discussed below.

43. The *Apologia* is the most sustained statement of Moisiodax's views in this regard. It was his main contention that the Greek curriculum be reformed to reflect the supremacy of scientific, empirical learning and arts at the expense of the neo-Aristotelian traditions favored by the earlier generations of logioi.

44. Iosepos Moisiodax, *Theoria tes Geographias*, (Vienna: Ioannes Thomas, 1781,) xiv-xv. Notaras in his *Eisagoge eis ta geographica kai sphairika* (1716), had nonetheless given the heliocentric position a fairly careful reading. In the end, however, it was not a position that the great cleric-logios could endorse. These issues treated more extensively in Chapter 5 below.

45. Moisiodax, 'Prologue, Ethike Philosophia,' 336.

46. Ibid, 335.

47. Moisiodax appears to espouse here a form of language reform that will later be known more generally as 'katharvousa,' (literally, purified). In an earlier passage of the Prologue he had noted how it was a natural tendency for the Greek language to acquire elements from "the nations within which each Greek city was located." Ibid, 335. Thus, depending on where you happened to be, one might find the presence of Turkish, Albanian or Italian influences in the spoken language. Reform of the language might be performed via a scientific comparison where "it suffices to recognize its (the demotic's) Hellenic mother, from which can be borrowed whatever is needed." Moisiodax, 'Prologue, Ethike Philosophia,' 336.

48. Ibid, 336.

49. The outcome of this early chapter in the 'language zetema' was the decision to use the common Greek, known since as the Koine.

50. This was especially true in regard to the dissemination of holy works, Christian teachings, etc. Numerous examples are contained in Eliou, *Prosthekes sten Hellenike Bibliographia*. See for example the bibliographic records of *Vivlion Kaloumenon Paradeisos* and *Triadeke Oktoexos* of the monk Agapios Landos, published in Venice in 1656. Ibid, 95-98.

51. The use of demotic works such as Mathaiou Kigalas's *Nea Synopsis diaforon Historion* (1650), in some of the instruction at the Flaggineo Schole of Venice did arouse opposition and criticism. Athansios E. Karathanases, *He Phlaggineios Schole tes Venetias*, 192.

52. Of course what Notaras and Meletios called the 'simple form' contained a great many archaic and New Testament fixtures. Both of these high-ranking clerics published the great majority of their works in the 'high' dialects.

53. Panayiotes Kodrikas, *Melete tes Koines Hellenikes Dialektou*, (Paris: Patrinou & Postolaka, 1818).

54. Of course as some of the writers below point out, there were significant differences between the 'ancient'

Greek spoken by Homer and Plato.

55. Kodrikas, *Melete*, 132. It is possible to speculate that Kodrikas's translation of the French vulgare to the Greek xydaion, one of its nearest but not precise equivalents, exerted an influence on how he believed Europeans judged the modern Greek language. Koraes was inclined to use the same word when dismissing the common demotic. The latter's introduction to his translation of Beccaria (1802) contains one of the clearest statements of his aversion to the common dialect. Konstanine Demaras is not alone among Greek scholars in emphasizing Koraes's persistent fear of seeing his homeland succumb to the "tyranny of the rabble." Demaras, *Neohellenikos Diaphotismos*, 19-20.

56. This raises an important question: who was intended for Enlightenment? The fact that men like Kodrikas or Doukas dismissed the obvious value of employing the language of the laos for the education of the laos, has led some modern Greek historians to raise the valid question of who it was therefore that these 'conservative' logioi sought to enlighten. See for example Dizirikes: "It is necessary above all to clarify that when they (the archaists) spoke about progress and education of the race (genos), they were certainly not thinking about the progress and education of the people (laos) who they ignored, disdained, held in contempt or viewed—as Koraes—as rabble, vulgar, savage and blind." *Ho Neohellenikos Diaphotismos kai to Europaiko Pneuma*, 76.

57. See Ioannes Kordatos, *Historia tes glossika zetema mas*, (Athens: Boukoumanis, 1973), 70.

58. Kodrikas had by this time emigrated to Paris where he spent the remainder of his life (1797-1827). It is significant that Kodrikas and Koraes, logioi who became enmeshed in French intellectual circles at a fairly high level, came to revile the xydaica, although important differences in their views on the language zetema turned them too into antagonists. (See below)

59. William Leake, *Researches in Greece*, (London: John Booth, 1814), ii.

60. Ibid, 49. The *Researches* was the outcome of the author's extensive travel in the Balkans and Asia Minor beginning in 1802 and became the precursor to his prodigious four volume work, *Travels in Northern Greece*.

61. Todorova, *Imagining the Balkans*, 98-100. See also below page 176.

62. Moisiodax begrudgingly alluded to the questions raised about his identity in a few writings, however he never used these occasions to acknowledge his ethnicity or elaborate in any way upon his personal relation to Hellenism. See below, page 167.

63. Kodrikas, *Melete*, oe-os.

64. Konstantas and Philippides, *Geographia Neoterike* 44. Note: The authors make the charge of economic exploitation on repeated occasions throughout this text, asserting at one point that Europeans take advantage of the incompetence and avarice of the local landowners to buy up the produce of Greece, leaving the people poor and hungry. Ibid 47.

65. Demaras for example is hesitant to place Moisiodax among the more 'ideological' movements and factions of the later period. See Demaras, *Neoellenikos Diaphotismos*, 11-16.

66. *Hermes ho Logios*, 1 January 1811, 3-4. Because of its attempt to bridge the distance between the ancient and modern languages, katharevousa was known as the 'middle way.'

67. These include the katharevousist, *Melissa* (1819-1821) that appeared in Paris, and in Vienna, the archaist

journal *Kalliope* (1819-1821).

68. See Neophytos Charilaou, *Ho Neophytos Doukas kai he symbole tou sto Neoelleniko Diaphotismo*, (Athens: Kybele, 2002), 169-185. Also, Demaras. *Ho Koraes kai he Epoche Tou*, 35-36.

69. 'Korakistika' refers of course to Koraes whose name had become associated with the katharevousa movement.

70. See 'Korakistika' in *Neoelleniko Theatro (1795-1929)*, edited and with an introduction by Giannes Sideres, (Athens: Vasike Vivliotheke, 1958), 55-66.

71. Demaras, editor's introduction, *Ho Koraes kai he Epoche Tou*, 34.

72. Ibid, 34.

73. Peter Bien, *Kazantzakis and the Linguistic Revolution in modern Greek Literature*, (Princeton: Princeton University Press, 1972), 50-1.

74. See Peter Mackridge, 'The Greek Intelligentsia 1780-1830: A Balkan Perspective,' 78. See also the dour epilogue 'Liberalism not Victorious' in Henderson's *The Revival of Greek Thought, 1620-1830.*

75. Ioannes Kordatos, *Historia tou Glossika mas zetematos*, 8. Kordatos had employed a similar approach in his famous Marxist interpretation of the 1821 Revolution, *He Koinonike Symasia tes Hellenikes Epanastaseos tou 1821*, (Athens, 1924).

76. Kordatos, *Historia tou Glossika mas zetematos*, 80.

77. Ibid, 51.

78. Moisiodax, *Apologia*, 3. The charge that his focus on mathematics amounted to 'Mbakalika' lessons implied that they were fit only for merchants and clerks, e.g. 'bean counters.' A 'true' education was founded on the basis of philosophy, such as one acquired through Voulgaris's *He Logike ek palaion te kai neoteron suneranistheisa,* (Leipzig, 1766), a standard specimen of the 'new Aristotelianism' which the 'illustrious Eugenios' (a reference to his former teacher that Moisiodax repeats with a certain sarcasm throughout the *Apologia*) was the chief proponent. The *Logike* was written in the ancient dialect, and therefore represents the prevailing assumptions regarding the unity of the substance and the medium of higher education that Moisiodax relates above. Nonetheless Moisiodax doggedly continued to advocate the demotic throughout the work based on his view of the "needs of the Race,' and the self-evident utility that the common idiom furnished in "facilitating the comprehension of the sciences." *Apologia*, 3.

79. Kodrikas, *Melete*, kd-ke. Kodrikas came to Moldavia in 1783 as secretary under the employ of the new Phanariot Hospodar Michael Soutsos. It was under these circumstances that he made the acquaintance of Moisiodax. Moisiodax had an erratic career at the local Academy of Jassy where he twice served as Director, first in 1765-66, and then again in 1776-77. See Kitromilides, *The Enlightenment as Social Criticism*, 52-3, 67-75. In both cases his tenure appears to have been affected by the resistance encountered to his scientific views.

80. Kodrikas, *Melete*, ke. When Kodrikas speaks of the 'Common Dialect,' which he advances as the choice for a universal 'national' language, he is speaking of the language used by the Greek Church: "The general form of Our Common Dialect we call that, which the Chiote, the Cypriot, the Cretan, the Peloponnesian, the

Thessalian, the Epiriotes, the Athenian, the Smyrnan, and in general all the leaders (prokritoi) of the race view as legitimate, and are in unison, and that is the form of the Great Church." Ibid, 1. For Kodrikas the language used by the Church, known as New Testament Greek or koine, deserved by virtue of its common usage throughout the Greek world (however narrowly) and what he believed to be its pure character, to be established as the 'national' language.

The passage above contains some interesting similarities with Leake's contemporary study of the Greek language, in which he had considered a style of writing called "the mixo-barbarous, which studies to employ Hellenic phrases, assumes many of the habits of ancient syntax, and endeavors to imitate its involutions, but is still combined with so many expressions of modern or foreign etymology." However such an approach only moved Leake, as it did Kodrikas, to question the competency of its perpetrators: "the style betrays itself, for that of men half learned in the literature of their ancestors, who unable to express themselves with purity in the ancient language, have yet been sufficiently acquainted with it, to write in a manner unintelligible to the vulgar." William Leake, *Researches in Greece*, 54-55. It is not clear if Kodrikas was familiar with Leake's work, however the inverse is true. Kodrikas was cited occasionally in Leake's *Researches*, where for example he noted the publication of Kodrikas's translation of Fontenelles 'Pluralite des Mondes.(1794)' *Researches*, 79. But Leake appears to have acquired his familiarity with Kodrikas's language views from the latter's *Observations sur les opinions de quelques Hellenistes touchant le Grec moderne*, (1804), although he disagreed with the author's opinion regarding the existence of an "Ecclesiastical Greek distinct both from Hellenic and Romaic." *Researches*, 440. Leake also included the books of 'Joseph the Moesodacian' in his 'Catalogue of Authors.' Ibid, 81.

81. Moisiodax, 'Prologue, Ethike Philosophia,' 336. Similar remarks were made by Daniel Philippides on the occasion of a letter to the French geographer Barbie du Bocage in 1801. "My friend, the more that a language is methodical, the easier it is to learn that language, and the facility of the language will put man on the path to knowledge at a faster pace. Vulgare Greek that is cultivated, corrected, reformed could perhaps become the most methodical language in Europe and, as a consequence, the best language, the philosophical language. I want to take charge of a reform project. I know well that the venture belongs to a Scholarly Society presided over by a Condillac, by a Kant. But I could only do what my powers allow me to do." Gazes-Bocage-Philippides, *Allelographia*, edited and with an introduction and commentary by Aikaterines Koumarianou, (Athens: Estras, 1966), 35.

82. A stormy defense of Moisiodax appears in the June 1819 (11/12) of the periodical, pages 530-531. However the editors do not respond to the ethnic elements of Kodrikas's critique in their defense of Moisiodax, nor do they even acknowledge them, limiting their arguments to the virtues of the reform faction to which they belonged and of which Moisiodax might be considered an early advocate. Nonetheless their silence on the issue of his ethnic identity is curious given that it played a central role in the offending piece. Of course Demetrios Katartzes, a Phanariot and yet an intense advocate of the demotic, was also criticized by Kodrikas in the *Melete*—in this case on purely ideological grounds. One can only speculate whether it was on these grounds too that the journal editors found it more comfortable or simply more convenient to concentrate their response. Finally, it is significant that Kodrikas does not single out Demetrios Darvares in his critique, for he too was a Vlach-Hellenizer and prolific writer who tended to feature the demotic in his work. In this case Kodrikas's focus on Moisiodax helps to show the latter's rather high status in the Greek 'Republic of Letters.' Darvares is treated with some depth below.

83. See Kitromilides, *The Enlightenment as Social Criticism*, 119-120. The work referred to above is Moisiodax's *Semeioseis Physiologikai* (Bucharest: Ioannou Lozarou, 1784).

84. Metropolitan Ignatios of Hungaro-Vlachia (1766-1828), was an important and controversial figure in his own rite. He will appear again in Chapter 4.

85. *Hermes ho Logios*, 1 January 1811, 59-60.

86. This is particularly true of Darvares. Of course the language debate broke out here too between those who favored teaching the Vlachs ancient Greek, such as Doukas, and those who favored the demotic. Of the latter one of the most interesting personages was Ioannes Velaras (1711-1823), author of a Greek-Albanian grammar of his own. See Angelike Konstantakopoulou, *He Hellenike Glossa sta Valkania (1750-1850), To Tetraglosso Lexico tou Daniel Moschhopolite*, (Iannina: University of Iannina, 1988), 36, 53.

87. See below in the examples of Daniel of Moschopolis and Demetrios Darvares. Language rationalization or homogenization as a means of Orthodox regeneration was also the principal theme of the fiery preacher and martyr Kosmas ho Aitolos (discussed below).

88. Raymond Detrez, 'Relations between Greeks and Bulgarians in the Pre-Nationalist Era: The Gudilas in Plovdiv,' in *Greece and the Balkans, Identities, Perceptions and Cultural Encounters since the Enlightenment*, edited by Dimitris Tziovas, (Hants, England: Ashgate, 2003), 39. The 'Gudilas' were Hellenized Bulgarians who had undergone this change as a "form of social promotion." Ibid, 35. Regarding the local Greek schools Detrz cites a passage from the work of Ljuben Karavelov (1834-1879) who once wrote that the disdain of the teachers "drove many Bulgarian children to feel ashamed of their name and nationality, and made them change their names and conceal their origin..." Ibid, 39.

89. These pragmatic motivations take precedence in Kitromilides, *Enlightenment as Social Criticism*, 120.

90. Of course, the claim that he was "proudly indicating his geographical origins in his surname," is pure conjecture. Peter Mackridge, 'The Greek Intelligentsia 1780-1830: A Balkan Perspective,' 71.

91. Phanes Michalopoulos, *Moschopolis: Hai Athenai tes Tourkokratias, 1500-1769*, (Athens: Ekdosis Perigegetikes Lexsies, 1941), 28.

92. Leake, *Researches in Greece*, 380.

93. See again here Hupchick (ed.), *The Pen and the Sword, Studies in Bulgarian History by James F. Clark*, 90-96.

94. Konstantakopoulou, *He Hellenike Glossa sta Valkania*, 52. Such attitudes were especially promoted by the economic developments of these years. See Darvares's *Eklogarion Graikikon* below. These points also discussed again in Chapter 4 below.

95. See Introduction to present work.

96. Father Paisii, 'Slavic-Bulgarian History of the Bulgarian People, Kings and Saints and of All Bulgarian Deeds and Events' (1762) cited in Marim V. Pundeff, 'Bulgarian Nationalism,' in *Nationalism in Eastern Europe*, edited by Peter F. Sugar and Ivo J. Lederer, (Seattle: University of Washington Press, 1969), 101. Pundeff implies that Paisii's 'nationalism' was encouraged by his experience in the Mount Athos monasteries where he was "often stung, according to his own testimony, by the ridicule Greek and Serbian monks heaped on Bulgarians for being backward, ignorant and lacking a great national past." Ibid, 100.

97. The author's full name was Daniil Mihali Adami Hagi. He was born around 1754 in the vicinity apparently of Moschopolis and of Vlach descent. The *Eisagogike* his only known work, was first published in 1802 while Daniel was a teacher at the Academy of Moschopolis. It was here where he worked closely with the great man of Moschopolis letters (and yet another former student of Voulgaris, whose language views he followed), Theodorou Kavalliotes (?-1789). Kavalliotes published himself a three language lexicon the *Protopieria* of 1770, in Greek (ancient), Vlach and Albanian. The year of Daniel's death has been put at 1822

or 1825. Konstantakopoulou, *He Hellenike glossa sta Valkania*, 32-33. For a summary of Voulgaris's influence on the language views of Kavalliotes see Stathes N. Kekrides, 'He Nea Academia tes Moschopolis kai he aktinovolia tes ston balkaniko xoro,'in *Moschopolis*, edited by Stavros Nkatsopoulos, (Iannina: Idrema Boreioepeirotikon Ereunon, 1979), 86.

98. The work has been reprinted a number of times. A long excerpt even appears in Leake's *Researches in Greece*, although Leake was not able to identify the author or the year of publication from the "small book" that he found so useful. Leake, *Researches*, 383-402. He himself found no small pleasure in "being furnished in the maxims and precepts of these exercises with a picture of some of the manners, superstitions, prejudices and opinions, of these secluded and unpolished nations." Ibid, 381. Daniel's text has also been reprinted several times in works of Bulgarian and Romanian authorship. See for example J. Kristophson's bibliography in 'Das Lexicon Tetraglossen,' *Zeitschrift fur Balkanologie*, 10, (1974): 128.

99. These and the following passages from the 'Eisagogike Didaskalia,'are taken from the most recent republication of the Lexicon in *Zeitschrift fur Balkanologie*, 10, (1974): 14.

100. Daniel, "Eisagogike Didaskalia,' 44.

101. "When you see some child that gets ashamed and becomes red in the cheeks, there is one who seeks to do good." Ibid, 80.

102. Ibid, 80.

103. Ibid, 49-50.

104. Ibid, 60-62.

105. The lexicon was followed by short lessons in Christian theology, the physical sciences, letter-writing, arithmetic and the Orthodox feast days. A description and analysis of the contents can be found in Eulogios Kourilas, *He Moschopolis kai he Nea Akademia avtes*, (Athens: Phoinekos, 1934), 300-5.

106. Daniil Michale Adame Xatze o Moschopolites, 'Eisagogike Didaskalia,' in *Bibliografia Romaneasca, Veche 1508-1830, Volume II*, edited by Ioan Bianu and Nerva Hodos, (Bucharest: Atelierele Socec & Co., 1909), 440-441. The publisher of the original text of the lexicon is not known, nor the place of publication. Clogg and Mackridge propose Constantinople, the Romanian editors above suggest Venice, as does Kostantakoplou, *He Hellenike Glossa sta Valkania*, 50.

107. Mackridge makes this mistake in his otherwise fine and frequently cited essay, 'The Greek Intelligentsia 1780-1830: A Balkan Perspective,' 70. The great Anglo scholar of Modern Greek history Richard Clogg also ascribes the text to Daniel in his 'Aspects of the Movement for Greek Independence,' in *The Struggle for Greek Independence*, 20. (Clogg also translated and included some lines from the verse in his collection of pre-revolutionary Greek documents, *The Movement for Greek Independence 1770-1821: a collection of documents*, 91-92.) Very recent works however continue to repeat this error. Daniel appears again as the author of the verse in Dimitris Livanios, 'Christians, Heroes and Barbarians: Serbs and Bulgarians in the Modern Greek Historical Imagination (1602-1950),' in *Greece and the Balkans* (2003), 74. Nonetheless, Sxenas was a man of some distinction in his times. He was a frequent contributor to *Hermes ho Logios* and eventually an ephoros (supervisor) of the famous Bucharest Academy. See for example his activities and pronouncements in connection with the Academy in *Hermes o Logios*, May 15, 1813, 53-61. One should also note his lengthy review of the logios Gregorios Zalekoglou's (1776-1827) *Galloelleniko Lexico* (1809) in the March 1, 1812 edition of the same journal. The review expresses Sxenas's intense desire to see the works of Enlightenment transmitted through the East and helps to explain his advocation of language consolidation,

e.g. language 'rationalization' as the handmaiden of enlightenment. *Hermes ho Logos*, March 1, 1812, 65-71.

108. The circumstances regarding how the verse came to be included in the work, or Sxenas's relation to Daniel, etc are not known.

109. In general, the remarkable severity of the cultural reproach lodged by Sxenas, delivered with a disarming absence of self-consciousness, has been under-emphasized. It certainly tells us much about the cultural assumptions and relationships of the time and the striking terms in which they could be expressed. A recent historian (Kostantakoplou) virtually passes over the subject in silence. *He Hellenike Glossa sta Valkania*, 50.

110. Eulogios Kourilas, *He Moschopolis kai he Nea Academeia autes*, Kourilas's critic Phanes Michalopoulos rejected such arguments by labeling the verse as the work of an 'outsider' to the region, adding that Greek learning needed no such propagandizing among the local inhabitants who already held it in esteem and counted themselves blessed to share in the faith, language, and even consciousness of Hellenism. Michalopoulos, *Moschopolis*, 28.

111. Konstantakoplou has nonetheless provided readers with an excellent summary of some key actors and milestones in the cultural conflicts of these times. She notes for example an episode in Pest in 1790 concerning the demand on the part of some members of the local Orthodox 'community of Greeks and Makedonovlachs' to have the liturgy performed in Vlach. She suggests some of the ambiguities of the dispute when writing that this movement was ultimately thwarted by "the Greeks or those Vlachs who felt themselves Greeks—here the boundaries are difficult to distinguish." *He Hellenike Glossa sta Valkania*, 39-40.

112. The author's decision for example to include people like Doukas in her analysis as a Greek writer is problematical for the simple reason that some question exists about his own ethnic background. Others such as Leake have identified him as a 'Vlachiote' *Researches in Greece*, 93. If so, Doukas would represent the example of a Hellenized Vlach who insisted on the diffusion of ancient Greek as the instrument of pan-Balkan enlightenment, not an entirely illogical outcome given the experience of Moisiodax. It was the latter's failure to advocate the ancient language for this purpose that left him vulnerable to his critics and perhaps foiled his efforts at assimilation. Unfortunately the important question of Doukas's ethnicity has yet to be resolved. One notes with disappointment the complete silence with which this subject is treated in a recent and by no means brief biography of the great logios, e.g., Neophytos Charilaou, *Ho Neophytos Doukas kai he symbole tou sto Neoelleniko Diafotismo*, (Athens: Kybele, 2002). It should be noted that Doukas is not alone in this regard. Regas Velestinlis, Daniel Philippides and Thomas Kavalliotes have all been subjects of similar questions ("he was a genuine Greek," Michalopoulos declared of the latter in his *Moschopolis*, 21.) It is apparently a difficult subject for Greek historians to address directly, being somewhat akin perhaps to 'giving up one's heroes.'

113. Stathes N. Kerkides, 'He Nea Academia tes Moschopolis kai he aktinovolia tes ston balkaniko xoro,'in *Moschopolis*, 90. Nektarios also financed the publishing of the *Eisagogike Didaskalia*.

114. Konstantakopolou, *He Hellenike glossa sta Valkania*, 49. Nonetheless, Michalopoulos is correct in saying that the pressure to demonstrate knowledge of ancient Greek was apparently felt by all, Greek and non-Greek alike, who wrote in the demotic, as often witnessed in the dedication pages of demotic works. *Moschopolis*, 26.

115. Editor's introduction to the reprint edition of *Sophias Apanthisma*, (Athens: Syllogos Pros Diadosin ton Ellenikon Grammaton, 1873), g. This work was originally published in 1811.

116. The 1 March 1811 featured a survey of some of his recent publications preceded by a lustrous introduction in which the editor declared, "Justly should the young men of our race call him Father." 76-77.

Darvares contributed at least seven articles to the journal. Emmanuel Fragkiskos, ed., *Ta Hellenika Proepanastika Periodica*, Vol B *Hermes ho Logios*, 1811-1821, (Athens: Kentron Neoellenikon Erevnon, 1976), 14.

117. *Hermes ho Logios*, 1 February 1811, 63-4. In fact Darvares's career reflects the manner and spirit of his contemporary Koraes more than Moisiodax. Moisiodax published few works and these of a rather dense theoretical nature while devoting equal energy to his teaching. It was more in the custom of Koraes and Darvares to stay put in the western capitals of enlightenment where they were clearly most comfortable, while keeping up a steady bombardment of simple, improving works on their eastern homelands.

118. Darvares frequently addressed himself directly to 'fathers' and encouraged them to take great care for this their first duty: the education of their sons. This quality is especially apparent in Darvares's, *Alethes hodos eis ten eudaimonian*, (Vienna: Georgio Vendote, 1796). In this piece Darvares draws together three 'instructive' writings from the ancients (Plutarch, Isocrates and Xenophon, with some fragments from Aristotle thrown in for good measure) on the subjects of upbringing and ethics, reminding fathers that "the mind of children resembles, according to Aristotle a white paper (levkon xarten) on which there isn't anything written, but it is possible with time for much to be written upon it." (iv) A good son of the Enlightenment Darvares returned often to the theme that "virtue and wickedness are not innate (emfetoi) in man, but are acquired,"(Ibid) He did caution to add in a later work however that human nature does "incline toward the bad rather than the good being hindered from its first-forming with a defect of hearing." He attributes this bit of wisdom to Plato. *Megale Katechisis, etoi orthodoxos christianike Didaskalia tes Anatolikes Ekklesias*, (Vienna: Georgio Vendote, 1805), v.

119. Hellenic luminaries are particularly present in the *Sophias Apanthisma*. Indeed the very first chapter takes its title from Socrates's grand injunction, 'Gnowthe savton.' However there are some surprises such as the chapter 'Time is money,' accorded to the "wise statement of Franklin." (79). Other chapters include 'Detest flattery,' 'Seek always to improve in your profession,' 'Don't boast of your virtues,' 'Don't make promises you can't keep,''Don't press your opinions fanatically,' etc

120. Darvares, *Sophias Apanthisma*, 85-6. Darvares appears to be speaking here of Casimir Perrier (1777-1832), holder of several ministerial posts in Restoration France.

121. *Syntomos Iera Istoria tes Ekklesias tes Palaias kai Neas Diathekes*, (Vienna: Ioannou Karolou Sxouenderou, 1800). This work is a synopsis of the Old and New Testament. See also *Megale Katechesis, etoi Orthodox Christianike Didaskalia tes Anatolikes Ekklesias*, (Vienna: Gergio Vendote, 1805). This work like the above was also translated from the Russian although the original sources are not identified.

122. Nonetheless, Darvares did put his knowledge of the ancient language on frequent display in his works, typically in the form of introductory epigrams. He also published an instruction book for ancient Greek "the mother of wisdom," composed in the form of dialogues between a father, student and teacher, e.g. *Eisagoge eis ten Hellenike Glossan*, (Vienna: Georgio Vendote, 1798).

123. This duty was actually specified by Darvares in one of his first works the *Cheiragogia eis ten kalokagatheia*, (Athens: Syllogos pros ton diadosin ton Hellenikon grammaton, 1876), 136. This book was originally published in 1790.

124. *Alethes hodos*, xii. And yet despite the discomfort that the awareness of this contempt inspired, it was nonetheless to Europe that the Balkans belonged and would perhaps find their salvation. Darvares was quite insistent on this point: "Europe, of which we live in, is the smallest (of the parts of the earth), but it is the most populous because it exceeds all the other parts in the arts and sciences and in just government." Darvares, *Eklogarian Graikikon*, (Vienna: Georgio Vendote, 1804), 20.

125. Darvares, *Eklogarion Graikikon*,, iii. Note use of 'omogeneis' translated here as 'common race' but used elsewhere by the author in different contexts. When thanking his brothers whose financial contributions to each edition he usually cites on the title page of his books, Darvares writes 'ton omogenon mou adelphon.' In a later work, he titles one lesson "Don't boast about your 'genos'," in which context he appears to again mean family. Darvares obviously did not have the troubles of future historians of Balkan nationalism in mind when he chose his words. *Sophias Apanthisma*, 36.

126. Darvares, *Sophias Apanthisma*, 82-84.

127. Note this revealing comment from a recent text: "What helped to establish ancient Hellas as one of the principal parts of the new state was the fact that it was implicitly suggested by Enlightened Europe which, as seen elsewhere, played a decisive role as a legitimizing factor. Had it not been for Europe's espousal of ancient Hellas as one of the high-points of human civilization and as one of its own three cherished antecedent heritages (the other two being the Roman empire and Christianity), it is not certain that the indigenous Greek elites of the time would have adopted it as their own." John S. Koliopoulos and Thanos M. Verenis, *Greece, The Modern Sequel*, (New York: New York University Press, 2002), 243. I would add that this study has also stressed the critical importance of the 'internal' dialogue between Greek 'elites' and their past.

128. Darvares, *Cheirogogia eis ten kalokagatheia*, (Athens: Syllogos pros diadosin ton Hellenikon Grammaton, 1876), 136.

129. This document is actually of significant historical interest as it marks the tension aroused among some Orthodox regarding the Habsburg re-conquests in the Balkans. For Voulgaris the "German armies" while liberating the local Christians (those living in Serbia) from the miseries they had long-suffered under the Turks were yet now subject to new persecutions and dangers at the hands of the "apostles of Rome." Eugeniou Voulgareos, *Propheteke epistole pros tous orthodoxous christianous*, reprint edition, (Athens: Orthodoxou Typou, 1969), 27.

130. Quote taken from Apostolos Tlavinas, 'He Symbole tou Moschopolite Nektariou Terpou sten anasxese ton exislamismon,' in *Moschopolis*, 30. *Pistis* had been published ten times by 1818. Ibid. There is also apparently some question regarding the ethnicity of Terpou whom another contributor to the volume identifies as a "Vlachophone" but yet "pure" Greek. See Michales G. Tritos, 'Nektarios Terpos, Ho Moschopolites Didascholos tou Genous,' 227.

131. Moisiodax, 'Prologue, Ethike Philosophia,' 325-26.

132. Kosma Thesprotou, 'Perigraphe Geographike Albanias,' *Geographia Alvanias kai Epirou*, 37.

133. Kosma Thesprotou, 'Prostheke eis ten Geographian tou Athanasiou Psalida,'*Geographia Alvanias kai Epirou* 77.

134. Markos Gkiolias, *Ho Kosmas Aitolos kai he epoche tou*, (Athens: Tymphestos, 1972), 27. Unlike Macedonia, Thessaly or Epeiros, Rumely (the part of the Greek mainland directly above the Peloponnesus), contained a less ethnically diverse and mostly Greek population.

135. Gkiolias, *Ho Kosmas Aitolos kai he epoche tou*, 137. Gkiolias asserts later in his biography that Kosmas himself had no "historical memory of his racial (fylogenetikes) descent." A claim that can only be treated with skepticism.

136. Kosma tou Aitolou, *Didachais*, edited by Ioannou B. Menounou, (Ahens: Tenos, 1979), 116-117. Kosmas's silence on his own background has not inspired a great deal of interest among his Greek biographers who rarely if ever venture an opinion on his ethnic origin.

137. This can be true of the biography of Phanes Michalopoulos, *Kosmas hos Aitolos*, (Athens: 1940).

138. Ibid, 19.

139. Kosma tou Aitolou, *Didachai*, 209-210.

140. In another teaching Kosmas thanks the villagers for guiding their children toward the Church but quickly turns to scolding them over their failure to provide schools: "Very well, you dedicated your children to me, but let's see, do you have a school where our children can read and study letters? You don't, God help us—illiterate children you dedicate to me? What kind do I want? I want a worthy donation. Children that are so many little pigs (gourounopoula) I don't accept, because I am proud. I want your donation. Should you like to donate to me a school here in your town where our children can learn letters, know where it is they walk, then will I bless them to live and to prosper." Ibid, 141-142.

141. Of course 'shame' held a prominent place in the rhetorical arsenal of many other national reformers, as we have seen above in the case of Koraes and Sakellarios.

142. Kosmas tou Aitolou, *Didachai*, 266-67.

143. Leake, *Travels in Northern Greece*, IV: 149. The circumstances of Kosmas's execution by the Turks remains in dispute. Certainly the tensions and climate of suspicion created by the recently concluded Russo-Turk War of 1768-74, and questions concerning his possible role or activities in the 1770 Orlov revolt, played a role in his death. See Menounu, *Didachais*, 26. No doubt too the aggressive proselytizing activities of Kosmas had long tested the patience of local Muslims. The fiery evangelist Nektarios Terpos, noted above, had himself narrowly escaped a similar fate, being the victim instead of a beating that left him scarred for life. G. Valeta, 'Nektarios Terpos: Ho agnoemenos megalos ethnophotistes, prodomos tou Kosma Aitolou (1690-1740),' *Nea Hestia*, 89, (1971), 577-581.

144. Raymond Pearson for example has written that: "Given the indisputable glories of the classical past, the modern Greeks and Italians were intimidated by the thought that any modern revival could only be a disappointment.... their Golden Age was as much a burden as an inspiration." Raymond Pearson, 'Fact, Fantasy, Fraud: Perceptions and Projections of National Revival' in *Ethnic Groups*, Vol 10 (1993): 55.

145. Koraes, 'Report on the Present State of Civilization in Greece,' 171.

146. Meniates as we have seen turned to the more sympathetic figure perhaps of the Virgin.

147. Denis Diderot, 'Foreword to Volume VIII of the Encyclopedia, in *Encyclopedia*, translated and with an introduction by Nelly S. Hoyt and Thomas Cassirer, (New York: The Bobbs-Merrill Company, Inc., 1965), 118.

148. Ibid, 117.

149. Anthimios Gazes, 'Meletiou Geographia,' in Demaras *Ho Koraes kai he epoche tou*, 320. This appeared in the prologue which he affixed to his 1807 reprint of Meletios's original work (first printing 1728). As noted above Gazes, a cleric, was also the editor of *Hermes ho Logios*.

150. Koraes, 'Report on the Present State of Civilization in Greece,' 158.

151. One of the angry criticisms of Gregory in his Patriarchal Encyclical of 1819 concerned the naming of Greek youth after ancient figures, a custom that violated the tradition of baptizing children in the name of Christian saints. See Gregorios V, 'Patriarchal Encyclical of 1819,' in *Ho Koraes kai he epoche tou*, 295.

IV. Culture and Revolution

> *Dear Greece, our common and affectionate mother turns her tear filled eyes to us and in a tender voice says 'my beloved children, seek always justice and glory. Hurry, but be prudent and virtuous, for history keeps watch on our work. The eyes of all well thinking Europe draw upon us, so reform yourselves, and appear to the end worthy of your ancestors...*[1]

The passage above, taken from the editor's introduction to the first number of the journal *Melissa*, contains an image of 'Mother Hellas' as she was often depicted in Greek texts prior to the revolution. This portrayal of Greece as an aggrieved woman, alternately mother or maiden, is a work of cultural and discursive shorthand, the 'national problem' rendered in the visceral image of violated womanhood. It represents too the 'vulgarization' of the discourse: all the intellectual dilemmas posed by decline and 'enlightenment' have been pruned down or put aside, reduced now to a simple image and message: duty.[2]

As Koraes's writings from the late Diaphotismos show quite well, the logioi found great utility in bartering these tragic heroines of enslaved Greece. Here after all was a symbol of unusual power and reach that projected with special urgency the message they had long labored to drive home. "Imagine if you can our mother, Greece," wrote Koraes in 1801, "old and famous to all peoples and all times, with black and shredded clothes, wounded in all parts of her body from the barbarous tyrants, her hair untied and tangled..." Though shoeless and nearly naked she runs toward us "her children," he continues, pleading for aid. With painful movements she shows us "her ripped clothing and one by one her wounds, she paints us with her blood, waters us with her tears..."[3]

These passages from Koraes's 'Trumpet Call of War' express the anxious sentiments of a patriot temporarily overcome with revolutionary enthusiasm. Such feelings had been inspired in the normally cautious logios by the victorious armies of France whom, he hoped, would soon free Greece in their liberating march through the East. It was already a time of heightening expectations for change given the ongoing and very visible erosion in the status of Ottoman power and influence. Within Greek society too were occurring developments that ran alongside these revolutions in the European balance of power. New classes were rising and asserting their influence on internal affairs, with the effect that larger and larger numbers of Greeks were engaged in the questions surrounding the 'national problem.' With time, the symbol of the wretched mother, and the implied duty of her sons to relieve her misery, became very much ritualized in the preamble of virtually every patriotic outburst and manifesto. This theme is in fact quite prominent in the 'Great Oath' of the Philike Etairia, the secret 'Society of Friends' determined on overthrowing Ottoman rule in the Balkans. "Finally, I swear to you, O holy and afflicted Motherland!" the new recruits solemnly declared, as they pledged themselves to the cause of the cursed nation:

> I swear by your long years of suffering. I swear by the bitter tears, which for so many centuries your wretched children have shed and continue to shed! By my own tears, which flow at this minute! And to the future freedom of my race I dedicate all myself to you! In the future you will be the cause and object of my thoughts, your name the guide of my actions and your happiness the reward of my efforts![4]

By the end of the eighteenth century therefore, the conception of the nation's awful plight and the accompanying insistence on rehabilitation had outgrown the narrow circle of the 'learned' and acquired a popular audience of some dimension.[5] The majority of the men, for example, who recited the fiery oath above were from merchant backgrounds. The 'national problem' had been vulgarized in the process and reduced to a caricature, something, admittedly, that it had always been prone to. This was accomplished through the publication in work after work of stock phrases, images and symbols, used to evoke the central themes of national degeneracy and infamy that very much defined the 'culture' of contemporary Greek discourse. Such images were circulated so generally in fact within Greece that they acquired an almost remote quality in the literature of these times.

The sources surrounding the creation and development of the Philike Etairia show that its members were obviously well versed in the rhetoric described above. It was this prevailing discourse that informed the ideology (to the extent one existed) and pronouncements of the Etairia, and furnished the Society with a stock of symbols ready made for incorporation into their oaths and declarations. Nonetheless, this is a point that has not been sufficiently emphasized in the past.[6] These men may have been uneducated, even illiterate, as some have written, but the discourse still found its way to them.

The three founders of the Philike Etairia were merchants, as were many of the first men drawn to the movement. This fact remains highly intriguing to Greek historians but would seem to hold some interest for students of nationalism in general. Given the composition of the Society, it may be possible to gain a closer glimpse of the motivations influencing these often young merchant-revolutionaries. It may even become clear that within its rhetoric and rituals the Philike was elaborating a revealing discourse of its own.

In pursuing these questions the present chapter aims to describe the manner in which the merchant element developed in Greek society and the subsequent role it came to play in the Neohellenic Enlightenment. Although works on this subject are not rare, there are important elements of the story that may yet be more fully explored, including the novel role that 'self-worth' came to play upon the earnest efforts of the 'friends' to rescue Mother Hellas.

The Rise of the Merchant Hero – Historical Background

Koraes's pronouncements of his later years and the example he himself presented as a young man determined to distinguish himself as the greatest Greek merchant ever to set foot in Amsterdam, derive from the very real fame that others before him had achieved in the rough and tumble world of the diaspora emboros (merchant). This fame was not simply based on the wealth such men had amassed, but the substantial contributions they had made to the revival of learning back in their 'patridas' (fatherlands). The impressive school and library building activities of the successful emboroi—efforts that reflected their desire to close the civilization gap between Greece and Europe—serve to reveal the often intense cultural self-consciousness that accompanied their experience of life in xeniteia (foreign parts), especially among the European centers of power and affluence to which they gravitated; it is an experience that they shared with the logioi in whose civilizing mission they very much collaborated.[7]

To explain the rise of the merchant classes we have to consider the pattern of European economic and diplomatic development over the seventeenth and eighteenth centuries. In a 1960 article in *The Journal of Modern History*, since become a classic in the field, Traian Stoianovich discussed the factors that he felt principally responsible for the rise of a new class of Greek, Armenian, Vlach, Serb and Bulgarian merchant over the early modern era.[8] One of the principal factors linked to this impressive growth in Balkan entrepreneurship was population recovery, both in European Turkey and those parts of her former territory newly-conquered by the Western powers. The Austrian conquest and re-colonization of Hungary for example led to an influx of Balkan merchants, men, according to Stoianovich who were better suited to exploit the opportunities that these rather rough and unsettled new territories offered.[9] The rise of European 'manufacturing' also proved advantageous to Balkan traders. Stoianovich noted that "the new textile factories of Austria, Saxony, Prussia, and Switzerland required the wool and cotton of Macedonia and Thessaly, and rising French, German and Italian demands caused the cotton production of Macedonia to treble between 1720 and 1800."[10] Greek traders were among the beneficiaries of these trends and gradually developed branches in the various European commercial capitals where such business was conducted. In time the growing presence of Balkan emboroi in the West earned them new privileges from their host countries. Certainly it was an important milestone in 1730 when Holland granted commercial equality to Greek, Jewish and Armenian merchants.[11] The important effects of trade liberalization and expansion were described by Koraes in his famous 1803 Memoir:

> Because of a new direction which various circumstances gave to the channels of commerce, many Greek commercial houses found themselves in a short time in possession of extraordinary riches... These newly enriched men did not take long to understand ... that far-seeing eyes were required to retain these gifts and render them fruitful. Accustomed hereto to use European agents in the management of their businesses... they now thought that they could replace them ... by native youth who thanks to the attraction of large salaries now found themselves tempted to study.[12]

It was through such means, Koraes adds, that commerce, "by spreading in the nation, saved from idleness a multitude of young Greeks, and scattered them into various regions of Europe."[13] He might well have counted himself among those "saved," as we found above, although the circumstances of his own unhappy experience as the young protege of a Chiot merchant do not so well conform to the events he depicted above.

We have finally to consider the influence of war and diplomacy on the fortunes of Balkan traders. In this sense the emboroi had benefitted from the Porte's unsuccessful wars against Austria. The negotiations following these conflicts had given the Greeks[14] increased trading rights, protections and access to European markets.[15] The eighteenth century witnessed furthermore the occurrence of frequent wars between the Russians and the Turks. The war of 1768, which ended in the Treaty of Kucuk Kaynarca (1774), holds great significance in the economic history of the late Tourkokratia, for it extended to Greek shipowners the privilege of flying the Russian flag and the protection of Russian consuls.[16] These new rights, combined with earlier compacts between the Austrians and Turks establishing the freedom of Ottoman nationals to trade in the

Habsburg Empire, set the stage for an impressive take-off in Greek commercial activities. Dakin asserts that "so important had Greek trade become that it is no exaggeration to say that Greece had a commercial empire before she had a state; and it can with equal truth be said that the Greeks as traders, just as the Greeks as Christians, formed a kind of state within the Turkish state."[17]

The mania for education and school building which became possible through the generosity of the merchants had a powerful shaping influence on the geography of the Neohellenic Enlightenment. This is illustrated by the fact that a great many of the major logioi from the late Diaphotismos came from the northern regions of Greece or European Turkey, that is Thessaly, Macedonia and Epiros, territories that were the main centers and beneficiaries of Greece's commercial development. From Thessaly for example we have Gregorios Konstantas (1748-1833), Anthimios Gazes (1758-1828), Daniel Philippides (1755-1832), Gregorios Zalikoglou (1776-1827), Theokletos Pharmakides (1784-1860), Konstantinos Koumas (1777-1836), Konstantinos Oikonomos (1780-1857), and Regas Velestinlis (1757-1798); from Epiros, the luminaries include Neophytos Doukas (1760-1845), Lambros Photiades (1752-1805), Athanasios Psalidas (1764-1829) and Ioannes Velaras (1771-1823). The Ionian Islands continued to contribute important logioi (Theotokes, Voulgaris, Vendotes, Solomos), so did the older commercial centers of the eastern Mediterranean, such as Smyrna and the Aegean Islands especially Chios, on the coast of Anatolia. From these lands we have of course Adamantios Koraes (1748-1833), as well as Konstantinos Nikolopoulos (1786-1841) Konstantinos Kokkinakis (1781-1831) and Neophetos Vamvas (1776-1855).[18]

The regions of Greece identified above continued to manifest an increasing commercial orientation and vitality as the eighteenth century progressed. The larger towns began to sprout schools, often endowed by the merchant sons of these provinces. From the Peloponnesus, where agriculture was dominant and the people dispersed, there was virtually no contribution at all to the ranks of the logioi. Nor did the coastal areas of the Peloponnesus, which included the relatively large Greek cities of Patras and Messalonghi prove particularly fruitful in schools or logioi. These factors have led historians like Ioannes Kordatos to conclude that Greece's intellectual awakening was a product of this steady but uneven commercial revolution.[19] This information also appears to reinforce what Miroslav Hroch said about the rise of nationalist movements in Europe, noting that: "the patriotically active territory lay in all the cases investigated either in part or entirely on the most productive and most market-oriented parts of the territory occupied by the oppressed nationality."[20] According to Hroch, a relatively high level of "social communication" was engendered in such a setting, leading him to conclude that "the market therefore had a more powerful impact than the educational system in spreading nationalist sentiments."[21] And yet one of the principal impacts of the 'market' or commercial revolution in these towns of European Turkey was the development of schools. Furthermore it was in these schools, existing entirely outside of the Ottoman state, that the writings of figures like Koraes, Benjamin of Lesbos or Philippides found an audience, as the surviving documents from the lightly educated men of the Philike Etairia serve to indicate.[22]

Regas Velestinlis, born in 1757, presents just one example of a young Greek intellectual who came of age in the middle of these developments. He was not a Phanariot but the son of a merchant from Thessaly who received his first schooling at the nearby town of Zagora, the birthplace of the merchant Ioannes Pringos. It was in fact at the library established there by Pringos that Regas studied as a youth.[23] Regas's path to education and status eventually took him, like others of his generation, to the Phanariot centers of Constantinople and Bucharest, where he ultimately became a 'secretary' to a succession of eminent men, and became himself a little wealthy in the process.[24] The year 1790 witnessed the publication in Vienna of Regas's first two books, where his work had carried him for a time, and which posting appears to have had a profound effect on his development.[25] "It isn't sufficient for me simply to lament the condition of my race," he wrote at the beginning of one of these works, "but to bring about its relief."[26] The words could have been uttered by virtually any logios of the period, although in this case they were only the prelude to a much more radical second act. In summary, the forces of commercial change and development, Phanariot penetration of the Principalities, and the excitement generated by the Enlightenment—both within Greece and without, all coalesced in the career of Regas, still young at the time of his execution in 1798.[27]

Ioannes Pringos, the 'Conquering Balkan Merchant'

During the years of Koraes's unsuccessful foray in Amsterdam as a man of commerce (1772-1775), there also lived in the city a Greek merchant of growing renown, Ioannes Pringos (1725?-1789).[28] From the few accounts and records that exist, it appears that Pringos's childhood was filled with hardships, including the loss of his parents at a young age.[29] In spite of these difficult circumstances, the resilient Pringos succeeded in gaining the notice of local merchants and by the age of fifteen (1740) was already embarking on his first journeys into xeniteia. In 1742 we find him in Venice, where he lived for almost ten years. Pringos's stay in Italy appears to have had a decisive influence on his consciousness. It was here that he first became acquainted with the 'Didachais' (Teachings) of Elias Meniates, a figure that wielded a considerable influence on him, as Pringos's own writings later show.

It was in Venice too, among the relics of Byzantium strewn about the city, that Pringos began to express an intense albeit wounded sense of cultural or national consciousness, as manifested in the angry outbursts contained in his letters. An enthusiastic even fanatical Orthodox Christian, he retained throughout his life a severe attitude toward the 'Frangoi' or the Franks, an old appellation applied collectively to all the Roman Catholic peoples of the West. Pringos regarded the Frangoi as the chief exploiters of Greece's misery.[30] "I saw the treasure at Saint Marks of Aghia Sophia," he wrote characteristically from Venice, "that was ours and that the Franks now have. And how much did I wither inside knowing that it belonged to us and that others have it for our sins. What great agony is this!" The image of Greece helplessly plundered from East and West, surfaces again in his angry declaration that: "The Greeks have two great enemies, the Turks and the Latins, would to God that she would be delivered from them."[31] These sentiments were not at all diminished by his departure from Italy in 1751 for the city of Amsterdam, or, as he came to call it, the 'emporium of the world.'

And yet for all his considerable activities on behalf of the 'race,' Pringos worked quite as diligently at his profession. His business affairs prospered to the point that he could well have fit Koraes's description of the new 'millionaire,' a word that "was for the first time heard among a people who had been accustomed to consider the small number of those who owned a capital of one hundred purses as men overwhelmed with the favors of fortune."[32] By the time of his death in 1789, as the sources clearly attest, Pringos had acquired a measure of the fame that Koraes himself had craved as a young emboros setting out for foreign parts. Perhaps he had even managed on some level to satisfy the desire aroused in him while a young man wandering in despair among the 'lost' relics of Byzantium: to become a benefactor of the race and an instrument of its renewal.

Celebrations of 'merchant-benefactors' like Pringos became something of a fixture in the inspirational texts of these times, for such men represented quite well the model of the good son of Mother Hellas.[33] No doubt these men served as the measuring stick for the young Koraes and those first recruits of the Philike Etairia. Even the English philologist William Leake felt obliged to note the contributions made by the emboroi in the various towns and villages of his travels. While touring Iannina for example in the Fall of 1806, Leake described the considerable funding provided to the city's newest school by the merchant Pikrozoi who "bequeathed 800 purses, the interest of which, together with other donations, affords a salary of 2000 piastres to the head teacher, Athanasius Psalidha, besides supporting 2 assistants, and giving a small yearly donation to each scholar. The same Pikrozoi built a church and hospital in the city."[34] Many of the growing merchant towns of European Turkey could boast of similar men. For Moschopolis, it was the famous Sinas brothers.[35] Another pair of famous brothers, the Zosimadon, were the Viennese publishers who produced Koraes's multi-volume *Hellenic Library* among numerous other works. Athanasios Psalidas himself, writing around 1809, singled out the Zosimadons in his geography of Epiros, praising their efforts to distribute books "not only to the young men of their fatherland, but to all the schools of Greece, as so many weapons to make war against the illiteracy of their race, and would to God that they would be victorious and Greece raise them up as trophies..."[36] The Zosimadons are also cited in Leake's passage on Zagora, in addition to the "library founded by a native named John Prinko, who made his fortune as a merchant in Holland."[37] Pringos and his 'exceptional' library were also the subjects of a glowing dedication in the *Geographia Neoterike* of Konstantas and Philippides:

> From Zagora came over time many worthy men, but only two who are deserving of being distinguished by name. Konstantinos Mavrikios, who served as an archon of Nicholas Mavrokordatos (1680-1730) and his son Konstantine (1711-1769), and benefitted his patrida very much, and Ioannes Pringos, who practiced business in Holland with great renown, and a benefactor of his patrida above all others, such that for progress and improvement and esteem, he sent from Holland an exceptional library, abundant with nearly all the Greek books and many of other languages.[38]

Pringos's correspondence shows that he was greatly influenced by the fame and good deeds of Mavrikios and "yearned" to "imitate him."[39] This veneration for the great men who preceded him and his zeal to prove himself too a champion of the race expressed itself in Pringos at a relatively early age. Indeed the intense respect that he felt for such men was exhibited in a remarkable ritual of homage, recounted by one of his biographers, when as a young merchant in Italy Pringos applied to the Senate of Venice for permission to see and hold in his hands the will of Thomas Flaggineis, the founder of the Flaggineio Schole.[40] Pringos's success in establishing himself among the pantheon of these emboroi-benefactors was acclaimed, finally, in the rapturous praise of the logios Anthimios Gazes in an 1811 edition of *Hermes ho Logios*:

> Let the virtue of the strong and rich be imitated! These accomplishments are the cause of the enlightenment of the race, when it esteems virtue and education, it is rewarded proportionately. Oh how indelibly it would remain in the souls of the later generations forever, O Benefactors of the race, the memory of these accomplishments. You would become the fathers of the race. The entire race would testify to the gifts, to all the good things that from you they enjoy. Would to God that all the prelates and shepherds of the flock of reason imitate the good Shepherd and heirarch IGNATIUS! Would to God that the men of business imitate those good benefactors the brothers Zosimadon! And Ioannes of Pringos![41]

Pringos, like these other celebrated men of commerce, was moved by the 'national problem' to an intense degree. This reaction was not so simply, as Marxist historians tend to exaggerate, an outcome of his 'class consciousness.' It is certainly true, as passages from Pringos's correspondence show, that his intense antipathy toward the Turks was powerfully motivated by the Empire's arbitrary legal and taxation policies. He made clear his 'bourgeois' grievances in a note from Holland in 1773. How can 'Tourkia' ever prosper, he asked, when the Sultan fails to see that "the wealth of the inhabitants is the wealth of his kingdom. These (Europeans) rule with justice however with the Turk everything is unjust and he seeks to do nothing more than to pillage." Pringos continued with an appeal, also typical for him, that God would annihilate the Turks and let good government prevail so that "everyone would have their own without fear of some injustice." He pleads for an end to the irrational despotism whereby "to seize ten it doesn't matter to him ('the Turk') that a hundred is wasted, that seizing the fruit he doesn't care that the plant is destroyed."[42] A similar letter from 1774 includes an appeal to God to "unite the Christian kings to free the Christians from the tyranny and despotism of the Turk, so that justice would rule... that everyone would be secure in his life and his own and not as it is now, where there is only terror, where you fear your own shadow..."[43]

One might ask why, if Pringos had been driven purely by economic impulses, did he remain so hostile to the Turks? After all, he had by this time in his career amassed a small fortune. He also enjoyed a measure of freedom in the West, where he had long made his home. But of course Pringos was moved by other sentiments: an attachment for his patrida, Zagora, to which he wished to return; a zealous attachment to his faith, which he felt to be threatened; and finally, a romantic attachment to his 'nation', which he longed to see lifted from the ranks of the ridiculed. Pringos's identity as an emboros was conditioned and attended by these other powerful forces. In this sense Pringos demonstrates very well Acton's maxim that "exile is the nursery of nationalism." Life in xeniteia, no matter how rewarding, served to provoke in him new resentments and grudges, alternately against both Turks and Europeans, and an intense sense of duty to the world he had left behind.

The commercial-oriented criticisms of Turkish despotism found in Pringos's journals were, furthermore, not limited to the merchant classes.[44] Logioi such as Meletios whose 'capitalist' motivations would seem to be rather tenuous, also tended to associate the strength of the West with its commercial vitality. Commerce appeared to be the root of the material and cultural efflorescence that distinguished the West from the East and was thus a central element in their notions of decline and revival. Similarly, Marxist interpretations of Pringos's 'nationalism' don't put adequate stress upon the cultural despair and self-consciousness over the loss of Greece's 'status' that appear so conspicuously in his writings. One finds in these passages an acute awareness of the national problem characterized by the sufferings of Greece at the hands not only of the Turks, but also the 'Franks,' as illustrated in Pringos's moody reflections on seeing the 'treasure of Hagia Sophia' at Saint Marks. On such occasions his sentimentalism over the plight of Greece approaches the feelings exhibited by the young Flaggineio scholars in the *Anthe Eulaveias*.

Pringos also expressed a clear awareness in his writings of the attitudes circulating in Europe regarding the modern Greeks and their condition. His bitter reaction to these attitudes is visible in the notes he made within a volume of Marcus Aurelius's *Meditations* found in the Zagora library. "I have never read," he begins, "a sweeter or wiser Italian book, as this one of the learned Emperor Mark Aurelius. He lived in a time when the Greeks gave learning to the Italians. Now the Italians give learning to the Greeks, a peculiar thing. That wisdom that blossomed among the Greeks of Greece, is no more..."[45] Far from being the promoters of wisdom, the Greeks had in fact become one of the 'ridiculed' people of the world, as he glumly observes below:

> This book testifies to what the Greeks were in wisdom. And now all ridicule the Greeks as ignorant, uneducated and illiterate. When someone has money, everyone is their friend. When he falls on hard times, no one is. For such reason, since we had once the treasure, the riches of wisdom, we had honor, love and respect from all the other foreign races. Now that wisdom has abandoned us and we have become barbarians, they ridicule and deride us as foolish and worthless.[46]

These notes aptly reveal the cultural self-consciousness of the author and his painful awareness of the division of the nations of the world into the esteemed and the "ridiculed." This term in fact surfaces frequently in his notes. When speaking elsewhere for example of the French and English he writes: "They are not ridiculed (den geliountai) but ridicule the other races... They are regarded, France and England, as the new Athens. France gives and the world receives from her."[47]

Pringos's writings therefore contain many recognizable elements of the larger Neohellenic discourse. This is perhaps not surprising considering that like the emigre-logioi of this study he too was a man of the diaspora and similarly exposed to the perceptions and judgements surrounding the terms 'East' and 'West.' His words reflect both the sting of these judgements and his eagerness to rebuke them. Greece's backwardness, Pringos frequently inferred, was owing to the difficulties obtaining from Ottoman despotism. His reaction in this case paralleled the defense of Greece often made by contemporary logioi. How similar, for example, are Pringos's words to the angry protests of Koraes in the passage below, sallying against those who "before the whole of Europe" heap scorn upon the Greeks:

> ...among European travelers there are some who, not having seen Greece, are apparently convinced that in order to know a nation it is unnecessary to move from one's study, and wishing to give a picture of the degeneration of the modern Greeks, have merely painted a caricature. They did not want to see among the Greeks but what has always been seen among all enslaved peoples; what in fact is seen today among many nations who are not nearly as arbitrarily governed as the Greeks of the present time.[48]

It would not be wholly accurate to say, however, that the words found in Pringos's diary were the spontaneous productions of his own experience or were otherwise sociologically determined. A close analysis of the emboros's writings shows that he imported arguments, images, and even whole passages from earlier Greek writers into his own work. The most intriguing example of this appears in an entry from the 'Chroniko,' the daily journal that Pringos contributed to while living in Amsterdam.[49] Using language recognizable from earlier texts, Pringos appealed to God in this document for the liberation of Greece. The immediate occasion of the appeal was the spectacle of a great celebration in Amsterdam. He begins by describing the dazzling sight of a city awash in opulence and civic pride:

> Holland 12 June 1768. The Prince goes about the cities and in each one they give him many and great honors and certainly too in Amsterdam where all night long there was a great overflow of light, the palace glowing from thousands of candles covering it and the dome with 6000 lamps...and inside the great parlor a ball was held and there were 8000 candles and as many as 400 noblewomen with innumerable diamonds dancing together with the princess.[50]

Unfortunately, such a sight can only raise up in him the contrasting picture of his fatherland. "If an orthodox saw such an array," Pringos writes of the scene, "the tears of the Greek would flow." The impassioned 'supplication' that follows provides a remarkable illustration of borrowing among authors separated by large intervals of time. In this case, Pringos's supplication of 1768, will draw heavily upon the item found in Meniates's 'Evaggelismon' (1688). As we have seen, Meniates was himself under the influence of the elder Skouphos, whose *Texne Rhetorike* (1681) was discussed in the second chapter. To illustrate the close parallels among these texts, translations of all three are included in the Appendix, arrayed chronologically from left to right.

Sin, anger, retribution and reprieve feature prominently in the three appeals.[51] Such themes gave shape to Skouphos's polemic in the *Rhetorike*, a text that the young Meniates studied at the Flaggineio Schole and whose form he obviously followed closely in his own address. It is not possible at this time to confirm that Pringos was familiar with the original work of Skouphos, however his connection to Meniates is clear.[52] He was an avid admirer of the great rhetorician and even underwrote the re-publication of some of his works. The Pringos library also contained many editions of Meniates's widely read 'Didachais.'[53] We see, nonetheless, in the Appendix, that Pringos directed the appeal for deliverance from the Virgin Mary, as Meniates had rendered it, back to God. This may reflect an effort on the part of the faithful Orthodox emboros to expunge the address of those stray Latin tendencies he objected to in Meniates.[54]

A phrase that appears in the beginning of all three supplications is the urgent question 'until when' or 'for how long' (os pote). This expression in fact surfaces repeatedly throughout the sources of the late Enlightenment. Regas's famous *Thourios* or War Song of 1797 for example begins: "Until when (os pote) must we live closed up and alone like lions in the cliffs and mountains?"[55] Koraes made the expression the central fixture in a similar call to arms, the *Asthma Polemisterion* (1800). This piece, like the *Salpisma Polemisterion* of 1801, manifests the revolutionary zeal that was, if only for a brief time, lit up in the great logios.[56] It too was written in verse form like Regas's *Thourios* and Koraes brings each of the nine stanzas of the piece to a close with the rousing cry

"For how long (os pote) tyranny? Long live freedom!"[57] Not surprisingly the expression appears in the sources of the Philike Etairia as well.[58]

The matter of Greece's 'sin' is worth noting as it is a subject that Pringos was given to question, despite the prominence accorded it in his own supplication. "Our sins didn't do it," he argued elsewhere, "poor administration did, and if God should see it to free us then this first lesson is the one we should take to heart." On another occasion he was moved to ask "all the others (nations) aren't sinners, only we, we are such sinners?"[59] These reversals were not rare for him; his appeal for example that God unite the Christian kings to liberate Greece conflicts with his many statements of acute Latin xenophobia, such as when he writes "two wild beasts are upon Europe: The Turk and the Pope."[60]

Pringos's skepticism in any case concerning 'sin' reveals his tendency to dwell instead on matters of government and education; these were the things that he had come to admire most about the West and to see as the source of its power.[61] The fall of Byzantium therefore resulted from the failure of its rulers to properly observe and practice these precepts. "Probably someone would say," he wrote in 1774, "that when the Turks took the City, that is Constantinople, there were so many wise men that when they left from there they enlightened Europe. Perhaps so, but it was only in the City, the remaining parts were completely ignorant and this brought about the disaster."[62]

The Pringos 'supplication,' while drawing heavily on the language and imagery of Skouphos and Meniates, contains, finally, an important addition. In the earlier texts, the fate of Greece had rested entirely on the compassion and power of God. Pringos attempts to move God here as well, however he expected the European powers and especially the Russians to be the instruments of God's will. This addition reveals the dramatic alteration that had been occurring in the Continental balance of power, and the excitement it engendered among nationalist-minded men like Pringos. Indeed this aspect of Pringos's thought acquired a new intensity when yet another war broke out between Russia and the Turks in 1768.

Pringos's entries in the 'Chroniko' from the war years brim with optimism for Greece's imminent freedom, especially upon news that a Russian force led by the enigmatic Orlovs had arrived in the Peloponnesus. He wrote excitedly in these passages of how the Maniotes, "a mass of people who live in the mountains of Mani and are of the race of the Lacedaemons (Spartans), and other Greek Orthodox, as are called Romaioi," had risen up to reclaim their liberty.[63] Of course the Orlov campaign led only to a new episode of devastation in the Morea. Pringos's final entries on the war therefore are bitter ruminations on the failure of

Russian resolve and the miserable acts of recompense undertaken on behalf of Greek refugees. Pringos even appears to incriminate himself for his own misplaced faith:

> Encouraged by the Russians they had fought to be free and did all they could, helping the Russians by any means, however their freedom did not arrive. Placing perhaps their hopes for freedom on the Russians rather than God they did not receive it. Russia looks after her own interests. She gave a free trip, in order to bring the Romaioi to her parts, to settle people in her wilderness. This is the freedom that suits her interest, that now they are to leave their vineyards, fields and homes, to go and make others, to leave their fine climate to live in a cold land. Russia should have taken hold of a part of the Dodecanese for a refuge for the Greeks. However, for her own interests did she concern herself.[64]

The final moody words of the entry recall the distrust that had always colored Pringos's view of the European kingdoms. It appears in fact that his hostility toward the great powers of Europe was never much ameliorated by his admiration for their prosperity and strength. These attitudes were shared by other Greeks, who, like Pringos, could live the majority of their lives in 'foreign parts' without ever losing their reflexive antipathy for the surrounding faiths and customs. Numerous examples of this tendency appear in the letters of Stamates Petros, the unhappy colleague of Koraes during the latter's brief turn as an emboros in the city of Amsterdam. Petros's letters from these years (1771-1774) contain many nasty asides on the mores of the Dutch and his dim view of the young Koraes, who seemed to be so terribly influenced by them. A letter from 1774 is characteristic:

> He (Koraes) has led his father to believe with his letters that his son has become quite devout here in Holland. But he doesn't know that two or three weeks go by between his visits to the Church and if some time he comes, he does so at the end. As much good as you have done here, so much the worse has he done by his poor example. Great harm has come to him since he came here, reading the satanical French books, he has become a prodigal son...[65]

Petros had summed up his thoughts on the matter in an earlier letter, where he ruefully observed: "I am sorry for the young people who come here. As is known to you, this place is not for Orthodox Christians."[66]

Well, it was at least not for those deprived of the gifts, or luck, that it took to succeed in the hard scrabble world of the diaspora merchant. Not everyone could become so rich and so beneficial as the good son of his patrida Ioannes Pringos. The savvy emboros died in 1789 having returned from his labors in xeniteia to spend his final years in the village of his birth. But the marketplace he had mastered would soon be convulsed by tempest and change. Like merchants of all times, the men who followed him were no strangers to fluctuation and uncertainty. But they now faced a trading environment made a good deal more volatile with the era of European warfare ushered in by the French Revolution. No doubt it was one that would have tested even the formidable skills of the 'all conquering' Pringos.

Boom and Bust

In 1814 three men, diaspora Greek merchants by occupation, though ones who, unlike their more illustrious brethren, had not made much of a mark in the world, formed the Philike Etairia (Friendly Society).[67] The three merchants in question, Emmanuel Xanthos, Nicholas Skouphas and Athanasios Tsakalof shared some interesting characteristics. They were men of little learning, though all had acquired at least a rudimentary education in their home villages before embarking on the path (they hoped) to fortune. It is even possible that Tsakalof may have studied for a time under the famous logios Athanasios Psalides at the Maroutsain Academy in Iannina.[68] All three men were also 'recent emigres' to the diaspora Greek merchant society in which they hoped to establish themselves. Unfortunately, all three had also, apparently, failed.

The founders of the Philike Etairia had left their patridas at young ages and were no doubt just as eager as the youthful Koraes to make themselves into successful emboroi on the order of Ioannes Pringos. Their enthusiasm may well have been encouraged by the latest boom in the business cycle accompanying the Napoleonic Wars. In perhaps a strange turn of events, Greek merchants and traders had seen their fortunes rise sharply with the outbreak of these wars, albeit from rather dubious causes. As summarized below by one historian, the conditions of war furnished new opportunities for the crafty 'Balkan economic man' who was not afraid of operating a little outside the rules:

> One of the main functions of the Aegean merchant fleet seems to have been the relocation of foreign imports and exports to and from the lesser ports of the Empire and the Black Sea. It reached the peak of its strength during the Napoleonic wars by quick and extremely profitable blockade running operations in which the Hydriots, who, according to a number of contemporary accounts, were perhaps the best sailors in the Levant, figured very prominently. It declined steadily following the re-establishment of general peace in 1815.[69]

Koraes also described the profitable windfall enjoyed by Greek 'blockade runners' in his famous Memoir of 1803. He noted how these opportunities were an outcome of the sudden exclusion of the French merchant marine from Mediterranean trade, combined with the extensive provisioning requirements of Napoleon's campaigns: "The deplorable state to which French commerce was then reduced, the scarcity experienced by the valiant Italian Expeditionary Army... all these brought a large number of Greek merchants and sailors to France. Here they sold their cargoes with large profits."[70]

However boom could, and did, give way to bust; nor were all of Napoleon's campaigns destined to have victorious endings. Perhaps it was such faith in Napoleon's invincibility that led Leon Leontides of Constantinople to hitch his fortunes to the Emperor's invasion of Russia, a gamble, it turns out, that ruined both. Of course Leontides's misfortune would surely have gone unmarked in history save for the fact that he appears in the surviving records of the Philike Etairia, indoctrinated in Odessa where events had conspired to leave him stranded. Like many early recruits to the organization, Leontides made no effort to conceal his difficulties from his fellow conspirators, succinctly identifying himself in the membership papers as a 'ruined merchant.'[71] In this sense Leontides's story is not unlike that of Philike Etairia founder Emmanuel Xanthos, who had recently presided over the demise of his own embryonic trading business.[72] Such tales of idle sailors, soldiers and boat captains are in fact an important feature of the historical literature surrounding the Philike Etairia, victims all of a boom and bust cycle that had left them out of funds and workless in various points around the Mediterranean.

The men of the Philike Etairia are popularly held today by Greek society as the fathers of national independence, noble and heroic men of vision and high ideals who risked everything to see their nation freed from the Turkish yoke. It is a picture that contrasts sharply however with the first portraits of the group rendered by their contemporaries. The earliest sources in fact often manifest a common contempt for the class of the men who formed and joined the organization. The English historian George Finlay, a Philhellene and participant himself in the revolutionary struggle, wrote of the Society: "The first members of the Philike Hetairia were bankrupt merchants and intriguing adventurers, possessed of some cunning and great enthusiasm."[73] The Society's attempts to win converts at first met with failure according to Finlay as the leading members of Greek society "generally despised the class of men who traveled as apostles of the Hetairia."[74]

One of the most virulent examples of anti-Etairia literature is represented by a letter of the Metropolitan Ignatius from October 11th 1821. As we have seen, Ignatius was a significant figure in the Diaphotismos, especially in the Principalities. In the letter of 1821, written in the aftermath of the outbreak of the revolution, he condemned the pretensions of those "brainless young men" who had destroyed his hopes for Greece's revival. For a great deal of time, the Metropolitan wrote, Greece had "quietly prepared itself for a better future." Fearing the people would not prove "worthy of freedom if the circumstances one day permitted them to throw off the yoke of tyranny and slavery," the wiser members of the nation had built schools and libraries. They had sent the brightest of their youth to the universities of France, Germany, England and Italy, he writes, with the intention of training a new generation of native educators for the multiplying schools of Greece. With such remarkable success were the Greeks busily enlightening themselves when:

> ... a secret society constituted of half-educated, adventurous and brainless young men having at their head the prince Ypsilantes carried the signal of a war of independence to the principalities of Moldavia in ignorance of the nation, that was unable to foresee or forestall such an unanticipated and untimely step, of which the results became fatal to all the Greek cities where the inhabitants are unarmed and exposed to the fury of their Turkish oppressors.[75]

Statements like these tend to support the view of the Etairia as consisting of desperate men, often of failed ambition, and looked down upon by their more established compatriots. Indeed the founders themselves did not hide the disdain and rejection they suffered at the hands of the rich diaspora merchants they originally appealed to for membership.[76]

From these humble beginnings, the Etairia would ultimately build up an organization of impressive scope, acquire perhaps a thousand members, and mobilize the forces behind the 1821 revolution.[77] Nonetheless, in one of the ironies of modern Greek history the Society virtually vanished from view with the outbreak of the revolution and had no influence at all on the course of events in independent Greece. True, some of its members, men like Alexander Mavrocordatos or John Kolletis, even Tsakalof, succeeded to important roles in post-revolutionary Greek life, however as a political organization the Etairia ceased to exist. In this regard, the Philikoi or Friends shared the fate of the logioi of the pre-independence period, many of whom appeared to exit abruptly from the scene in the aftermath of the revolution, succeeded by a new generation of men with new preoccupations.[78] Perhaps both were victims of their own success. Once the revolution broke out the natural leaders of Greek society, the primates, clan chiefs, klephtic 'captains' and town elders, became the rallying point of political action and authority. The original founders of the Philike Etairia, who had managed with great difficulty (and some guile) to win such men to the Society, failed to supplant them when events took on a new and critical course.[79]

Because the merchant quotient in the membership of the Etairia was so great it became fashionable at one time to see the Greek Revolution as a vivid demonstration of the laws of Marxist historiography. Here was an ascendant bourgeoisie seeking to sweep away the feudal barriers that impeded its conquest of political and economic power.[80] However, this view does not take into account a full picture of the 'merchants' in question. As George Frangos has written "a close examination of the Etairia's membership reveals that the members of the major social groups that joined the society were not representative of their group as a whole."[81] The Greek merchant class included men of great wealth to be sure, however these did not typically join the Society.[82] Frangos came to find that "in determining the character of the early membership" one characteristic rose above all others: "nearly all of them were first generation merchants who had emigrated from their native areas but who failed to achieve the economic success which had prompted their move."[83]

We have already met with one of these unfortunate men, Leon Leontides of Constantinople who was indoctrinated in Odessa in 1816. Another example is furnished by Emmanuel Glykoudes, a thirty year old 'ploiarxos' or shipowner from Ithaca who joined the Society while in Galatzi in 1818. He explained his predicament in his 'devotional letter':

> I find myself here my friend without work, so weak is business, and the reason that I am not at sea is that I owe ten thousand grosia and struggle to find work in order to pay it off. I reside in Santorini and am married, my patrida is Ithaca; I was however a shipowner doing business with my own capital. It hurts me now, that I have met you, that I don't have work in hand to indicate my worthiness, since when someone has work in hand, he is more esteemed among men and much better listened to. Me, if I had work in hand and were at sea, I could win (for the Fatherland) many good and beneficial patriots.[84]

In Constantinople the Society recruited another young emigre, Demetrios Mamounes, a native of the Aegean island Psara. He too took the occasion of his 'devotional letter' to describe the difficult state of his affairs:

> After so many years wandering away from my patrida from Psara a captain with my ship and I am twenty five years old I haven't succeeded to do anything good. Now however learning all the clear truth from Mr. Panayiote Demetropoulo Spartiate I am sending you with this letter three hundred grosia, to use in the new school and whenever you command me to bring the (?) for the school I am ready with my ship to go to the place where you appoint me to carry the timber.[85]

Demeterios Dordos, who also joined the Society in Constantinople, was an emigre from the island of Patras. He expressed in his letter a note of frustrated philanthropy similar to the examples above:

> Coming to the age of 38 I was never able to appear beneficial to the school of our patrida, now being able, thanks to God, I am sending you through Mr. Panayiote Avagnostopoulou one hundred and fifty grosia, of which receiving from the same you would use to assist the poor youth of our patrida, following this it is pledged that I would like to help them with all my power and circumstances...[86]

Finally, a letter from the initiate Ioannes Svoronos, who wrote from Zakynthos in 1819. This particular letter actually refers to the sudden 'bust' in the wheat market following the Napoleonic Wars. Perhaps Svoronos was one of those ambitious young men originally drawn into the trade by its earlier boom phase:

> It is known to you, my friend, and from many letters, that I practice my profession as a sea captain and have been away from my patrida Cephallonia for three years and now I have arrived from Constantinople here in Zakyntho and intend to pass on to my patrida. However know, friend, that I am a 27 year old man and the losses that I suffered this year, on account of the decline of wheat, were such as I have never experienced before.[87]

In addition to the letters and oaths, each initiate to the Society had to submit to a series of interrogations or 'confessions.' The confession consisted of a number of questions which the Society presumably felt essential to determining the trustworthiness, character, conspiratorial potential, etc, of the recruit. In this case they provide an intriguing insight into the minds of the makers of the Society. Intriguing but far from conclusive, for the questionnaire is as enigmatic and peculiar as the Society itself. Like other sources from the Etairia, it too appears possessed of a kind of social self-consciousness that leads one to speculate on the role of self-worth in the development of the Society's nationalism. The questions have been translated below:

> How do you live and from where are you from?
> What relatives do you have, what is their profession and what condition are they in?
> Have you ever broken with one of your friends, or another?
> Did you reconcile with him, and how did these things happen?
> Are you married, do you want to marry?
> Are you in love, were you ever, did you break it off and when?
> Have you suffered any loss or a change in your situation?
> Are you satisfied in the profession that you find yourself, and which do you desire more?
> Do you have some faithful friend, who is he?
> How do you plan to live now, and how in the future?[88]

One can only guess at the intent of these questions and the information the interrogators were seeking to glean. What value, for example, did they place on the desire for marriage? Was this a sign of the initiates moral character or did it have negative implications? Were they seeking men who would not be distracted from their duty to the Society over the difficult days ahead?[89] Because several questions relate to personal and romantic schisms, it seems however that the founders put an emphasis on loyalty, stability, commitment and reliability in relationships. They appear on the look-out for divisive individuals.[90] The evil of 'stasis,' discord, was even cited in a surviving piece of the Society's literature as the cause "that brought our race down to our wretched state."[91] Perhaps they were seeking above all men who would be able to "strive together" in the interests of the Motherland.[92]

These considerations of fidelity mingle with others that appear to be focused even more determinedly on the initiate's social circumstances. The questions even intimate certain assumptions about the confessor's situation: "What is your profession and financial condition, are you satisfied, is there something you want to do more, have you suffered any damage, or changes in your personal circumstances/state of affairs?" Again, what value did they attach to the man whose affairs were in disarray, a situation which their questions were particularly determined to fish out? It does not appear to be a coincidence that the men asking such questions were themselves not at all content with their station in life. It is not clear however what this connection means. Perhaps they considered a man in such straits, down but not defeated, as likely to possess something of that bold patriotic spirit that they recognized in themselves. Certainly the founders could not have been seeking to exclude men like themselves from the Society—although it is an intriguing question in the context of the 'self-contempt' manifest throughout the Society's sources.[93]

Here as elsewhere the 'discourse' occurring within the Etairia was highly concerned with the issue of status. Of course by the act of forming and joining a group one manufactured a kind of status for himself: membership alone conferred the distinction of being part of a morally select company of men. One acquired the status of a patriot, a good son, status as an officer of the Society, a leader of men, etc. Because the acquisition of status was one of the 'effects' of the Society's creation, it does suggest that on some level the desire for status was a cause of its creation.

Finally, presuming that the recruit had answered the questions in a suitable fashion and had, additionally, satisfied the ensuing oaths and initiation rituals, he was asked to provide the Society with a 'dedicatory' letter. The instructions were set down by the founders as follows:

> ...you say to him that he should offer to the Society a certain amount of money, such as his patriotism and means allow. His offering must be accompanied by a letter addressed to whatever name and city he wishes near or far (not however so far that it will arouse curiosity and suspicion). In this he should reveal his age, profession, his place of birth, and the amount of his offering, commissioning the other to send this sum to his unfortunate friend, or to the newly founded school, or for the publishing or purchasing of books, or to some monastery, or for the marriage of his sister, signing and indicating the date and place.[94]

This instruction serves to indicate the way in which the Society cloaked its activities under the guise of the good works practiced by successful emboroi, works that were so common they had become cliche.[95] Records in the Greek state archives even include a form letter to be shared with the initiate. It reads: "Dear _____, I am ____ years old and travel about to various places and am occupied in the work of a merchant etc."[96] But it shows further the founders' awareness, an indication of the no doubt widespread awareness, of the philanthropic contributions and projects undertaken by men of rank in society. These were social contributions, even duties, that were simply beyond the reach of the men of the Etairia. Still they were contributions that they felt responsible to make and their failure to make them was probably a source of self-consciousness, as the documents indicate.

The "failure to achieve economic success" as these materials indicate, led Frangos to make a tentative assertion about the real motivations of the men involved: "They found a solution to their alienation," he concluded, "in the promise of a nation-state that would recognize them as its redeeming sons."[97] The devotional letters, oaths and rituals of the Philike Etairia do appear to reveal the force of "failure" upon these men and, subsequently, their intense desire for personal rehabilitation, esteem, or in so many words, to be "better listened to."

Frangos is not the first to suggest a relation between self-contempt and 'redemption through action' when writing of revolutions and those who make them. [98] The symbolism surrounding the Etairia is in fact so suggestive of this theme that it veritably impels the historian toward such conclusions. Here are a group of men who appear moved as much by their own plight as that of Mother Hellas. Perhaps these tensions supplied the motive force that revolutionized the 'enlightenment movement' Ignatios exalted and carried it to its violent climax.[99] Such are the conclusions inferred by Frangos's remarks, even if it is obviously not possible to confirm that by striking at the Turks the men of the Etairia were really manifesting a kind of sublimated rage, or that, living in revolutionary times, they had seized upon an idea, a mission, that promised a way out of their own predicament (as much as the nation's). Their sources of course do not say these things. What they do say however is that they strike in order to be dutiful sons, and in this the Etairia reveals at least one side of itself to the historian—it shows the marks left upon it by the Diaphotismos.

In the case of the Diaphotismos, the relation between self-worth and national action has also been suggested to play a role. The logioi demanded for example that 'ridiculed' and 'wretched' Greece wake up, become enlightened and join the ranks of the civilized nations. This activity on behalf of the nation had a personal motivation: it was the logioi after all who were most conscious of the contempt that Greek society elicited, circulating as they did as intellectual emigres in foreign lands. This contempt attached itself to them and it was not unnatural that they conceived its remedy, its only lasting remedy, in the improvement of the race to which they belonged.[100]

However for the Philike Etairia the connection between self-contempt and action appears to have a different character. The poor merchants of the Etairia sought not so much to redeem themselves in the eyes of enlightened Europe, but in those of their own countrymen. The inadequacies of such men was similarly defined by an 'other' that served to magnify their failure, self-consciousness and self-contempt: this other was the universally lauded 'all conquering' emboros-benefactor.

The soaring praise lavished upon these men, exalted by Koraes and Gazes as veritable 'Fathers of the Race,' had an obvious effect upon the founders of the Etairia. It was in fact as such men that they pose within their sources. They emulate them in their rituals and letters, doing and saying the things that (successful) men of their kind were expected to do.[101] Everywhere in fact within the sources of the Etairia is raised up the ideal of the merchant benefactor glorified by the Diaphotismos.

The Philike Etairia and the Diaphotismos

The intersections between the Diaphotismos and the Philike Etairia are not inconsiderable. We have already noted the appearance for example of key imagery, such as the tortured figure of Mother Hellas, from the late Enlightenment in the rhetoric of the Great Oath. Another example was furnished in the repetition of that common phrase 'os pote' (until when), observed in the circulating epistle of the Etairia. This document in fact contains many other elements of interest. At one point the author throws down a challenge that will be familiar to anyone acquainted with the rhetoric of men like Sakellarios and Koraes:

> Let's either give up as undeserving the Hellenic name for the softer one of Persians, just as actually many of our race continue wholeheartedly to follow their customs and turn away from the Hellenic; or remain always strong and worthy sons of the patrida and (Greek) name let's be, striving together, with all our strength for her rebirth.[102]

These lines resemble passages cited earlier from the preamble of one of Koraes's volumes in the Hellenic Library.[103] Of course to be a good son of the patrida meant to follow the example of those great men celebrated throughout Diaphotismos literature and culture. This theme is brought out in another passage from the source above:

> Her (Hellas) tormented children feeling the anguish of their wretched mother, struggled in every manner to relieve her pains each utilizing the means that their ability allowed, some through the construction of schools, others through the publication of books and others in myriad other ways ...[104]

The author does all but mention in name the great emboroi benefactors, the builders of schools and publishers of books celebrated in the texts of this period.[105] Frangos may have more heavily emphasized the impulse to be a 'redeeming son' if he had considered the degree to which this image had been dispersed throughout Greek society in the preceding decades.

Among the interesting items to be found in Valerios Mexas's compilation of the papers of Panayiotes Sekeris, are the dedicatory letters addressed by some of the merchants to logioi. Demetrios Rodiates, a thirty five year old merchant from the Peloponnesus, indoctrinated in Ismail in 1818, addressed his dedication letter to the logios Benjamin of Lesbos.[106] A thirty one year old school teacher from the prosperous 'mercantile island' of Hydra, Demetrios Koulopoulos, addressed his to Koraes.[107] Koraes was in fact the 'recipient' of several false letters. These included one from the thirty two year old merchant Anastases Androutsos, and the thirty six year old 'ship captain' Giakoumakes Toumbazes.[108] The logios Konstantinos Koumas was also the recipient of a dedication letter, his from the thirty three year old merchant Spyridon Tzanakes.[109] Of course the founders of the Society had a similar familiarity with the Diaphotismos and its luminaries.[110] They were in fact ultimately successful in winning several high profile logioi to the cause. These included the aforementioned Benjamin, in addition to Neophytos Doukas and Daniel Philippides.[111] These 'intersections' help to explain the incorporation of Diaphotismos imagery and symbolism into the sources of the Etairia.

The absence of the Diaphotismos from Frangos's study deprives his text consequently of a main source of the Society's rhetoric. But more importantly, it tends to conceal the basic cultural contiguity and even unity of this period. Frangos's description of the muddled 'nationalism' of the Etairia would for example have been better informed if greater consideration had been given to the general pattern of Greek thought during these times—it too offered little more than 'muddled' ideas on this point. Similarly, the question he poses regarding whether the Society's nationalism "was a function of their own social experience, or whether it was learned indirectly from western European examples," omits the essential internal sources of the Etairia's 'doctrine.'[112] If it was, finally, a 'nationalism' in which there was "an apparent absence of any developed political position," or of a kind where "they spoke of their nation's betterment but did not once clearly propose the political form a modern Greek state might adopt," then the Etairia reflected very well the Diaphotismos, if not the even older tradition of Skouphos and Meniates, whose impulses, vague though inspiring, their declarations imitated.[113] Virtually the only visible addition to the rhetoric of these older apostles of liberation, and it is a significant one, is the abandonment of the faith in intervention. Here 'history' had played a decisive role. We have even witnessed the germ of this attitude in the diary entries of Pringos.

Summary

This study has attempted to describe how early modern Greek national consciousness was influenced and perhaps conditioned by the notions of civilization and backwardness then circulating in Europe. The decline of Byzantium, the rise of the West, the celebration of antiquity, all helped to cultivate the tense cultural self-consciousness one finds in Greek letters. If the emigre-logios found exposure to the West a thrilling experience, it was one that might very well arouse too a melancholy sense of national inadequacy. It was no different for the failed emboroi in the presence of so many Ioannes Pringoses. If imitation is indeed the highest form of flattery then the logioi and the emboroi should have been well pleased by the countless acts of mimicry they inspired from the founders of the Etairia.

Of course the 'Friends' are distinctive for their emphasis on revolutionary action.[114] They may have taken inspiration from important historical precedents, such as Regas's execution, the ongoing revolutionary unrest in Europe, including the Serbian revolt of 1804, and the breakdown of authority within the Ottoman Empire itself. This latter factor tends often to be overlooked, yet it was significantly to rogue pashas and insurgents such as Pasvanoglou that Regas had appealed in his own *Thourios*.[115] The social circumstances of the men involved has also been considered above, circumstances that suggest the close mingling noted earlier of national feeling and self worth. There are in fact widespread notes of failure in the Philike Etairia documents. Such predicaments prevented them from fulfilling the image of the merchant benefactor so highly exalted within the discourse of 'decline and duty.' Being unlucky and unlettered, what else did they have to offer Mother Hellas, this line of reasoning suggests, save action?

These are intriguing arguments, however I have declined to press them too far. The intent of this section has been rather to use the Philike Etairia as a vehicle to demonstrate how well diffused and pervasive the 'national problem' had become in Greek discourse; to show the contiguity of the Etairia's 'literature' with native sources both distant and contemporary.

If the Society's leaders, finally, coopted the material circulating amongst them, then their acts of appropriation were no different from those performed by Pringos, Koraes, Regas or even Meniates; they all borrowed freely from a well worn stock of words and images inherited from the past. What Frangos's otherwise valuable analysis of the Etairia omits to emphasize is exactly this heavy presence among the Philikoi of the Diaphotismos—not only in their texts and pronouncements, but in their very reduction of themselves into a caricature of the great men it exalted.

Notes

1. *Melissa*, I (1819), 7.

2. There must be some obvious significance in the characterization of maidenly or motherly Greece as an icon for male action. One scholar has concluded that such symbols are perpetuated by "ethnic or national leaders" to "create nationalist identities, using ethnic symbols to mimic the cues that originally evoked a genuine kinship/group-defense response—hence the 'motherland' and 'fatherland' symbols commonly used by nationalists to combine the notions of territory and family." Stuart J. Kaufman, *Modern Hatreds. The Symbolic Politics of Ethnic War*, (Ithaca: Cornell University Press, 2001), 30.

3. Drawing close she then addresses herself to her children in terms that the reader will recognize from past sources: "My beloved children, whoever calls themselves Greeks, in any century, in any place on the earth, compared to me your mother, neither a more fortunate nor brighter one appears. My first children, your ancestors, were the most enlightened, the most vital people of the world. Of liberty, the sweetest name, from them was founded, in those first ones it was heard, from their mouths it was first given voice. These first ones founded and increased the arts and sciences, which up to now testify the books... In me, Greece, were first born poetry, rhetoric, philosophy...." Koraes, 'Salpisma Polemistirion' in Apostolos B. Daskalakes,(ed.), *Keimena-Pegai tes Historias tes Hellenikos Epansataseos, Vol. 1*, (Athens, 1966), 33. Koraes's portrayal of Mother Hellas could well have served as the model for the woman who appears in the *Rossagglogallos*, a famous work of satire from 1805. See Konstantine Demaras (ed), *Ho Rossanglosgallos*,(Athens: Poreia, 1990), 22-26. This piece bears a chronological and thematic relation to the *Hellenike Nomarchia* (1806), and presents another example of the heightening unrest within Greek society and perhaps the sense of expectation fostered by recent events.

4. 'Great Oath' of the Philike Etairia from Emmanuel G. Protopsaltes, *He Philike Hetaireia*, (Athens: Academy of Athens, 1964), 29. Note: there are at least three versions of the 'Great Oath' available in manuscript, however the differences between them are negligible. The version above, which also appears in Daskalakes (*Keimena-Pegai*, 51), was taken from the General State Archives of Greece. A second manuscript exists in the state archives of Romania, (published in 1960 by the Romanian Academy, Institute of History). A third version appears in the document section of Ioannes Philemon's classic history of the Greek Revolution,[*Dokimion Historikon peri tes Hellenikes Epanastaseos*, (Athens: P. Soutsa, 1859)] drawn in large part from the personal papers of Alexander Ypsilantes (since lost). Note also another glimpse of Mother Hellas from one of the Etaireia's circulating epistles: "...our wretched motherland Hellas for so many years in agony from the most odious despotism and ignorance never ceased to incessantly appeal to her genuine children in a wretched voice and showing to them her wounds to plead moaningly for aid." Protopsaltes, *He Philike Hetaireia*, 29.

5. However this 'limitation' was not so much intentional as defacto. Skouphos had certainly attempted to transmit this 'dialogue with the past' to his readers. So too had Meniates. One notes the introductory lines from one of his 'teachings': "I follow the example of the great teacher of the nations, the blessed Paul, who says 'To the learned and unlearned I am obliged, as much as I am able I teach simply, in order that all understand me.'" Meniates, *Didachai*, I: 44. However the social diffusion of any 'improving' work, no matter how simple the idiom in which it was written, was subject to the very finite limits imposed upon it by the conditions of life and literacy in Greece.

6. I will be seeking throughout this chapter to add more dimension to the portrait of the Philike Etairia

presented in George Frangos's, The Philike Etairia, 1814-1821: A Social and Historical Analysis, (unpublished dissertation, Columbia University, 1971). Frangos published a summary of his findings in Richard Clogg (ed), *The Struggle for Greek Independence*. See 'The Philike Etairia: A Premature National Coalition,' 87-103.

7. The growing participation of the emboroi in the Diaphotismos has already been alluded to in the case of their support for the subscription drives that accompanied the publications of Greek books such as Moisiodax's *Ethike Philosophia*. The cultural presence of the emboroi is witnessed elsewhere in a survey of the subject material from Neohellenic journals such as *Athena*, published in Paris. The 1819 edition featured several articles of interest to businessmen in addition to the typical selection devoted to history, world news, philology etc. The former included 'Business customs in England and America,' and 'Business news from France, Spain and Portugal.' *Ta Hellenika Proepanastika Periodika*, Index, (Athens: Kentron Noellenikon Erevnon, 1971), 49-51.

8. Traian Stoianovich, 'The Conquering Balkan Orthodox Merchant,' *Journal of Modern History*, (1960): 234-314. It is an intriguing phenomenon captured for example by the numbers Stoianovich cites of "Ottoman merchants" practicing their trades in Vienna. The estimate of fifty to sixty in 1760 had risen to one hundred and thirty four in 1768 and "several times this number in 1783." Ibid, 301.

9. Ibid, 242-3, 265-7. Stoianovich notes that the Balkan merchant's ability to triumph in these areas lay in his dependence on "wile rather than science," Ibid, 297. Indeed these were the characteristics that described "Balkan economic man," a shrewd, adaptable, figure always ready to "move from one place to another as a shepherd moves with his flocks..." Ibid, 290.

10. Ibid, 260. Of course in the long term this pattern in east-west trade proved harmful to prospects for economic development and modernization in the Balkans. See Nikos Mouzelis, *Modern Greece, Facets of Underdevelopment*, (London: Macmillan, 1978), Chs 1-3.

11. Ibid, 271.

12. Koraes, 'Report on the Present State of Civilization in Greece,' 161.

13. Ibid, 162.

14. It should be noted again that these rights were not given to the 'Greeks' by name but simply to Turkish subjects. However as the Turks tended not to be active in such trades or actually discouraged them, the benefits of these agreements fell defacto to the Greeks and others within the Empire.

15. The Treaty of Karlowitz (1699) between Austria and Turkey was particularly advantageous to Balkan traders as it provided them with new levels of commercial freedom and access within the expanding territories of the Habsburg Empire.

16. The treaty included provisions for the establishment of Odessa as a trading center with special privileges extended to Balkan immigrants. These benefits had nonetheless been secured at great cost, coming in the aftermath of the disastrous Russian inspired Orlov revolt of the war years. See Douglas Dakin, *The Greek Struggle for Independence*, (Berkeley: University of California Press, 1973), 22-26. Tales of the destruction that followed the Turkish reprisals, carried out by Albanian irregulars, fill the pages of the *Geographia Neoterike*, (1791). See below Chapter 5.

17. Dakin, *The Greek Struggle for Independence*, 21-2.

18. Does this new 'breed' of intellectuals form a sharp break in the history of Greek thought? These writers, whose careers will mature in the latter decades of the eighteenth century, certainly do become a force to be reckoned with. For George Dizikirikes they represent the spirit and vitality of the triumphant 'urban intellectual', a species of Greek intellectual whose social condition separated them from the Phanariot or clerical writers of the past, and carried them closer to the philosophes with whom they became so deeply attached. See for example Dizirikes's notes on Holbach, *Ho Neohellenikos diaphotismos kai to Europaiko pnevma*, 19.

19. "Where there existed trading centers, in Epiros, Thessalia, Pelio and elsewhere, grew up one by one the schools, some lower and others higher, Hellenic societies, academies..." Kordatos, *Historia tou Glossike mas zetematos*, 43.

20. Hroch, *The Social Preconditions of National Revival*, 172.

21. Ibid, 174. Note that Hroch's analysis concerned societies that were dissimilar in important political and social contexts from those of European Turkey (most of his case studies came from Scandinavia and the Hapsburg lands of Central Europe). In his study, teachers (and clergy) were likely to be reasonably influential in patriotic movements, however they were prone to drop-out when nationalist commitments conflicted with state authorities, on whose resources they were dependent. Ibid, 145. Of course in eighteenth century Greece no such conflicts existed given the complete absence of the 'state' in educational affairs. Greek schools and educators consequently operated in complete independence of state control. Leake was in fact so startled by the "liberty of opinions" he found in Greece that he was moved to write: "The Turkish government is no obstacle to such a proceeding (spread of education), being too blind or too careless of distant consequences to oppose the education of its Christian subjects, and rather pleased perhaps to see them engaged in such peaceful pursuits, though in the end they may be the most formidable of any to the Ottoman power." Leake, *Travels in Northern Greece*, IV: 388.

22. Discussed below.

23. A. Nikarouses, 'Ho Regas, he schole kai he vivliotheke tes Zagoras,' *Deltion tes Historikes kai Ethnologikes Etaireias tes Ellados (nea seira)*, I, (1928): 53-88. Vranousis's comments on Regas's studies are also worth noting. See editor's introduction, *Regas*, 8-10.

24. Ibid, 38. Of course it was here too in Bucharest that Regas met some of the leading men of the Neo-Hellenic Enlightenment.

25. The first was a translation of a popular French romance entitled, *Scholeion ton delikaton eraston* (School of Delicate Lovers). The second, *Phisikes Apanthisma*, was a survey of western scholarship on the subject of natural philosophy, rendered in the form of a dialogue between a father and son. This was a typical form for the times, as witnessed earlier by the works of Darvares.

26. Regas Velestinlis, 'Physikes Apanthisma,' in *Regas*, 268.

27. These developments in the structure of Greek society and learning, leave out the important external factors that would play an influential role in Regas's thought and activities: the French Revolution and ensuing wars together with the deterioration of central authority within the Ottoman Empire.

28. There is no documentary evidence to confirm that the two men ever met, however it is not implausible.

29. Vaggeles Skouvaras, *Ioannes Pringos: He Hellenike paroikia tou Amsterdam*, (Athens: Historikes kai logographikes etaireias ton Thessalon, 1964), 28. It was this event that deprived him evidently of any chance

at education, a situation that he ruminated bitterly on later: "When they were studying in reading and writing in school, I, being an orphan, was hauling wood, and now I am burning that I didn't learn." N. Andriotes, 'To Chroniko tou Amsterdam,' *Nea Estia*, 10 (1931): 850.

30. Pringos's enthusiasm for Meniates and his contempt for the 'Frangoi' came together in 1760 when he personally reprinted from Amsterdam 2000 copies of Meniates anti-Catholic diatribe 'Peri Skandalou.' The copies were sent to the Aegean Islands to combat what he feared were aggressive efforts at Catholic proselytization in those parts. Skouvaras, *Ioannes Pringos*, 159. One notes the obvious similarities with Voulgaris, who had undertaken efforts of his own to counteract what he perceived as an attempt to Catholicize the newly reconquered 'Orthodox' domains of Serbia and Croatia. See above Chapter 3. Pringos was in fact familiar with Voulgaris's anti-papal polemics. See again Skouvaras, *Ioannes Pringos*, 160.

31. Ibid, 37, 181.

32. Koraes, 'Report on the Present State of Civilization in Greece,' 161.

33. In fact those merchants who failed to fulfill these obligations to the race were among the targets of scorn in the polemical pamphlets *Hellenike Nomarchia* and the *Rossangglogallos*, the latter of which acknowledged "there are those who throw a lot of money upon the race and schools in order to awaken it, but they are few, and their money is not sufficient..." More typical of this class, according to the satirical author of this pamphlet, was the avaricious individual depicted in the text. *Ho Rossanglogallos*, 19-20.

34. Leake, *Travels in Northern Greece*, IV, 148. We will encounter the logios Psalidas again in the following chapters; he is the author, along with Kosmas Thesprotos of the *Geographia Alvanias kai Epeirou*. The new school described above by Leake served approximately '100 scholars." Note also that there was in addition an older school in Iannina which, as Leake mentions, was financially supported by the brothers Zosimadon.

35. See Antones M. Koltsidas, 'Hoi oikonomikes drasteriotetes ton Moschopoliton os paraontas diaphotistikes kai politismikes metakenoses ston Hellenismo', in *Moschopolis*, 117-8. See also Stoianovich, 'The Conquering Balkan Orthodox Merchant,' 302.

36.Athanasiou Psalidas, 'Perigraphe Geographike tes Epeirou,' *Geographia Alvanias kai Epeirou*, (Iannina: Society for Epirot Studies, 1964), 53. One of the three founding members of the Philike Etairia, the unsuccessful merchant Tsakalof, may well have been a student of Psalidas during his years at the Ioannina Academy. See below.

37. William Leake, *Travels in Northern Greece*, IV: 394.

38. Konstantas and Philippides, *Geographia Neoterike*, 120.

39. From a note sent by Pringos from Holland accompanying a shipment of books he was donating to the village school at Zagora. Skouvaras, *Ioannes Pringos*, 30.

40. Ibid, 34. See also Karathanases, *He Phlagineios schole tes Venetias*, 124. Flaggineis's activities were not restricted to Venice. He also contributed financially to the establishment and support of schools within the Ionian Islands as well, especially Zakynthos. Flaggineis's lucrative law practice was the principal source of this wealth, not all of which he lavished on philanthropy; his richly furnished home included a considerable library and an art collection that featured two works of Tintoretto and three of Jacomo Palma. Ibid, 38-43.

41. *Hermes ho Logios*, 15 March 1811, 91.

42. Andriotes, 'To Chroniko tou Amsterdam,' 851.

43. Ibid, 852.

44. Meletios's geography of 1728 presents an early example of the observations made here. These works discussed more fully in Chapter 5. Of course we have already confronted this critique of the 'wages of subjugation' in Moisiodax's preface to the *Ethike Philosophia*. The great logios had described the smothering effect of arbitrary taxation on civilization: "...burdened to provide not only for the means of life, but similarly the tax of captivity, nothing could they take care for... and so much so that in a little time they found themselves, priests, citizen, nobles, all reduced, all fallen into primitiveness." See above Chapter 3.

45. This note probably written ca. 1759. Skouvaras, *Ioannes Pringos*, 191.

46. Skouvaras, *Ioannes Pringos*, 197-198.

47. Ibid,187. Notes taken from a volume of Aristotle in the Zagora library.

48. Certainly Koraes's phrase "before the whole of Europe" speaks volumes viz the acute self-consciousness that such works aroused in the emigre-logios. Koraes, 'Report on the State of Civilization in Greece,' 155. Koraes refers here to the 1788 *Philosophical Researches Concerning the Greeks* by de Pauw who dared to "prophecy before the whole of Europe, with the tone and confidence of one inspired, that 'among the Greeks ignorance and superstition have put down roots so deep and so tenacious that no force, no human power could extirpate them.'" Ibid 159. Unfortunately new voices appeared to challenge Koraes's claim that such observations were the work of men who were not personally acquainted with Greece. The most extreme of these was Bartholdy who actually charged that the Greeks had regressed over the last century. The *Rossangglogallos* serves as another example of this 'protest' literature. In this piece a trio of Russian, English and French travelers are making their way through Greece and commenting upon its rude state of affairs, before receiving a rebuke from Mother Hellas who lectures them on their own culpability in the country's fate.

49. The 'Chroniko' was a series of notes kept over the years 1755-1774 at the local Orthodox church in which Pringos recorded events of interest to Greeks of the city (Amsterdam). Pringos frequently copied news from local and foreign sources, to which he often added his own observations. Pringos's notes were collected and published by Andriotes in *Nea Estia*, 10, (1931), 846-853 and 914-920.

50. Ibid, 852.

51. The mention of John Chrysostomos (347-407C.E.) in the texts above suggests an even older source of influence surrounding these themes. Chrysostomos's Divine Liturgy, still used today by the Orthodox Church, features the appeal: "Lord, save your people and bless your inheritance; protect the body of your Church... do not forsake us who hope in you."

52. Skouphos's *Texne Rhetorike* does not appear in the catalogue of the Zagora Library. As a zealous Greek Orthodox it is likely that Pringos would have had a conflicted view of the convert Skouphos. Pringos even grumbled at times over the hint of Catholic influence within his otherwise much-adored 'Didachais' of Meniates. Skouvaras, *Ioannes Pringos*, 33. No doubt Skouphos would have fallen in the category of those youths who as students in Italy came "inside the embrace of the Pope" and teachers who strove "more to teach them the dogmas or the superstitions of the Latins, rather than reading, writing and sciences... as it is known that so many children sent from Greece to Italy, to Padua and Bologna and certainly to Rome in order to study, have many (teachers) who struggle to cloud their minds with Latin opinions and speak falsely to them… who don't know what their church teaches them, the eastern and the orthodox, and so easily are they

frankicized." Andriotes, 'Chroniko tou Amsterdam,' 916. One notes similarly the failure of one of Meniates's most prominent biographers and editors to note the obvious influence of Skouphos's 'Supplication' on Meniates's Euagellismos. The author in question, the Orthodox cleric Anthimios Mazarakes (1800-1868), must certainly have known of the Skouphos piece, yet remained conspicuously silent on the *Rhetorike* and its writer when discussing Meniates's work. Anthimios Mazarakes, *Viographiai ton endoxon andron tes nesou Kephallenias*, (Venice: Phoinekos, 1843), 66-67. This 'silence' on the influence of Skouphos is not true of later historians and biographers, e.g, Paparregopoulos, Papadopoulos, Karathanses, Tatakis, Kasines, etc.

53. Skouvaras, *Ioannes Pringos*, 125-134.

54. "This Meniates was a good listener of his Italian teachers," Pringos commented once to a correspondent. Ibid, 33.

55. Regas Velestinlis, 'Thourios,' in Daskalakes, *Keimena-Pegai*, 21.

56. These declarations were excited again by the French army's advances in the East under the triumphant Napoleon—one who inspired no small faith in Koraes. Koraes makes mention in his 'Autobiography' of the hopes he once nourished for the Emperor, a man for whom he appears still to possess some sympathy: "Adorned with monumental governmental and martial virtues as history attests, and created by nature to inspire fear in agitators, and respect in those who yearn for peace, in this only did he err... instead of liberating the suffering peoples of Europe from their despots, he preferred to become himself the despot of the despots. Instead of spreading happiness in all of Europe and establish himself a god upon the earth, blessed by immortal hymns by present and future infinite generations of people, he preferred the odorous incense of the vile flatterers. He erred the tormented one!" Koraes, 'Autoviographia' in *Ho Koraes kai he Epoche Tou*, 243. The Autoviographia was originally published in 1833.

57. Adamantios Koraes, 'Asthma Polemisterion,' in Daskalakes, *Keimena-Pegai*, 27-31.

58. From a circulating epistle of the Society: "...let's awake Greek friends, for how long (os pote) will we be justly accused by all the nations, for how long (os pote) to look with indifference on our rude, insignificant, without form or beauty, much afflicted patrida Greece..." Protopsaltes, *He Philike Hetaireia*, 30.

59. Skouvaras, *Ioannes Pringos*, 190, 189.

60. Ibid, 181.

61. In this sense Pringos represents exceptionally well those Greeks described by Koumarianou who "obliged through historical and economic necessity to live outside their own land, were helped by their contact with other ways of life to formulate their national demands, based on their historical tradition and enriched by elements taken from Western civilization." See 'The Contributions of the Intelligentsia,' in *The Greek Struggle for Independence*, 77.

62. Skouvaras, *Ioannes Pringos*, 191. Note the similarities here with the observations of Konstantas and Philippides. As with other Neo-Hellenic writers Pringos adhered to the assumption that the West was spiritually heretical, but that this was no cause to deprive Greece of its innovations or under certain circumstances, its power.

63. The Maniotes were frequently heralded as embodying the living spirit of Free Greece in texts from these years, as Pringos writes "always free they remained up in their mountains and haven't been subjugated to the yoke of the Hagarenes, as the remaining Christians of the Morea and the rest of Greece." Andriotes, 'To Chroniko tou Amsterdam,' 853. See similar passages from the *Geographia Neoterike* below.

64. Andriotes, 'To Chroniko tou Amsterdam,' 920. Similar disillusionment was expressed by Emmanuel Xanthos, a founder of the Philike Etairia, in his memoirs. Xanthos cited these events as a motivating factor in the creation of the revolutionary society. *Apomnemonevmata peri tes Philikes Etaireias*, (Athens: Hetairia Historikon Ekdoseon, 1956), 141. Kaisarios Dapontes (discussed in the previous chapter) also lived to see the Russo-Turkish War of 1769-1774 and like many others believed that the old prophecies foretelling the liberation of Greece at the hands of a 'blond race' were about to be fulfilled. In an earlier text (1738) Dapontes had recorded the experience of a prophetic dream where he saw "a double-headed eagle (symbol of the Byzantine Empire) high in the heavens, shining like the sun, from above it there the venerable church, a kingly crown on its head, with a cross, as customary, on its peak. Eagle, crown, cross, with innumerable shining stars forming all around. Nearby the eagle Constantine the Great, together with his mother, and he too with a cross." See 'Oneiron,' in *Hoi Prodromoi*, 20. His disappointment over the failure of the Orlov campaign became the occasion for the bitter lines in 'Ekstithi fritton, ourane!': "It is for the Russians to lament now for the wretched Romaious, their brothers, who remain slaves and again ruined!" This poem was part of the *Geographike Istoria*, unpublished in Dapontes lifetime. Selections from the larger work including the above published in the anthology *Hoi Prodromoi*, 25. Pringos was also quite familiar with these prophecies as noted in chapter l.

65. Stamates Petros, Adamantios Koraes, *Grammata apo to Amsterdam*, edited and with an introduction by Philippos Eliou, (Athens: Hermes, 1976), 41.

66. Ibid, 25. Letter is dated March 1773.

67. The naming of the society furnished an early indication of the founders' humble backgrounds and the difficulties they would have in attracting men of a higher class to their group. They had intended to call their organization the 'Society of Friends,' but had succeeded only in 'Friendly Society.' See Frangos, The Philike Etairia 1814-21: A Social and Historical Analysis, 1.

68. Ibid, 35.

69. Yannis Yannoulopoulos, 'Greek Society on the Eve of Independence,' in *Balkan Society in the Age of Greek Independence*, 30. Stoianovich also described the influence of inter-European warfare on the rise and fall of Balkan trade, especially in relation to the elimination of French traders and shippers from the Mediterranean. These events had the effect of helping to build Odessa, birthplace of the Philike Etairia, into a "great grain emporium." See 'The Conquering Balkan Orthodox Merchant,' 275, 289.

70. Koraes, 'Report on the Present State of Civilization in Greece,' 180.

71. Leon Leontides of Constantinople joined the Society in 1816. Leontides had apparently set out to serve as a supplier to Napoleon's great invasion of Russia. However 'the ill-fated end of the campaign," Mexas writes "had brought about his economic catastrophe." Valerios G. Mexas, *Hoi Philikoi*, (Athens, 1937), 1.

72. Frangos, The Philike Etairia 1814-21: A Social and Historical Analysis, 33-34.

73. George Finlay, *History of the Greek Revolution and the Reign of King Otho*, (London: Zeno, 1971), 98.

74. Ibid, 76.

75. In Tasos Vournas, *Philike Etairia*, (Athens: Afon Totide Solomos, 1982), 149-150.

76. Mexas, *Hoi Philikoi*, 1.

77. The most authoritative account of the number of people who became members in the organization has been produced by George Frangos from a compilation of those first published in Sekeres, Philemon, and Mexas. From these Frangos accumulated a list of 1093 names. Of the 910 members who reported their occupation, the majority or 53.7 percent counted themselves as merchants, followed by 'professionals,' a group that included physicians, teachers, lawyers and students. These accounted for slightly over 13 percent of the members. The remainder of the organization was drawn from clerics, of all levels, and the small class of Greek notables or primates from the Peloponnesus. Frangos, The Philike Etairia 1814-21: A Social and Historical Analysis, 87.

78. Alkhes Aggelou's *Hoi logioi kai ho Agonas*, (Athens: Syllogos pros ton diadosin ophelimon vivlion, 1971), is perhaps the only work devoted to this subject. A short and somewhat esoteric piece the author nonetheless shows that the logioi were not absent from the revolution. Their contributions were most often made as 'secretaries,' or perhaps more accurately scribes, in the service of military chiefs and political leaders. This theme is also considered by Henderson in *The Revival of Greek Thought*. Note for example his conception of the 'tragic view of Koraes,' page 154.

79. One of the best analyses of this subject remains Nicholas Kaltchas's *Introduction to the Constitutional History of Modern Greece*, (New York: Columbia University Press, 1940). As Kaltchas notes on page 42, "the indigenous ruling classes—Peloponnesian landowners, Hydriot shipowners and merchants, and higher clergy—hesitated to plunge into insurgency at the behest of rootless idealists and, at worst, irresponsible adventurers." The attention and support of the primates was gradually obtained via the Etairia's success in winning adherents among the corps of kapetanioi, whether klephts or armotolos, as both Mexas and Kaltchas note. This may in turn have caused the Peloponnesian landowners to join the Society as a way of maintaining an interest in the course of events, a kind of 'hedging' of bets. Frangos's analysis demonstrates how carefully worded were the initiation papers of the Peloponnesian notables and concludes that "A bargain had been struck: the Maniotes would... come to the aid of the 'general fatherland' in return for the recognition of their traditional political and social position in their particular 'fatherland.'" Frangos, 'The Philike Etairia: A Premature National Coalition, *The Struggle for Greek Independence*, 98. Frangos also does not fail to note the influence of the Etairia's false claim in these negotiations that it had acquired the backing of the Russian Empire. The actual outbreak of the revolution ultimately forced the hand of the remaining elites. As Kaltchas writes perceptively again: "The upper clergy and the ruling oligarchy, confronted with the dilemma of answering with life and property for the insurgency of their humbler co-religionists or of blocking the path of national liberation, were virtually compelled to assume the leadership of the revolt." *Introduction to the Constitutional History of Modern Greece*, 43.

80. The best representative of this literature is Ioannes Kordatos's famous *He koinoneke semasia tes Hellenikes Epanastaseos tou 1821*, (Athens, 1926).

81. Frangos, The Philike Etairia 1814-21: A Social and Historical Analysis, 89.

82. A notable exception was the wealthy Constantinople merchant Panayiotes Sekeris, who provided the resources needed to sustain the group's activities over its fledgling years. Panayiotes was the eldest of three brothers. He was recruited into the Society in 1818, sometime after the initiation of his two younger (and less successful) siblings. See Frangos, The Philike Etairia 1814-21: A Social and Historical Analysis, 105.

83. Ibid, 123. He summarizes his data later: "In total, 75.4% of the merchant members of the Philike Etairia joined the society in non-native areas. In tis respect they were surpassed only by sailors, 89.3% of whom were initiated away from their native areas. Sixty two percent of the professionals and 57.9% of the military men were also recruited in non-native areas." Ibid, 235. As noted above 'merchants' were by far the largest membership category within the Society.

84. Philemon, *Dokimion Historikon peri tes Hellenikes Epanastaseos*, I: 334. Note the term 'ploiarchos' may not necessarily mean 'ship owner.' Sailors might apply the title to themselves by virtue of the custom of profit-sharing then common on these trading vessels. See Koraes 'Report on the Present State of Civilization in Greece,' 168.

85. Protopsaltes, *He Philike Etaireia*, 255. Note: The translation here as elsewhere is intended to give a true and unadorned sense of the language and craftsmanship of these letters.

86. Ibid, 255-6. Note: it cannot be confirmed whether the funds specified in these letters were actually received by the Society or were merely pledges, as the letter noted here appears to indicate. This subject discussed in Ioannes Philemon, *Dokimion Historikon peri tes Philikes Hetaireias*, (Nafplion: Th. Kontaxe, 1834), 161.

87. Protopsaltes, *He Philike Etaireia*, 258.

88. Daskalakes *Keimena-Pegai*, 48-9. Taken from the Bucharest Archives. The 'Confession' that exists in the Greek State Archives (and printed in Protopsaltes), contains some slight differences. Question 1 above for example, appears in the Greek archives as "How do you live and what is way of your livelihood," question 7 asks "Are you burdened with some great loss, or change (turnabout) in your condition of life?" Question 8 is also slightly modified: "Are you satisfied in your profession and do you desire more from it?" See Protopsaltes, *He Philike Etaireia*, 246.

89. The question of marriage could also have socio-economic significance. This was a commitment that was influenced by a man's economic means and those of his family. Obviously a man in financial distress could not marry. There were other potential difficulties: the practice of giving dowries led to the custom of young men delaying marriage until their sisters had been provided for; a situation influenced of course by the relative affluence or means of the family concerned. Note below that one sample act of philanthropy in the dedication 'form letter' of the Society included a contribution toward the marriage of the recipient's sister.

90. The oaths of the initiates to the Society appear to reinforce the emphasis on individuals who were steadfast, loyal and not given to ruptures in personal relationships: "I swear that wherever I find a comrade, I will help and aid him to the extent of my strength and means, that I will offer to him my respect and obedience if he is greater in rank, and if he was before my enemy, the greater was our enmity, the more will I love him." Daskalakes, *Keimena-Pegai*, 58.

91. See below.

92. Frangos had an interesting if speculative interpretation of his own. He believed that "such searching questions could not but have weakened a prospective member's ties to the traditional world which he was being asked to abandon. Perhaps not unlike religious confession, the exomologisis bared the initiate's soul, in this instance his social being, and thus made a fundamental conversion easier to accomplish." He appeared to relate the effect of this shock treatment to the observation of "anthropologists ...that members of traditional and family centered societies strongly resist individual questioning by strangers on personal matters." Such insights confer considerable intellectual dexterity upon men whose sophistication Frangos was not otherwise given to praise. Frangos, The Philike Etairia 1814-21: A Social and Historical Analysis, 54-6. Note: the author's source for anthropological data is cited as: Ernestine Friedl, *Vasilika, A Village in Modern Greece*, (New York, 1962).

93. It does appear that the Etairia sought first to win the prosperous merchants to their cause. The Society's oath also exhibits some concern over financial fidelity, a virtue that might be compromised by one in difficult circumstances: "...whatever obligation/debt I might have in the world, even the very greatest, I will count as

nothing before the Society... I swear that in no way will I benefit from the funds of the Society, but I will consider it as a holy matter and a needful pledge to all our tortured nation, as also the letters received and sent." Daskalakes, *Keimena- Pegai*, 57, 58.

94. Ibid, 72.

95. In time 'mouseiou' and 'school' became code words for 'Etairia' and 'revolution.' Philemon, *Dokimion Historikon peri tes Hellenikes Epanasataseos*, I: 157-8.

96. Protopsaltes, *He Philke Etaireia*, 251. Translation could possibly be understood as "I work in the service of a merchant," an even more telling indication of the apprentice nature of the men involved.

97. Frangos, The Philike Etairia 1814-21: A Social and Historical Analysis, 291. He did not elaborate further however upon the idea of 'redemption.'

98. Perhaps the men described in the devotional letters resemble those that Frantz Fanon once wrote of in the post-colonial societies of Africa, the "classless idlers" seeking to be "rehabilitated in their own eyes and in the eyes of history": "these classless idlers will by militant and decisive action discover the path that leads to nationhood...these workless less-than-men are rehabilitated in their own eyes and in the eyes of history ... all the hopeless dregs of humanity ...will recover their balance, once more go forward, and march proudly in the great procession of the awakened nation." Frantz Fanon, *The Wretched of the Earth*, translated by Constance Farrington, (New York: Grove Press, 1963), 130.

99. Once again, these impulses have been used by scientists to explain historical phenomena. In his recent study of ethnic conflict, Stuart Kaufman borrowed rather often from psychological studies to explain modern episodes of ethnic violence in the Balkans as well as other regions of the world. Kaufman's theory for example of the 'Symbolic Politics of Ethnic War' drew upon research that has some relevance to the subjects considered above: "Research shows that people experiencing any negative emotion are more prone to feelings of anger and aggression if ideas justifying anger and aggression are brought to mind." *Modern Hatreds, The Symbolic Politics of Ethnic War*, 29. This conclusion derived in part from: Leonard Berkowitz, 'On the Formation and Regulation of Anger and Aggression: A Cognitive-Neoassocianistic Analysis,' *American Psychologist* 45, no.4 (1990), 494-503.

100. These 'negative' sources of group identity are key elements in the works of Geertz and Kaufman cited above.

101. Much as the emigre logioi hoped to bring modern Greek culture closer to the ancient model so loved by Europe. See comments of Koliopoulos and Veremis from Chapter 3 above.

102. Protopsaltes, *He Philike Etaireia*, 30. 'Striving together' in this case in order to avoid, as the narrator goes on to say, the "internal conflict and discord" that "brought our race down to this wretched state." Ibid, 30. Of course this is one of the most prominent themes in Neo-Hellenic discourse. Moisiodax emphasized discord in his *Ethike Rhetorike* as noted above; it appeared earlier in Meletios's geography and earlier still among the teachings of Meniates. See Konstantinou Paparregopoulou, *Istoria tou Hellenikou Ethnous*, Volume 15, (Athens: Kaktos, 1993), 170.

103. See chapter three.

104. Protopsaltes, *He Philike Etaireia*, 30.

105. The author of most Etairia literature is generally considered to be Tsakalof, one of the three original

founders. Frangos, The Philike Etairia, 1814-1821: A Social and Historical Analysis, 66. In many ways he himself presents the figure of a frustrated logios, a judgement derived from his ambiguous claims of once being a student in Paris, his apparent authorship of the Etairia texts and his activities during the Revolution in the service of a politico-military chief. Protopsaltes, *He Philike Etaireia*, 23-4.

106. Mexas, *Hoi Philikoi*, 27.

107. Ibid, 76.

108. Ibid, 10, 19.

109. Ibid, 10.

110. The founders had early on even attempted to recruit the logioi into the Society, as Skouphas's 1816 meeting with Gazes in Odessa demonstrates. The persistent efforts in fact of the Society to recruit the well known logios do not appear to have been completely successful. Xanthos, *Apomenemonevmata peri tes Philikes Hetaireias*, 142. Plans were also made to approach Koraes himself in Paris, but there is no evidence that Koraes was ever contacted by the Society or knew of its existence prior to the start of the Revolution. Frangos, The Philike Etairia 1814-1821: A Social and Historical Analysis, 45-6.

111. The initiation letters of Doukas and Benjamin are included in Philemon, *Dokimion Historikon peri tes Hellenikes Epanastaseos* I: 337-8. Passages from the Doukas letter appear in the preface of this study.

112. Frangos, The Philike Etairia 1814-21: A Social and Historical Analysis, 291. Frangos was more intensely drawn to the vestiges of Freemasonry and the Carbonari he detected in some of the Etaireia rituals and customs. These do appear to be significant. Ibid, 64-5.

113. Ibid, 79.

114. This too comes with caveats given the revolutionary declarations made earlier by Koraes, and the precedents set by Regas and the Orlov revolt.

115. Regas Velestinlis, 'Thourios,' in *Regas*, 393. Many other Greeks watched this ongoing deterioration with great interest and expectation. One notes the comments of Pharmakides, then a young scholar in Leipzig, in a letter from June 1820. "We wet ourselves for joy when learning of the Sultan's mobilization against Ali Pasha." Georgios Laios (ed.), *Anekdotes Epistles kai Engrapha tou 1821*, (Athens: Diphos, 1958), 25. Pharmakides went on to play an important role in the ecclesiastical affairs of the Greek kingdom.

V. Neohellenic Geography and the National Problem

> *Kerkyra and the other islands are all inhabited by Greeks (Graikous), illiterate and without arts on account of the previous Venetian administration, now under the governance of France... as for the end of the war, and what will come after, nobody knows...*[1]

This passage from Athanasios Psalidas's geography of Epiros alludes to the unsettled political state of affairs in the Balkans in the years surrounding the creation of the Philike Etairia. The fate of Kerkyra (Corfu) was finally determined in 1815 by the establishment of the Septinsular Republic of the Ionian Islands. It was of course in the year before that the leaders of the Philike Etairia had pledged themselves to the cause of a free Greece, in part out of frustration over these diplomatic outcomes of the Napoleonic Wars.[2] But what did this 'free Greece' consist of?

In the previous chapter George Frangos proposed that the founders of the Etairia were men who had undergone a "profound social and psychological transformation" that led them to the "creation and adoption of a new social, political and individual identity—the nation."[3] But one looks in vain for those features that would distinguish the Etairia's conception of the nation from others.[4] Upon the vaguely defined terms nation and race had been deposited several centuries worth of literary matter. We have sampled some of it here. The 'nation' that the Friends spoke of is a similarly un-evolved creature, having no clearly delineated form or organs. What the records of the Etairia more accurately reveal is the manner in which new ranks and classes of men came to bind themselves to the cause of this forlorn entity, and secondly, the extraordinary degree to which the declarations of these later redeemers had been alloyed with the rhetoric of the logioi.

Another example of the influence that the intellectual culture of the Greek Enlightenment exerted upon the Etairia, is presented by the case of a young initiate, the twenty seven year old Jassy merchant Panayiotes Panos. Following the policy set down by the founders, Panos disguised his donation to the secret organization as an act of philanthropy. However his choice of medium was significant: Panos proposed that his money be used to fund the publication in

Greek of a new book of geography.[5] By doing so, this young merchant helps to indicate the high place that this science had acquired within Greek culture over the course of the Enlightenment.

The heavy emphasis placed by the logioi on the study of geography naturally leads one to seek the cause of their attraction. The short answer may be that through geography they found the Enlightenment to speak most directly to their situation and needs, as I will try to show below. This phenomenon may in fact have something important to teach us regarding the nature of borrowing, or 'ideological piracy' according to some, that occurred between national cultures during the Enlightenment—a topic that has drawn the special attention of modern scholars of nationalism.[6]

The Greek intellectuals of the eighteenth century were not unlike those of other 'nations,' the Americans perhaps or the Bohemians, who experienced the Enlightenment as a foreign world of thinkers and thought radiating out from the 'West.' In some parts of the world the effect was significant, in others, negligible. Writing of the Swedish experience, for example, one historian has said that the Enlightenment "never formed a truly coherent current of ideas or became a unified movement." This, he argues, was a consequence of the "political and social" conditions obtaining in Sweden and the "resulting intellectual climate." Frangsmyr concludes that "Ideas never arise in a vacuum; there has to be the right soil for their germination and growth. Quite simply, they must have an application—it must be possible to assign them a function."[7]

These assumptions bear an uncanny resemblance to those expressed by an eighteenth century central European scholar cited in the same volume. Mikulas Teich's essay on Bohemia includes a brief portrait of the Prague University philologist Josef Dobrovsky (1753-1828). Dobrovsky's consciousness of himself as a European intellectual on the periphery of the Enlightenment, as well as his awareness of the cultural factors guiding the processes of encounter and "application," is exhibited in a remarkable passage from his correspondence:

> I read Raynal in German translation; and I could not make up my mind to read the patriarchs of French philosophy Voltaire and Rousseau. Why that? Because I shall certainly not find that what I should like to find. In time I shall do it in order to see whether on German soil it is possible to arrive there, where these gentlemen had arrived. There are things said by others that we should never believe, but we should always first think for ourselves, and then compare our thinking with that of others.[8]

Dobrovsky's remark that we prefer to find 'that what we should like to find,' has obvious resonance in the Greek case. In the study of geography the

Greeks found much of what they wished to find, for reasons I hope to explain below. Furthermore, in the case of the Greeks, the Enlightenment did become a movement of formidable force and one that expressed a level of cohesion and unity perhaps absent in other lands. Why did this happen? The Greek world was certainly every bit as tradition-bound as the one described by Frangsmyr, a largely rural society that would not have figured as an ideal setting for the spread of Enlightenment ideas. Nonetheless it was a world virtually free of state imposed censure and, furthermore, one that the logioi were quite at liberty to leave.

In explaining the participation of the Greek world in the European Enlightenment a few additional factors should be considered. The first was its 'posture' toward the West as it had evolved over the preceding centuries. This posture, one which generally deferred to Europe as the center of all new learning and knowledge, was aptly symbolized in the stream of students from the East who had for centuries sought to complete their educations in its universities.

The genesis of the assumptions described above concerning the relative merits of East and West extended back to late Byzantium, and the growing self-consciousness of the sinking status of the Greek world that becomes apparent in the sources from that period. The West might be heretical and wicked as the more zealous Orthodox Greeks insisted, however even these would have been obliged to acknowledge, like Pringos, that it wielded immense power. The Diaphotismos was unified therefore around the basic impulse to 'catch-up.' And even though this impulse existed to a certain degree in Sweden, as Frangsmyr notes, it never acquired the weight and scale of the Greek case.

Nor were the Swedes the targets of the kind of disillusionment and even invective found in Holderlin, de Pauw, Poqueville, etc, indeed an entire host of European writers. "Is this the renowned Athens?" Lord Charlemont shrugged in dismay and disappointment upon his arrival in the city after a long and tiring pilgrimage.[9] Indeed it was. So did the greatness of its past and the completeness of its collapse make Greece an essential subject for all interested in the phenomenon of decline—an intellectual preoccupation of some weight within the Enlightenment and the gradually forming antithesis to its enchantment with progress.[10] For educated Greeks, these desultory and embarrassing judgements had a counterpart in their own native sources, the writings of predecessors who dwelt not infrequently upon the same themes. The urgency of the national revival was animated in no small part by that golden past, under the tyranny of which the logioi of succeeding generations had long labored to prove themselves. This 'tyranny of the past' may alone serve to distinguish the reception of the Enlightenment among the Greeks from other peoples.[11] So common was this attitude that even the Orthodox Church became a participant in the struggle, however reluctantly or unwittingly, as witnessed by the tremendous amount of 'enlightenment' activity conducted by clerics.

In this sense the 'gatekeeper' factor in Greece was remarkably porous, much less an obstacle to the diffusion of Enlightenment than the obstacles implied by the physical condition of Greek society. The urgency of the 'cultural problem,' the self-consciousness that attended the inescapable fact of decline, lent the educational reform of Greece a legitimacy that was difficult even for the established Church, the cultural guardian of the Greek world, to resist or resist with unanimity. For all the celebrated outbursts directed by high officials against the dangers of the new learning, this 'mission' yet penetrated the Church to a profound degree. Furthermore the Church could not sit idly by as illiteracy took its toll on the spiritual integrity of the Orthodox faithful or left them defenseless against the rhetoric of its enemies. As discussed above these fears were considerable motivation in drawing the Church into the struggle against the national problem.

The Enlightenment, finally, did not have to go to Greece to make its presence felt; more accurately, the Greeks went to the Enlightenment, and in a number and frequency that merits notice. The culturally and intellectually restrictive environments within which other thinkers may have been enclosed was overcome in the Greek case by the steady flow of students and scholars to the Enlightenment centers of Europe. This tradition was of course much older than the Enlightenment as discussed in the second chapter. But it certainly increased in scale during these times, for the scholarly interchange was being steadily augmented by the entry and participation of new social classes in the process. The entire mosaic was re-composed by the old klepht Kolokotronis, as he looked back on the times preceding the Revolution:

> ...the merchants in the kingdoms and the many young men studying in the universities and so many others of us in foreign parts... living there we lost the lethargy and torpor of slavery and the fear of tyranny and we saw the gentility and greatness of the other nations and learned that we had ancestors of formidable power and we yearned ourselves for our own regeneration and for the ancient glories of Greece. Schools were started in Smyrna, Iannina, Athens... and they brought out learned clergymen and laymen and the people were enlightened.[12]

Finally, the ambivalent position which the Ottoman authorities took on the educational activities of the Greeks is also a significant factor in explaining the ability of the Enlightenment to gather strength in the East.[13] To a degree, the

Greek logioi were able to operate completely outside the reach of the 'state' and had more to fear from their own co-religionists in Constantinople than Ottoman censors.[14]

For the reasons discussed above, the Diaphotismos was permitted room to operate and expand, as witnessed by the steady increase in Greek publishing activity over the eighteenth century.[15] This growth and dispersion of print culture was reflected in the rise of Greek language newspapers and periodicals. It was through such means and mediums that the Diaphotismos accomplished its diffusion over time and (social) space.

Throughout this study it has been my intent to consider the extent to which the Greek Enlightenment and its intellectual preoccupations were influenced by Western forms, ideas and idioms. Both parties brought something to this transaction. We see the 'Greek' quotient in the things that the logioi tended to seize upon and the manner in which this was done. I have referred to this elsewhere as the cultural appropriation or nationalization of the Enlightenment. The Enlightenment after all constitutes a vast range of thinkers and themes. Which parts did the Greeks, like others, find themselves especially attracted to?

Writing of Italy Owen Chadwick described the Enlightenment as characterized by "its tendency to be very practical. Italians thought about practical problems, economics, prosperity, government, penal reform, education. For the first time they applied to political philosophy that phrase, 'the greatest happiness of the greatest number.'"[16] A basic 'practicality' is equally visible in the thought of the logioi, however the search for the character of the Greek Enlightenment must often consider what it translated rather than produced. There was no Greek Beccaria, or Vico or Muratori. On the whole, the Enlightenment took little notice of its Neohellenic acolyte: the Greeks made no original contributions to European thought and their works were rarely translated into European languages.[17] Nor did the logioi delude themselves in the conceit that they *could* make an original contribution to the Enlightenment.[18] These intellectuals were experiencing and participating in the Enlightenment on an entirely different level, their efforts and activities conditioned by an overwhelming national preoccupation. This activity swallowed up all the energy of the logioi and they gave little thought to original speculation in the purest sense except as it concerned the sources of national decline and revival, although here too they were inclined toward a synthesis of the modern (Western) and native (Hellenic) traditions.

Neohellenic Geography: Roots of Discourse

The Greek fascination with geography is clearly visible in the publishing activities of many of its greatest Enlightenment figures.[19] This is apparent in the work of one we have already considered in depth, Iosepos Moisiodax, whose *Theoria tes Geographias*, was published in Vienna in 1781. But Moisiodax was himself following in the footsteps of several important predecessors. These included Meletios (Metros) the Metropolitan of Athens (1661-1714), whose *Geographia palaia kai nea* was written around the close of the seventeenth century and published posthumously in Venice in 1728. This was also the year that the second edition of Chrysanthos Notaras's *Eisagoge eis ta geographika, kai sphairika* was published in Venice, following an earlier edition that appeared in Paris in 1716. In 1749 another Greek, Marcos Antonios Katsaites published his *Geografia in dialogo*, the same year in which appeared the *Odon Mathematikes*, a joint work authored by Methodios Anthrakites and Balanos Vasilopoulos. In 1760, again from Venice, came Giorgios Fatzeas's *Grammatike Geographike*. The *Geographia Neoterike* of Philippides and Konstantas appeared in 1791, a work highly inspired by the close association of the authors with that great figure of the Neohellenic Enlightenment, Demetrios Katartzes. It was in fact on the occasion of one of his 'exhortatory essays' that Katartzes indicated the primacy that history and geography had attained among the logioi of the period:

> One must study before anything else the two eyes of history, chronology and geography, sciences that we chiefly need. Chronology, a new science, can be found in French; geography was around from the beginning, however the numbers of books we have don't fill all of our needs. Like the geographer, let's divide geography into two parts, ancient and modern, as is done in history; for the ancient, let's speak of the nations (ethne), the states, countries that used to be, and in the modern, those that are. The Eisagoge of Chrysanthou and the Grammatike of Fatzea are excellent writings for their times, and yet they aren't taught in our schools or homes. The wise young man must also make maps, for the same reason that chronology has for history, so are maps to geography; in the first one sees the connection between events in time, in the second the connection of countries in space.[20]

By the second half of the eighteenth century geography had found its way into the curriculum of the Flaggineio School and the University of Padua.[21] Publishing activities continued at a steady pace into the nineteenth century. In 1807 Anthimios Gazes (1758-1828) published *Meletiou Geographia* (a reprint of Meletios's work), also in Vienna; yet another edition of the work was published by Konstantine Koumas in 1819. Gazes had earlier, in 1804, edited and published

Nikephoros Theotokes's *Stoicheia Geographias* which had been written in 1774.[22] The important logios Athanasios Psalidas wrote a geography of Albania and Epiros in 1819, as we have seen above, and, finally, Koraes was also active in this field.[23] It is noteworthy that one of Regas's own projects was a translation of the popular French work of historical geography, the *Voyage du jeune Anacharsis en Grece*, first published in 1788 by the abbe Barthelemy (1716-1795). The appearance of Barthelemy's *Anacharsis* led to the publication of Regas's famous *Map of Greece* in 1797, which was intended to serve as an aid to readers of the young Scythian's (Anacharsis) travels through the eastern Mediterranean.[24] Beyond these original monographs and translations we have also to consider the numerous surveys of geography and geographical studies found in Greek newspapers and periodicals of the era.[25] This growing emphasis upon geography as the basis of a modern education was stressed finally by Gazes in the prologue to his republication of Meletios:

> Geography and History not only cultivate the man, but also establish him as a citizen, and beneficial to civilized society. On the one hand Geography takes him around from place to place, shows him all the spheres of world upon which we dwell, the sites, the divisions, the parts, the kingdoms and their peoples; History bears on all of this and follows from the beginning all of the events of the world, the changes of nations and powers, the virtues and achievements of great men, excites the soul towards imitation of their virtue, discernment and prosperity; and toward aversion and avoidance of the bad. Two sciences therefore necessary to every person! Sciences of which, before any others, are necessary for the young people of our race to study in our schools. Sciences that every parent must teach to his children....[26]

Gazes's 1807 republication of Meletios's *Geographia*, nearly one hundred years old at the time, serves to demonstrate the admiration this work elicited among later logioi. Konstantas and Philippides cited from the *Geographia* and spoke glowingly of its author in their own geography, as did Psalidas.[27] Theotokes, as we will see below, lifted whole passages from it. The republication and citation of texts such as these by later generations of logioi helps to illustrate the internal unity of the Neohellenic Enlightenment and offers important insights into how key elements of its thought were internally inspired and transmitted. It is not entirely true, as some writers are too quick to claim, that the logioi made contact with their 'golden past' only upon emigration to the West.[28] The unity of the Greek Enlightenment was partly the outcome of a tradition of 'internal borrowing' of great vintage, into which the contributions of succeeding generations of logioi was steadily assimilated.

"It is apparent dear reader," Meletios wrote in the preface to his geography, "that nothing better adorns and enriches a man than the knowledge of Geography and certainly too of History.... Isn't it a great shame for a man, who would call himself the keeper of his house, not to know the ways in and out of that house..to be ignorant of its upper and lower floors, the gates, the gardens and whatever else is there...?"[29] The general inference of Meletios, and certainly Katartzes and Gazes, whose words are highly reminiscent of those above, is that an awareness of the larger world is an essential condition of enlightenment and civilization. Meletios's opening declaration, similar to others we have encountered, is an assault upon mental insularity and isolation, marks, he infers, of the small mindedness and ignorance that characterize a people dwelling in darkness. The civilized man, Meletios implied, was one who knew the world. But his geography is not only a geography of space, it is also one of time ('palaia kai nea'). Cicero had declared that to be ignorant of the world that existed before one's birth was to remain forever a child. To know the world, 'one's house,' was equally for Meletios to have a perspective on its past. And it is here that geography functioned as an instrument of cultural revival and consciousness raising, for it is in this perspective on the past that the modern Greek encountered lessons of obvious significance.

Meletios emphasized at the very beginning of his geography the obligation he felt to help spread education within Greek society.[30] His publisher felt called upon nonetheless to reinforce this message, and so we find an additional dedication at the beginning of the volume praising all those devoted to the "spread of letters," a duty, the author added with great pathos, that has an almost holy character for "our fallen race."[31] It was for such a people and in such a spirit Meletios, tells us himself in the preface, that he wrote this work "in the common dialect... as a gift toward the majority of our race."[32]

As the century progressed works of geography continued to appear both within the Greek world and without, works that added greater depth to the manner in which this science was understood and practiced. Here as elsewhere the Enlightenment made its influence felt, and it is in this context that one can perceive the way in which the traditions of Greek thought were gradually augmented with the European.

Notaras's *Eisagoge eis ta geographika, kai sphairika*, as its title suggests, was intended less as a stand alone work of geography than as a primer on the proper terminology and plan of study to follow when producing works of this kind. In this case Notaras's *Eisagoge* reflected its author's rather wide ranging knowledge and familiarity with the principal Greek and European texts.[33] Notaras does nonetheless occasionally depart from the general pedagogical format of the

Eisagoge to make his own thoughts known on matters of culture and civilization - observations that often serve as excellent examples of the national discourse we have been describing.

As an item of intellectual history, Notaras's *Eisagoge* is valuable on many levels, not the least of which is the exhibition of scholasticism present throughout the work. This is displayed especially well in the lengthy section on cosmology.[34] The great question for Notaras, even at this late date (1716), remained the geo versus the heliocentric structure of the universe.[35] Notaras gives due regard to the 'proofs' of contemporary astronomers, and his appendix contains a series of vivid illustrations depicting their arguments. However he himself held to the older position, which he defended through a lengthy exposition of pagan and Christian texts.[36]

The first printing of Notaras's *Eisagoge* occurred in 1716, or two years after Meletios's death. The *Eisagoge* furthermore was probably written after Meletios's *Geographia palaia kai nea*, however the latter was not published in Notaras's lifetime.[37] Meletios and Notaras make no reference therefore to each other in their works. Who do these writers consequently draw upon for inspiration and instruction? From the Greek tradition come Herodotus, Plato, Aristotle, Dionysios, Polybius, Plutarch and Ptolemy, this last of whom Notaras declared the "summit of Geographers."[38] Strabo also appears prominently throughout both works. These are old figures to be sure, a point that is worth noting. As the Diaphotismos approached its mature stage, these ancient Hellenic authorities were gradually supplanted by contemporary ones; citations of Aristotle for example start to give way in the later sources to those of Meletios or Voulgaris. In this sense Notaras and Meletios could be fit within the intellectual-historical space occupied by Skouphos, who, like them, drew heavily upon the 'fathers' of Hellenic culture for inspiration. However in a striking departure from Skouphos, Meletios and Notaras make extensive use of European authors in their geographies as well. Of these, Philippe Briet (1601-1668), Philippe Cluver (1580-1622) and Gerardus Mercator (1512-1594) were noteworthy influences.[39]

As the geographical sciences progressed in the eighteenth century, a growing preoccupation with 'cause and effect' became increasingly evident, especially in the context of cultural affluence and decline. Montesquieu was perhaps the most often celebrated figure here and he will have a considerable influence on Greek thought. However Montesquieu's *Considerations sur la grandeur et la decadence des Romains* (1734) and *Esprit des lois* (1748) appeared long after the publications of Notaras and Meletios.[40] One may be surprised therefore at the presence in these earlier works of ideas that contain elements of the principles associated with later philosophes and ideologues. An interesting example occurs in a section from the *Eisagoge*—"On the results and properties of the zones"(climactic divisions of the earth)—where Notaras linked the "ethics and nature of the people who find themselves in the inhabited parts and the condition of the air."[41] Notaras proceeded to illustrate this principle with the following examples:

> And so those who find themselves in the torrid zones are dry, dark, ugly, have twisted hair, wrinkled flesh, blood of high temperature and are melancholic, so that they are given to rage, inhumane, wild, crude, bestial and many of them cannibals. Those who live in the temperate zones, and especially in the middle of them, so too are they balanced in their humors, ruddy, light haired, domesticated, diligent, studious, humane, hospitable, intelligent, pious ... those again inhabiting the frigid zones, are for the most part white, careless, barbarous, small bodied, dull, long haired, very cold, slothful in the mind and cannibals.[42]

The kind of linkages that Notaras makes above between climate and culture were long a tradition of Greek thought. Nonetheless they may well have served as the nucleus of the more far-reaching enquiries to come.[43] For Notaras there were additionally four parts of the world, Europe, Asia, Africa and America.[44] The geographer's task therefore was to investigate each of these parts and delineate the "human" properties from the "natural." Regarding the "natural," he explained that "every place has something of its own, and exceptional, of which cannot be found in another or doesn't have the same force, quality or superiority... the same is always true of the human properties."[45] Notaras goes on to specify the human attributes that should properly feature in a work of geography:

> The people of a place, of what size are they and color are they most inclined, what kind or law of morals do they have, in what studies, arts and trades are they occupied in, which are their languages, which religion, what type of polity do they have, Monarchical, Aristocratic, Democratic, mixed, how much capability do they have in matters of war, and is it only on land are also at sea? Which famous men and from which times came from the place, and in which parts occurred some great triumph, as for example the war of Hannibal with the Romans, the War of Alexander, the War between Caesar and Pompey. Which are the famous cities. Which are called metropolises, in which are the thrones of the Kings, the Dukes, the Princes, the Rulers? Are there found any exceptional remains of antiquity, aqueducts, exceptional churches, convents, palaces, fortresses, hippodromes, theaters, statues of artistic note, Academies, schools, hotels, homes for the poor, great bridges, special paved roads, magnificent tombs...[46]

By seeking those attributes that make a particular kingdom or people exceptional, Notaras's human geography perhaps inevitably dwells upon matters of power, fame and grandeur. Perhaps it is no coincidence that Notaras chose to illustrate this lesson through a survey of Europe. In the section that follows he describes how natural and human properties collaborated to make Europe the dominant civilization in the world, providing, along the way, a revealing example of the assumptions that inform Neohellenic geography and thought.

Essential to Europe's dominance was the fact that "nearly all of Europe is located in the temperate zone," a condition whose advantages Notaras described earlier.[47] His ensuing survey begins with a word of caution: "diverse historians and geographers, both Greeks (Hellenes) and Latins have written in length, if often confusing matters geographical, natural and human. On this it is necessary for the reader to think on and discern."[48] He proceeds to give a correct description of the human element of European geography:

> The people of Europe are energetic, courageous and intelligent. In Europe has been born so many wise men, so many lawmakers, so many physicians, so many orators, so many generals who pacified, educated and conquered all the other peoples of the world with the power of their minds, their language, their arms. In Europe stood the two famous kingdoms of the Greeks and the Romans. In here rose, bloomed and now flourishes all the sciences and arts, the heroic exploits, morality, nobility, of which it would accurately be to call her the decency of the world. The Europeans are particularly exceptional in the present century in the field of navigation. They are diverse in their languages, in their customs, in their religion, in the size of their bodies and their color.[49]

What is left for him but to conclude that "in the area of general happiness and numbers of virtuous men, and in the abundant fruitfulness on account of the conditions of the air, and the nearly everywhere well allotted waters and the variety and profusion of excellent fruits and necessities of life and all other products, Europe is much superior to the other two (Asia and Africa)."[50]

A subject of particular interest for historians concerns the geographical space that Greece occupied in the early modern Hellenic consciousness. In his division of the world Notaras locates Greece, "Hellas," in Europe.[51] Notaras's assumption of the physical extent of Greece is however difficult to determine as he goes into no detail on these matters. Constantinople for example is included as a "European" city.[52] However it is not clear if the city is a property of Greece or "Turkey," for the latter is divided into European and Asiatic zones. Europe also includes 'Dakia' (Transylvania, Wallachia, Moldavia), which were, like Greece, territorial dominions of European Turkey.[53]

These subjects were treated more authoritatively in Meletios. Like Notaras,

Meletios also placed Greece in Europe. This might in some ways be considered a significant act, as to place Greece in Europe was to move her within the sphere of what he (and Notaras) described as the advanced world, to declare her independence from Asia, etc. Perhaps more significantly, Meletios's Greece extends up to and includes the city of Constantinople.[54] Such assumptions concerning the extent and 'belongings' of the Greek world, however vague, help indicate the roots of the territorial disputes that came to dominate Eastern Mediterranean history right up to the present. This indefinite yet extensive sense of Greece's boundaries will be equally visible in the geographers who follow.[55] Of course the conception of this 'Greater Greece' has led historians to question the 'national' character of the movements led by Regas or the Etairia, seeing not so much the demand for a 'nation-state' as a revival of the Byzantine Empire.[56]

Meletios's geography also contains the enthusiastic and wholly unscrutinized Westernism that was exhibited in the *Eisagoge*. "Europe holds the first place in the world," he declared, in terms reminiscent of Notaras, "due to the fertility of the ground and the temperate air, and because of the magnificence of its buildings, similarly does it exceed others in the numbers of its people, and rare their inabilities ...in them is always lit virtue and morality and science and arms and all those things that benefit the people; found here are nearly all the admired arts..."[57] In sharp contrast, the interior of Asia Minor "was formerly a place of culture and men of great Christian faith where there were many great cities, of which four thousand were devastated by the Turks and its former luminosity and nobility has been completely transformed into a barbarous and desolate valley..."[58]

Proceeding from his study of Europe, the *Geographia*, a heavy work of six hundred and twenty split-column pages of text, conducts a dense examination of all the great kingdoms and empires of the world. Once again the capital cities of Europe are described with the type of reflexive admiration that would typify the first reactions of later Greek pilgrims such as Koraes and Kazantzakis. Amsterdam for Meletios is:

> a new city, and an exceptional one, with the most famous commerce in all the world, for more than a hundred years at least the greatest and richest, as to be judged one of the exceptional cities in Europe and in every way it stands out brightly; it has the best and most spacious harbor, and exceeds all the other merchant centers of Europe with its number of ships, the progress of its trades, the wealth of its citizens and the skill of its sailors.[59]

It is probably important to note that Meletios had never been to Holland, a fact that does not appear to temper in the least his enthusiasm. He had however spent time in Venice, which he describes as "a large city with a great population of people, magnificent, rich, a famous center of business in which are occupied people from every place and ethnicity..."[60] Finally Paris, another city he had not visited, was the "greatest city of Gallia and most luminous, rich with a great crowd of people, always increasing, and formidable merchants, home of a famous university founded by Charles the Great in 790 and the high parliament..."[61] As an example of internal transmission, one notes how Theotokes found it convenient to simply adopt Meletios's description of the city of Paris for his own work. In the much later *Stoicheia Geographias* Paris was thus the "grand city, heavily populated, rich, commercially-oriented, nourished by the muses, Charles the Great was the first to establish in her an Academy around 790..."[62]

Meletios's descriptions of grandeur, dwelling on population, vitality and commerce (this last especially), contain the principle features found again in the geographies which follow. Of course, these images serve to bring into sharp focus the poor figure cut by Greece, which Meletios turned his geographer's gaze upon over the second half of the book.

Beginning his survey of the Greek world (the title, 'Peri tes Ellados,' was reprieved by Konstantas and Philippides in 1791), Meletios sounds the first notes of what will be a consistent lament: "Greece, the great and legendary name of ancient times, the slight and deplorable one of the present."[63] This introduction was followed by a wistful rumination on antiquity:

> Before any other place in Europe, or Asia there was established in Greece a people of ancient greatness and incomparable glory and luminosity in all their acts and works; here was secured the home, the residence of Wisdom, and from her came the sciences, and to the other parts of Europe and other places from Greece were sent colonists to many different lands .... and so did Greece light up the world.[64]

In the author's mind Athens comes in for special attention and he described the ancient polis in the same lavish terms that expressed his admiration for the great cities of modern Europe:

> Mother and nurse of all the sciences and disciplines and histories ... to her ran crowds of people to study and to teach for Greece was the center of the world and Attica was the center of Greece and Athens was the center of Attica, the city was in truth the residing place of the wise, the very Hellas of Hellados, the home of its spirit, heart, eyes and every other good and praiseworthy thing.[65]

Unfortunately this era was brought to an end by a succession of internal wars and invasions, concluding ultimately with the Turkish conquest: "From these and so many wars, comes the deplorable condition, what was once so luminous has been almost completely darkened and rendered into a state of barbarity."[66] Meletios's words here sound out the themes of 'stasis,' or discord, and conquest that are recognizable in many succeeding (and preceding) accounts of Greece's decline. His survey in fact of Greece's rise and fall into barbarism bears a close resemblance to the saga retold in the prologue of Moisiodax's *Ethike Philosophia.*

Beyond these images of greatness and decline, the cultural self-consciousness that recognized both Greece's plight and the supremacy of the West, Meletios's geography provides additional clues regarding other matters of interest in the sphere of Balkan intellectual history. The remarkable variety of ways in which Meletios divided and categorized the inhabitants of the earth surely counts as one. His consciousness was fully alert to the myriad bases upon which peoples could be separated and understood. On language for example, "There are four dialects in Europe principally, from which are derived the others, the Greek, Latin, Teutonic and Slavonic."[67] Of religion, the world was "divided between Christianity in which the inhabitants follow the Gospel, Islam, where the teachings of Muhammed rule, Judaism and Buddhism." It is partly from these faiths' differences in law and custom, he intimates, that the peoples of the world are differentiated, but they are also organized into diverse political entities.[68] These include the "Turkish Empire, the Kingdoms of the Persians, French, Spanish and in this manner is divided Italy in many parts and ruled by various princes" and occasionally too there are "free cities" such as those of Germany. Meletios even describes England's experiment under Cromwell with "aristocracy." The events surrounding the fall of the Stuarts and their restoration were no doubt a subject of great interest and speculation in his own lifetime.[69]

Given the variety inherent within the political and cultural estates of Europe, Meletios was confronted with a problem of organization. 'England,' 'Portugal,' 'Spain' and 'France' presented themselves as subjects for study organized around political lines. 'Germany' and 'Italy' however were cultural entities, like 'Greece.' Greece was a cultural and historical object, connected to Europe on the basis of time and space but distinct too from its neighbors as its neighbors were distinct from each other.[70] It is tempting to say, based on the above, that Meletios found it most convenient to divide the geography of Europe by its 'nations'; sometimes political boundaries complied in this design and sometimes they did not.[71]

Another item of interest concerns the use of the term 'freedom' that appears periodically in Meletios, especially in the context of the Balkans. In the section

'Concerning Dacia, or of Moldavia, Vlachia and Transylvania,' Meletios describes the various cities that had been "liberated" by the "Kaisarean Forces." In such manner was the city of Baradin in Moldavia, "conquered by the Turks in 1662, and liberated by Imperial Forces in 1694."[72] In similar manner was Hungary "liberated" and the city of Strigonion, "conquered by Sultan Sulieman in 1543, taken back with great trouble by the Christians in 1595, again by the Turks in 1605, and again abandoned by them in 1683."[73] Buda was "liberated by the Kaiser in 1686," as was Pest "liberated by the Christians with great effort in 1604," only to be lost again.[74]

Although Meletios and Notaras reveled in the achievements of classical Greece and contemporary Europe, they were largely silent on matters of 'cause.' In this case both works are absent of those deeper enquiries that moved the geographers who followed.[75] The instructional or enlightenment value that Meletios perceived in geography is also only vaguely articulated, though he clearly means, like Katartzes, to enlist the forces of geography in the struggle against Greece's mental isolation and atrophy.

At least one scholar of the Enlightenment has argued that geographical studies in early modern France accompanied state-led initiatives intended to take stock of and mobilize the kingdom's resources.[76] The Greeks of course had no living kingdom to concern themselves with, however their geographical initiative was similarly based on an intent to "know one's house." Perhaps it is significant that Katartzes would wax upon the merits of geography and history in an essay entitled, 'Know Thyself.' By the study of history and geography, he implied, one knew himself: his present, his past, his place in the larger world—it is a consciousness and identity-engendering work of a national character. Meletios's own world geography devoted a disproportionate share of its bulk to Greece; the later work of Konstantas and Philippides dispensed with the world completely and encouraged those who followed them to do the same. If one's character and identity were powerfully influenced by place, as later works were prone to emphasize, then to know one's geography was to know oneself. As the century progressed, Greek geographers came in fact to associate people with place in an increasingly explicit manner. Theotokes's *Stoicheia Geographias* even features a kind of picture gallery of national stereotypes in which the Germans are "chivalrous, sincere, brave, diligent, excellent soldiers..."[77] The Dutch are "serious, prudent, diligent," the English are "melancholy, magnanimous, having a lively and restless mind."[78] England's neighbors the Scots "are burly and warlike" while the Irish "are affable, courageous, practitioners of the musical arts," although the common people are "dim-witted and vengeful."[79]

Meletios's flushed almost propagandistic celebration of the West was augmented by future geographers with a more determined enquiry into the sources of this vitality. Where Meletios inferred a connection between commerce and prosperity, those who followed were more explicit, linking with great confidence the interplay of environment, commerce, morals and government in the alchemy of civilization. Nonetheless these later writers will continue as well to adhere to the consciousness-raising "duty" set down by their predecessors Meletios and Katartzes, as exhibited in the *Geographia Neoterike* of 1791. "We have a duty," wrote the collaborators Konstantas and Philippides, "to tell that which we know, teach others who don't know, and thus give examples to our other men of letters..." Those who come after them, they advise, should seek as well to:

> ...describe each place where they grew up, not mathematically and precisely, such as in length and width; such a form the backwardness of our people's condition does not permit; I don't speak mathematically or geographically, but narratively, remarking each on the regions and villages of his area, its administration, how many souls each village has, what peoples, what customs, what religion, what trees, income, animals, which sea it neighbors, what other provinces it borders; speaking without bias on however commendable or contemptible his compatriots...If all commit themselves in such a praiseworthy and honorable way so we will acquire a description of our area, a necessary thing and beneficial to all, and if not with great erudition and precision - but which nation (ethnos) so succeeded in the beginnings or in the rebirth of their knowledge? Time improves everything, and it is sufficient only for a people to love to learn, to be inquisitive, to examine, and not to condemn that which is simple to learn.[80]

Geography meets the Enlightenment

The Greek attraction to the study of geography presents us with the analytical challenge of determining why this field of learning was singled out for special attention.[81] The convenient answer is that the Greeks found something here that corresponded to their own experiences or perhaps in the words of Frangsmyr could be "assigned a function." Geography was held to be instructional, it had important lessons to teach the Greeks about their history and their predicament.

When one surveys geographical works from the eighteenth century it appears that the authors were performing a grand work of investigation and analysis that crossed over into many fields of study, such as history and anthropology. Geography was more than simply a description of the earth, its properties and its peoples; it concerned deeper speculations regarding the connections culture and environment. David Livingstone has written "that the issue of human diversity, its cause and consequence were part and parcel of geography's domain during the period of what is called the Enlightenment."[82] These developments had in part been provoked by the Enlightenment's search for a new pedagogy, with memorization and repetition giving way to analysis and critical-thinking in the new order of values. Eventually a hierarchy of disciplines began to emerge based upon this rearrangement of merit. These developments conspired to confront Geography with a "loss of status" Anne Marie Claire Godlewska argues, and thus its future depended on its ability to acquire the virtues of an analytical science.[83]

The momentous discoveries of the previous century had revealed how natural laws perfected the motions of the planets and kept the universe in order. That one might seek in nature laws governing human life became a major preoccupation of the Enlightenment. "We have for quite some time needed a reasoning age," Diderot declared in the *Encyclopaedia*, "when men would no longer seek the rules in classical authors but in nature." The eighteenth century was "permeated by this conviction," wrote Ernst Cassirer in his classic study of the age, "that in the history of humanity the time had now arrived to deprive nature of its carefully guarded secret, to leave it no longer in the dark to be marveled at as an incomprehensible mystery but to bring it under the bright light of reason and analyze it with all its fundamental forces."[84] The master attempt within this "reasoning age" at an explication of the natural laws of human civilization was represented by Montesquieu. Begun in the 1720s and published for the first time in 1748, *The Spirit of the Laws* ultimately appeared in twenty two editions and certainly rates as one of the most spectacular publishing phenomenons of the eighteenth century. Regarded to this day as a milestone in the history of Western political science, *The Spirit of the Laws* was to become in the eighteenth century a kind of template for the 'geographies' of the era.[85] Regas's own exposure to the work during his first visit to Vienna in 1790 had a decisive effect on him, and he immediately took to translating an edition for Greek readers.[86]

Montesquieu's researches led him to consider the possible determining effect of nature on human life, including population, culture, happiness and even laws. In the second volume for example, in a chapter entitled 'Of the Productions of the Earth which require a greater or less Number of Men,' Montesquieu wrote of how particular lands were disposed to particular crops. These basic factors ultimately determined the number of humans who could feasibly inhabit such a territory.[87] The same regulating function was performed by culture, which,

Montesquieu appeared to suggest, forms itself around similar exigencies of space, subsistence and population.[88]

However to reduce a work as long and rich with analogies as Montesquieu's into a single 'law of civilization' would be a challenging and perhaps fraudulent enterprise. Nonetheless, the determining power of place, of geography, was one of the lessons that readers were prone to fix upon. It was a compelling idea, to be sure, possessing a quality of the 'great law' that has excited minds throughout history. It was also an idea that lent a deeper analytical capacity to the staid old science of geography, a discipline after all that was undergoing an identity crisis. These verities of interpretation and emphasis aside, it is nonetheless clear that Montesquieu's approach to the study of civilization had a considerable influence on the emerging cultural understanding of Greece's decline, a subject that I would like to turn to below.

Despotism and the National Character

A revealing testament of Montesquieu's influence on his times is provided by the young Irish nobleman and philhellene, James Caulfield, known also as Lord Charlemont (1728-1799). The diaries from Charlemont's travels through Greece and Turkey are in fact filled with observations that bear a direct connection to Montesquieu's teachings. Like other philhellenes, Charlemont's dreamy vision of antiquity broke hard against the modern reality of Athenian life.[89] And yet for all his distress, Charlemont found occasion to acknowledge a survival or two of the ancient virtues among the current inhabitants. "This similarity between the manners of the modern and ancient Athenians," he observed, "affords me an opportunity of mentioning some other coincidences of a like nature, such indeed as might induce us unreservedly to subscribe to the opinion and fundamental maxim laid down by the great Montesquieu, that 'physical causes never cease to operate, and to produce their effects, notwithstanding the total subversion of every moral cause.'"[90]

Montesquieu had applied such "maxims" himself to the question of Greece's plight. However his view of the causes of its ascent and decline could not be reduced to physical environment; after all this had not changed. The answer must therefore be sought in human actions and history. It is within this context that Montequieu discussed the distorting moral and material influences of conquest and despotism. He wrote for example that "Italy, Sicily, Asia Minor, Gaul and Germany were nearly in the same state as Greece; full of small nations that abounded with inhabitants."[91] However this happy epoch was brought to an end with the rise of Rome: "All these little republics were swallowed up in a large one, and the globe insensibly became depopulated: in order to be convinced of this, we need only to consider the state of Italy and Greece before and after the victories of the Romans."[92] Here as elsewhere, Montesquieu tended to use population as a kind of empirical measure of happiness. The subject of how to repair the damage wrought by these distortions and set society back upon the path to prosperity, and growth, proved the occasion for one of his characteristic soliloquies:

> This evil is almost incurable when the depopulation is prepared beforehand by interior vice and a bad government. When this is the case men perish with an insensible and habitual disease; born in misery and weakness, in violence or under the influence of a wicked administrator, they see themselves destroyed, and frequently without perceiving the cause of their destruction. Of this we have a melancholy proof in the countries desolated by despotic power, or by the excessive advantages of the clergy over the laity.[93]

These sentiments were echoed by Charlemont, whose sojourn through contemporary Athens brought to view a people reduced by circumstances, political tyranny and want of education "into low cunning and knavery, from whence it follows that the people of Attica are generally addicted to the most refined species of cheating, and the countrymen of Aristides are now perhaps the keenest and most accomplished rogues upon the face of the earth."[94]

A final example of the prevailing 'cultural understanding' of the Greek character comes via the novel *Anastasius, or, Memoirs of a Greek*, by the English writer Thomas Hope. In this lengthy work (three volumes), Hope tells the story of a young Greek who comes of age, like the character in Holderlin's *Hyperion*, amid the upheavals of the late eighteenth century. The Orlov Revolt of 1770 features in fact quite prominently in both texts.[95] The passage below is only one of the many insights offered by Hope on that puzzling subject that equally fascinated Charlemont, Leake, Montesquieu, indeed an entire host of Western observers: on what basis, if any, could the modern Greeks be truly judged descendants of the ancients? "Credulity, versatility, and thirst of distinctions from the earliest period formed, still form, and ever will continue to form, the basis of the Greek character," Hope says, before illustrating his argument with a series of proofs:

> The ancient Greeks worshiped an hundred gods, the modern Greeks adore as many saints. The ancient Greeks believed in oracles and prodigies...the modern Greeks have faith in relics and miracles... The former were staunch patriots at home, and subtle courtiers in Persia; the latter defy the Turks in Mayno, and fawn upon them at the Fanar... Does not every modern Greek preserve the same desire for supremacy, the same readiness to undermine by every means fair or foul his competitors, which was displayed by his ancestors? Believe me, the very difference between the Greeks of time past and the present day, arises only from their thorough resemblance... When patriotism, public spirit, and preeminence in arts, science, literature and warfare, were the road to distinction, the Greeks show the first of patriots, of heroes, of painters, of poets, and of philosophers. Now that craft and subtlety, adoration and intrigue are the only paths to greatness, these same Greeks are what you see them.[96]

Observations such as these contain much of interest not only to the historian of the Tourkokratia, but for broader enquiries too into the intellectual assumptions of the early modern period. Hope's general view of Greek society resembles what Montesquieu dismissed above as a community entirely possessed by "avarice."[97] This was in fact a typical theme within both the foreign and native sources from the era.[98] As the modern Greek historian Vacalopoulos once wrote, foreign observers of Greece shared "a fairly steady consensus on the Greek proclivity towards guile, his changeableness, self-esteem, craftiness, as well as ingenuity, verve, natural eloquence and deft mimicry."[99] However the linkage of despotism and morality, the influence of what Montesquieu called "bad government" and "wicked administrators," served to occasionally leaven such views and excuse this wanton creature, as Vacalopoulos does, as the product of "an atmosphere of terror, torment and persecution." The modern Greek was the creation of an environment, Vacalopoulos added, "which bred a new sort of graeculus, the raia, a pitiful creature who trembled before the conqueror and who was always eager to serve, flatter or curry favor with him."[100]

An Act of Synthesis: The Geographia Neoterike

The evolution and influence of the themes described above is quite visible in the *Geographia Neoterike* of Konstantas and Philippides. This work stands in fact as an especially good specimen of the Diaphotismos in its late stage. Like others of its type, and such a list could include the *Apologia* of Moisiodax and Koraes's 'Memoir,' the authors pay homage to both ancient and 'modern' Greek letters while drawing on the new ideas emanating from Europe.[101] In this sense the *Geographia Neoterike* offers a view of the Diaphotismos as having arrived at a certain consciousness of its own existence.[102] Finally the *Geographia* is also a work rendered in the simple dialect and is in fact an important polemic from the language 'zetema.' It was in the course of arguing their views on this subject that the author's acknowledged their debt to the "great" Montesquieu.

"A nation that neglects and scorns its national language," the authors declare, in the spirited manner that typifies their work, "neglects and scorns its humanity." They go on to describe the damage that such neglect inflicts on the progress and enlightenment of such a nation:

> Some study French, Italian, Latin, German, but all these other languages are not our own, they are foreign, and they don't remove from the ledger of the barbarous those that study them... five educated people don't a nation make, from these no one could say that such a nation was educated, of such a nation one could more justly say that they were barbarous and ignorant... The great Montesquieu speaks ironically of the Spanish that they find numerous places in the other hemispheres, and yet there are places in Spain which they don't know still, what would he say of one of our learned who knows so many aged verbs used two thousand years ago in Athens and of the many used now that he doesn't know?

"The first and natural lesson of the young," they conclude, "must be the study of the mother language, then geography and history, after this the young man can proceed with greater ease to every other language that he would use, to every course of study, to every science.[103]

The *Geographia Neoterike* contains many passages such as the above in which the authors mock the self-contempt of their fellow Greeks and the actions it sometimes drove them to. In this case they have singled out those learned men who instead of shouldering their duty to lead the race out of the 'labyrinth of ignorance,' attempt instead to strike themselves from "the ledger of the barbarous" by adopting a European tongue. These errant Greeks, who scorn their language and thus their humanity, are condemned by Konstantas and Philippides in terms reminiscent of the *Nomarchia*.[104] Though admirers of Western thought, the collaborators shared the intense national self-consciousness that animated Skouphos's vehement defense of the Hellenic legacy in the *Texne Rhetorike*. Skouphos, Katartzes, Konstantas and Philippides in fact all appear to place their faith in revival on that ancient maxim: 'know thyself.' It was additionally a lesson best taught through that potent linkage of language, history and geography.

Finally, one encounters in this text an almost gratuitously harsh and relentless critique of the backwardness of modern Greek society, making the *Geographia Neoterike* a vivid example of the ritualization of self-contempt within the late discourse. Nonetheless, Konstantas and Philippides's steady account of the inadequacies of Greece are accompanied by an equally sustained plea for revival. This plea was prone to tap into the 'shame and duty' complex that appears so often in these late sources, as when the author's exclaim "What a disgrace it is to the ancient Greeks to have such descendants!"[105] Geography, and its allied science history, were of course especially good mediums for inflicting this kind of guilt, for they were sciences that dwelled heavily upon the golden world of the past. These lessons were in turn carried out in a spirit of irreverence that is surely another outstanding feature of the geography, and one that Leake himself found so remarkable. The boldness of the authors' critique, and it bears keeping in mind that they were both ordained churchmen, is illustrated in a passage on that most hallowed land of Orthodoxy, Mount Athos:

> Our fortunate kings looked to fill their kingdoms with crowds of good monks and not soldiers thinking that with their rosaries they would ward off the Arabs from the middle parts, the Turks from the East, the Skythians from the North and the Italians from the West. Besides the mountain (Agios Oros) the whole of Greece was full of richly endowed monasteries. In Constantinople and its environs were a crowd of wealthy and densely populated ones and so it appears to me that this was the cause of her destruction.[106]

The *Geographia Neoterike* begins by announcing its intention to correct the errors of past works. "Describing Greece," the authors explain, "I would like to give her a greater size than that given her by Europeans, and accordingly much greater than that given to her by the ancient geographers." In addition to Attica and the Peloponnesus, "European Greece" includes Thessaly, Epiros, Albania, Macedonia, Thrace, Krete and the Ionian and Aegean Islands. There is also "Asiatic Greece" which includes Ionia and the "islands of Asia Minor."[107]

The dispersion of the Greek population over these lands was explained by the geographers as a natural consequence of the south Balkan landscape. "We are like frogs around a pond" Plato famously remarked when speaking of the city states arrayed along the rocky coasts of the Aegean Sea. So they were, Konstantas and Philippides affirm, but this element of Greece's geography played a vital role too in the rise of its civilization: "The place the ancient Greeks inhabited wasn't contiguous, but parceled out by Seas, and so a nation of commerce, civilization and freedom grew and spread itself prodigiously and established itself all around."[108] Commerce looms large in the *Geographia Neoterike* as an essential instrument of material and cultural development. In this case the author's reflect the intellectual preoccupations of their immediate predecessors. Having come to associate commerce with the vitality of the modern West, Greek geographers were prone, as if guided by Croce's famous maxim, to consider it too as the source of the ancient world's affluence. We have for example this passage from the geography of ancient Corinth:

> Corinth was known in the past for its prosperity. But what was the source? It isn't the good and fertile soil that makes for the prosperity and happiness of the inhabitants; man himself does everything; the Corinthians not hoping for anything from the earth, turned their eyes to something else, fixed their hopes on the sea and became stupendously rich... so did ancient Tyre and Athens, and now Venice and Holland, situated in poor habitats become in such ways wealthy.[109]

The soil may have been poor but the Greeks were blessed according to the geographers with a climate designed to promote mental acuity. As noted in an earlier section, they followed the precepts of Hippocrates that the changing seasons preserved the Greek mind from the torpor or narrowness that fell to those who inhabited lands of unrelenting heat or cold. But if the ancient Greeks had made so much of these natural conditions and advantages, why not their descendants? It was in the pursuit of this larger enquiry that the *Geographia Neoterike* becomes finally a work of political and social criticism. It cannot be said however that the authors present the reader with a consistent argument. In this sense the geography resembles the narratives of foreign travelers who were equally prone to pin the blame for Greece's plight on both native and Turkish deficiencies. These latter included the evils of arbitrary power and the absence of a rational system of law. The disastrous flight of capital and talent from Greece and her resulting impoverishment were counted as one of the chief outcomes of poor administration, as the authors explain below. They do so in terms that are highly reminiscent of the criticisms made by Pringos in his journal entries from Amsterdam:

> The despotic, arbitrary rule of the Sultan is an example to be followed by all those below him until finally everyone in Tourkia becomes fretful over their lives and property, and certainly the rich, in large numbers pick up and leave and establish themselves in neighboring countries where the laws rule, as does the respect for life and individuality, and sigh continuously remembering the beauty and fortuitous climate of their fatherlands.[110]

This was not the first time that the term 'despotism' was applied to the Ottoman administration in the Greek geographical sources. In fact Konstantas and Philippides adopt a definition that is not too remote from the one used by Theotokes in the earlier *Stoicheia Geographias*. A "Despotic" system of government the older logios had written, exists wherever the laws of the state are the same as the leader's will, "such as with the Ottomans."[111] Theotokes went on to describe the implications for the citizens of such a regime: "The one called the Sultan, by the Europeans, grand seigneur, or great Despot" he wrote, "is the master of Turkey, independent of control, autocephalos, having absolute power over the life and property of his subjects, who from birth are counted as his slaves."[112]

The natural gifts of Greece were therefore neutralized by despotism, for "prosperity requires first of all good government." Konstantas and Philippides devote numerous pages therefore to the deficiencies of Turkish rule, having its most obvious manifestation in the commercial underdevelopment and depopulation of the country.[113] Of course the resemblances here to Montesquieu and the larger 'cultural understanding' of Greece's plight discussed above, are quite evident. From these inadequacies proceed the backwardness and cultural delinquency that forms the narrative unity of the book. Of the ethics and morality of the Greeks, the authors ask:

> What can you say about the enlightenment of a people who are under the yoke, lacking schools, books, breeding, education? And yet despite all this, the long-lived yoke to which everything is tied and perishes, the Greek mind that animated their ancestors is not yet extinguished; it doesn't wait for more than a free wind to blow and light again the theater of the world.[114]

Here again appears the term 'freedom' although, as elsewhere in the sources from this era, it is an airy concept that is left dangling without form throughout the text. Nonetheless the emphasis on freedom as a precursor to enlightenment, at least at this moment in the narrative, contrasts sharply with what had been written earlier by Moisiodax. The most explicit discussion of this subject in the *Geographia Neoterike* occurs in the section on the Mani—that region of Greece, not far from ancient Sparta, where Turkish rule had never been completely imposed. Enclosed in the rugged mountains of this region, they write, "are 365 villages, the inhabitants of which are brave people, freedom loving in the extreme, accustomed to hardship, and true descendants of those Lacedaemons."[115] Although the authors acknowledge that the people of the Mani had suffered of late to recognize the suzerainty of the Turks, this was, they hoped, a temporary setback: "Very little stops the Mani should they seek to rise against the Turks, it is only sufficient for them to understand what they did, and what they have to do."[116]

The discussion of the Maniotes became finally the occasion for another lesson on the cause of Greece's moral decline. The author's were especially moved to comment on the notorious banditry for which this region was known. And yet they choose not to condemn the inhabitants, judging their actions as an outcome, however unfortunate, of their intention to remain free.[117] The authors do acknowledge that it would be better if the Maniotes found another art to exercise their talents upon. These are "vigorous people" after all who inhabit a land rich with trading potential. Should such people only "fix their hopes on sea-going and trading...they could in truth be like Venetians or Dutchmen."[118] So too would they become not only rich, but "enlightened" through their intercourse with other peoples and these two qualities combine to "make them the pride of the wretched Greek nation." And yet this happy vision must remain unrealized as the Maniotes, like the other Greeks portrayed in the text, are lost again in the "labyrinth," as Psalidas would say, of isolation and ignorance:

> What is it that impeded them and impedes them still? Ignorance and ignorance alone causes them to be pygmies when they could be colossuses, for this they don't need foreign examples, having such famous ancestors. But can there be found amongst the Maniotes even two or three that know they have such ancestors? What pleasure it would be in a new Greece to hear (the words) 'Principle,' 'Authority,' 'Power,' all that remains of the glory of that once ever glorious and now wretched people.[119]

Summary: Geography and Function

A survey of early modern Greek geography helps to illustrate the thematic unity of the Neohellenic Enlightenment. On an immediate level, these works articulated the preoccupations and assumptions that distinguished the larger discourse, especially as it concerned the 'national problem'—and this was the subject after all that gave unity and life to the movement. The fact that works of geography serve so well to represent the Neohellenic Enlightenment should not be too surprising given that many of the most notable figures of the Diaphotismos were contributors to this literature.

It is also within the Greek literature surrounding geography that the 'processes' of the Diaphotismos become visible, that is, the collaboration of internal and external sources in the shaping of its thought. The internal transmission of ideas and traditions is visible in the repetition of words, values and imagery that takes place from work to work. But the external influences show themselves too. A survey of Greek geography from the eighteenth century serves to reveal the manner in which European ideas were integrated within or had an important "clarifying" influence upon Greek thought.

The traditional elements of Greek historiography appear in the numberless laments on the evil of discord that surface throughout the sources from this era. "Alas," Moisiodax exclaimed in a work discussed earlier, Nemesis had "forged her (Greece) with envy, and after she ran rampant with civil wars she was compelled to put her neck into the yoke of the Romans." These remarks from mid-century were echoed by Konstantas and Philippides at the century's end. They too saw the fall of Greece as an outcome of stasis. And although this lesson had already become a standard fixture in Greek letters, it was one that they still felt called upon to repeat:

> At the time when the Romans conquered the kingdoms of the successors of Alexander, the inhabitants were Greeks (Hellenes). In Asia Minor, Syria, Egypt the Greek language flourished. Alexandria surpassed Athens, Tarsus and other cities were renowned for their schools. The Hebrews that were in Alexandria their natural language was Greek. With every reason then all of Asia Minor, Lower Egypt... could have all been called Greece, since in all of these parts the inhabitants were all Greeks... Nonetheless now everything is changed and those who could be the first nation in the world, their discord has lowered them into a miserable condition, shrunk them into a confined space, and nearly nothing remains to them of their ancestral traditions save the discord, which is their first characteristic everywhere.[120]

But as we have seen throughout this study, these eighteenth century writers were themselves successors to a much older tradition. Note for example this remarkable passage from one of Elias Meniates's teachings, 'On Envy' (Peri Fthonou), a text that was a hundred years old when the *Geographia Neoterike* was published:

> I have said up to now that which I knew to say, let him finish the teaching the blessed Paul. 'Let's not be vain,' he says, "disputing and envying each other." Let's not become vain, let's recognize each as our own, let's not criticize each the other, let's not envy one the other, because, he proceeds to tells us the Apostle, that if you devour each other, look, surely you destroy your very self in the end ... This is a prophecy, and it fulfills itself in us. How great was our Race. What glory our empire. Do you know how it came to be destroyed? Read our histories. Not from the power of the Persians, nor from the sword of the Hagarenes, but from our envy. We destroyed ourselves, because we devoured ourselves, disputing and envying each other. And if we arm ourselves, each against the other in order to fall upon ourselves like hail, we don't have need of other enemies nor even the devil.[121]

"Read our histories" Meniates urged his readers in terms that are reminiscent of the advice issued by Katartzes in "Gnowthe Savton" (know thyself). History and geography were invaluable materials for acquiring a deeper awareness of one's past and thus oneself. Clearly the fixation on history and geography was intended to raise the cultural consciousness of Greek society. It bothered men like Katartzes that the Greeks did not sufficiently know their land or their history. Konstantas and Philippides complained similarly of the modern Peloponnesians: "Can there be found amidst the 120,000 or more Maniotes even two or three that know they have such ancestors?" These writers approached their subject matter with an intent and spirit that recalled the 'Art of Rhetoric' of the much earlier Skouphos. Here too was an 'improving work' that became a vehicle for the author to unburden himself of a kind of intense ethnic restiveness. Like the geographers and historians of the eighteenth century, Skouphos's lessons in rhetoric were made to serve a higher purpose: to lead the reader on a tour—and one that had geographical and historical qualities—of the glittering luminaries of the Hellenic tradition.

Of course works of geography that dealt with the Greek past were naturally prone to confront questions regarding the rise and decline of civilizations. Again, Greek tradition supplied a number of answers to this quandary such as sin and stasis. But new ideas were afoot: it was in fact on this subject that the European intellect of the eighteenth century, untethered to such traditions, continued to busy itself and came ultimately to propose somewhat more scientific explanations. These new directions in thought emanating from Europe proved attractive as well to the logioi.

The early geographical texts had articulated a curious symbiosis of people and place, as witnessed in Notaras. People were shaped by their environment, their way of life, mentality, etc all an outcome of some peculiar arithmetic of climate and culture. These ideas found a place in the late geography of Konstantas and Philippides, however they are not the object of great emphasis. We find instead a more penetrating enquiry into the interplay of political, economic and cultural factors in the rise (and fall) of civilizations and peoples. These complex linkages were responsible for the power amassed by modern Europe, which they accepted as reflexively as Meletios and Notaras, as well as that of ancient Greece. In geography, therefore, was an old way and a new way of seeing the national problem.

Geography was finally a science that served, intentionally or not, to mark the differences separating the regions and inhabitants of the earth. Notaras had instructed his readers to do this very thing in their future works, to fix on the differences that distinguished one place and one people from another. Employed in this fashion, geography was a spectacularly vivid medium for portraying the 'national problem.' Knowing one's "house" its entries and exits, its surroundings, provided a means of locating oneself in the larger picture. This new perspective on the world was one that made clear the relative virtues and inadequacies of its inhabitants, not a small motivation for enlightenment. Geography functioned therefore as an assault upon mental isolation, complacency and apathy.

This assault became more graphic, the characterization of national delinquency more severe, as the Diaphotismos matured. The evolving view of 'geography' engendered a cultural understanding of Greece's plight that imbued the whispy dreams of revival in the verses of the *Anthe Eulaveias* with a striking 'modern' pragmatism. The first step to progress Moisiodax lectured his readers was not to shrink from the awareness of their situation. See the greatness of Europe, he had declared, in her model Greece must find its renewal. So too did Konstantas and Philippides when writing of the Mani dream aloud of a Greece aware of itself and possessed of a mission, a Greece participating in the larger European world of commerce and intellect, an interplay itself of enlightening consequence. But of course ideas such as these were not necessarily prone to lead Greek society down the path of cosmopolitanism. The emphasis put on 'place' in the oath to "know thyself" expressed the primacy of the interconnections between a people, a culture and a land, without which one had no identity, "no humanity." The implications of this linkage for the elaboration of nationalist ideology are obviously immense.[122]

There was at last a more visceral and mysterious national quotient to the attraction and practice of geography than even those intimated above. This has to do again with the fixation upon the Greek space that became more intense and pronounced as the century progressed. This fascination was first evident in the considerable amount of text devoted to 'Greece' in Meletios's *Geographia palaia kai nea*. The later *Geographia Neoterike* omitted the world completely and confined itself to "Peri tes Ellados." But their work too, the collaborators believed, was insufficient, and so they encouraged others to finish the task by authoring new books on their particular homelands and regions; in this way would all contribute to the great work of bringing 'Greece' back into form and light, re-composing and reclaiming her, as it were, patrida by patrida.[123] These later works expressed an intense desire to imagine 'Greece' as a physical entity, to chart its contours and extent, to give it shape and depth, indeed to give it life. Perhaps by so joining the parts of Greece together geography served to encourage the notion that all belonged to a common homeland, that is, this work had a national consciousness raising function.[124]

The ultimate example of this intense impulse to geographically conjure

Greece into form was the famous "Map of Greece" (1797) of the revolutionary nationalist Regas. It may be that for such men the fabrication of Greece into a physical object articulated in an especially vivid way the very thing that their manifestoes could not. In his map Regas created an entity that tangibly expressed the goal of his revolutionary rhetoric, the thing to be possessed. All of these images were strewn together, indeed this is no doubt the way they were experienced, in the words of the logios Giorgios Tertsetes, when recalling the feelings of past days:

> So many times, young friends, it happened to me when seeing the Geographical Map of Regas that it was like seeing open the last will and testament of a careful father, who marks the ancestral property, shows the titles of the owners and places to be held in guardianship for the minors the name and glory of ancient civilization. As the excellence of a woman can't be hidden, but as soon as she appears her young comeliness shows, accordingly Regas couldn't hide his amorous passions, and his extreme virtue led to his slaughter in the Danubian city.[125]

Tertsetes suggests that looking on the map of Greece was for Regas, and perhaps for himself too, like looking on the figure of a woman. But had this not been the very intent of the Diaphotismos? It was exactly into the figure of a woman that Greece had been ritualized as the Diaphotismos matured.[126] As an object of imagination and fabrication this woman, this figure, was surely a most extreme extension of that impulse to conjure Greece into form that animated the map-making of Regas or the geography of Konstantas and Philippides; nonetheless they are products of a similar impulse. This woman, naked, shoeless and covered with wounds, was the physical personification of the impoverished and abused nation depicted in the *Geographia Neoterike*. She was perhaps too the distillation of the Diaphotismos and its works into that singular expression of contempt and duty: the indictment of manly honor. She was not to be absent therefore from the proclamation issued by Ypsilantis, as he led his small band of insurgents across the River Pruth. "What will you do, O Greeks," he asked, "to whom the Motherland, naked, shows its wounds and, with broken voice, calls on the help of its children?"[127]

Notes

1. Athanasios Psalidas, 'Perigraphe Geographia tes Epeirou,'in *Geographia Epeirou kai Alvanias*, 63. Psalidas's geography was written around 1809, though not published in his lifetime. Beginning in 1797, Kerkyra and the remaining Ionian Islands, found themselves alternately occupied by French, Russian and Turkish forces. This turbulence persisted until the creation of the Septinsular Republic of 1815 mentioned above. From this point forward the Islands were administered by the British until ceded to the Greek Kingdom in 1864.

2. Note again Xanthos, *Apomnemonevmata*, 141. Regas had been inspired by similar events. As one of his biographers writes: "The inglorious conclusion of the Austro-Russian campaign (1787-92) had dissolved the chimera of the 'xanthou genous' (blond race)." These developments had turned his hopes toward a pan-Balkan uprising. Vranousis, editor's introduction, in *Regas*, 59.

3. Frangos, The Philike Etairia 1814-1821: A Social and Historical Analysis, 24.

4. It is in fact entirely without form—much less realized as an idea than even the fanciful Hellenic Republic of Regas. See Regas Velestinlis, 'Nea Politike Dioikesis,' (1797) in *Regas*, 369-377.

5. Mexas, *Hoi Philikoi*, 16.

6. This term used by Benedict Anderson to illustrate one of the central elements of his theory in *Imagined Communities*, 81.

7. Tore Frangsmyr, 'The Enlightenment in Sweden,' in *The Enlightenment in National Context*, edited by Roy Porter and Mikulas Teich, (Cambridge: Cambridge University Press, 1981), 164.

8. Mikulas Teich, 'Bohemia: From darkness into light,' in *The Enlightenment in National Context*, 161. The French philosopher Guillaume Raynal (1713-1796) was an important influence upon Konstantas and Philippides as well. See editor's note to 'Peri tes Ellados, in *Ho Koraes kai he Epoche tou*, 76.

9. Lord Charlemont, *The Travels of Lord Charlemont in Greece and Turkey*, Edited by E.J. Finopoulos and W.B. Stanford, (London: Trigraph, 1984), 134. Charlemont toured these lands in 1749.

10. Of its enchantment for example Ernst Cassirer wrote: "Perhaps no other century is so completely permeated by the idea of intellectual progress as that of the Enlightenment." *The Philosophy of the Enlightenment*, Translated by Fritz C.A. Koelln and James P. Pettegrove, (Princeton: Princeton University Press, 1979), 5. Charlemont's diary entries depict the reflexive nature of this process. "I find in my notebook," he wrote, "the following fantastical flight on my first contemplating the ruins of Athens." These included the awareness that "Cities, kingdoms, empires, as well as men, though the period of their existence be somewhat longer, finally perish and fall to decay, and the huge skeleton alone demonstrates the vastness of the once tremendous giant!" Lord Charlemont, *The Travels of Lord Charlemont in Greece and Turkey*, 134-5.

11. This theme was evident in Italian culture as well, as Pearson observed in Chapter 3. One notes how the greatness of Rome served as a rallying point for generations of Italians including Machiavelli, who ended his 'Exhortation to liberate Italy from the barbarians' with a dash of rhetoric from Petrarch: "Virtue against fury shall advance the fight, And it the combat soon shall put to flight; For the old Roman valour is not dead, Nor in the Italians' breast extinguished." Certainly the kind of statement that would not be out of place in a Greek

text. Nicolo Machiavelli, *The Prince*, Translated by W.K. Marriott, (Chicago: Encyclopaedia Britannica, 1952), 37

12. As told to Giorgios Tersetes, 'Logos 25 March 1851,' in *Ho Georgios Tersetes kai to evriskomena erga tou*, edited by Ntinos Konomos, (Athens: Library of the Parliament of Greece, 1984), 397.

13. Note the comments of Leake upon reading the *Geographia Neoterike* of Konstantas and Philippides, a work which showed that "the liberty of publishing their opinions has been for many years greater among the modern Greeks, than it is now among the inhabitants of the Continent of Europe." *Researches in Greece*, 172.

14. Of course by operating outside the Ottoman Empire they placed themselves under the auspices of others. Indeed the activities of the Greek logioi and publishers in Vienna came under increasing scrutiny by the Habsburg authorities with the outbreak of the French Revolution and Napoleonic Wars. We have seen how this led to the death of Regas. But Kokkinakis, Gazes, Vamvas and Koumas were also watched closely by the Austrian police (the latter two actually jailed after the outbreak of the Revolution). See Laios, *Anekdotes epistoles kai engrapha tou 1821*, 113, 181, 232-34.

15. 749 books were published in Greek over the years 1776-1800, compared to 107 during the period 1700-1725. Of equal significance is the sharp decline in the number of religious titles that comprise these totals. Over the earlier period, religious works represented 75% of the total; by the end of this period the ratio had fallen to 53%. Aikaterina Koumarianou, 'The Contribution of the Intelligentsia towards the Greek Independence Movement, 1798-1821,' 70. Overall these numbers testify to the existence of the Enlightenment as a historical phenomenon of wide dimension. Upon this subject Leake himself had observed that "the progress of intelligence has followed the same course of improvement in Greece as in the rest of Europe, although with unequal steps." *Researches in Greece*, 231.

16. Owen Chadwick, 'The Italian Enlightenment,' in *The Enlightenment in National Context*, 90.

17. As the distinguished Greek scholar Panayiotis Kondyles himself once asserted, "the Neohellenic Enlightenment did not create any original philosophical ideas." Panayiotis Kondyles, *Ho Neohellenikos diaphotismos: hoi philosophikes idees*, (Athens: Themelio, 1988), 9.

18. Koraes's Memoir is again revealing. He implies in the very first lines of this text that the significance of the Diaphotismos is to be found not so much in what it produces as what it represents: a demonstration of the historical processes of a people's decline and regeneration. Koraes, *Report on the Present State of Civilization in Greece*, 153.

19. Observations regarding the geographical interests of the logioi can be found throughout Manuel Gedeon, *He pnevmatike kinisis tou genous kata ton IH kai ITH aiona*, edited by Alkhes Aggelou, (Athens: 1976), and Paschalis M. Kitromilides, *Neohellenikos Diaphotismos*, (Athens: Morfotiko Idrima Ethnikis Trapezis, 1999), Chapter 3.

20. Demetrios Katartzes 'Gnowthi Savton,' in *Ta Evriskomena*, edited by Konstantine Demaras, (Athens: Hermes, 1970), 188-9. Those familiar with Notaras's *Eisagoge* will recognize immediately the influence of his thought on Katartzes. Koumarianou has suggested that Philippides and Konstantas were later guided toward geography under the influence of Katartzes in whose circle they worked and studied over the years 1780-1790. See Koumarianou, editor's introduction, *Geographia Neoterike*, 22.

21. The teaching of geography began in Padua in 1767, around the same time that it was introduced at the Flaggineio School. Several copies of Fatseas's *Grammatike Geographike* were found in the old library of Flaggineio and it is believed that Meletios's text was also used. Karathanases, *He Phlagineios Schole tes*

Venetias, 202.

22. The text had been originally written and produced for the instruction of Theotokes's students at the Academy of Jassy.

23. Koraes produced a French translation of the ancient geographer Strabo at the behest of Napoleon. See below.

24. Vranousis, *Regas*, 'Map of Greece,' 359-369. I have omitted from the list above the fanciful account of Greek life rendered by Kaisarios Dapontes (1714-1784) under the title *Geographike Istoria*. The work was unpublished in the author's lifetime.

25. See *Melissa*, Vol I (1819). Surveys and excerpts from geographical works (and closely allied fields such as Archaeology and History) were featured in virtually every edition of the Vienna periodical *Hermes ho Logios*.

26. Anthimios Gazes, 'Meletiou Geographia Palaia kai Nea' in *Ho Koraes kai he Epoche Tou*, 320. He adds that the neglect of these disciplines derives from the poor quality of instruction in Greek schools, under which the youth of Greece consequently lose their curiosity and "appetite for learning." He urges that the methods of instruction change and quickly if Greece is to have "educated and diligent sons," adding for emphasis: "Be sorry for your sons, that you don't hear consequently curses from them, when they come of age, and don't have any longer that golden time for proper learning!" Ibid, 360. The Phanariot 'Countess' Roxana Stourtza made similar points in her correspondence with Metropolitan Ignatius regarding her efforts in Germany to prepare Greek youths for higher studies in Europe: "our compatriots... don't have even the bare minimum of learning when they come to the universities... They don't have any idea of Geography, History or even the ancient language." Vournas, *Philike Etairia*, 360.

27. Konstantas and Philippides, *Geographia Neoterike*, 86, 87, 93, 126. Psalidas, 'Perigraphe Geographike tes Epeirou,' 54.

28. See for example Elie Kedourie's introduction to *Nationalism in Asia and Africa*, 40. On this same subject Benedict Anderson wrote: "As western scholars made new use of classical material, published it, wrote about it, exalted it, they lit emotional fires among Greek intellectuals who lived or traveled through their domains. This inspired dreams of a return to cultural glory," *Imagined Communities*, 80. The quote above from Kolokotronis may serve to promote this point, however the exigencies of life had left the old klepht far removed of course from the intellectual culture of his times and 'nation.' Notaras for example studied Aristotle and Ptolemy, among other Hellenic luminaries of the past, while a student at the Patriarchal Academy in Constantinople from 1680-1 (if not before). He also studied here the 'modern' works of Mavrokordatos, Korydalleos, Vlachos, etc. The logioi did not have to leave Greece to encounter 'their past,' they had already made contact with it long before setting out for the West. Penelope Stathos, *Chrysanthos Notaras*, (Athens: Syndesmou ton en Athenais Megaloscholiton, 1999), 56, 80-1.

29. Meletios, *Geographia Palaia kai Nea*, preface.

30. He was himself a teacher for many years in Iannina, which was also the place of his birth. Meletios began teaching here in 1687, shortly after his return from Venice. Like others before and after him, Meletios had studied at Padua (ca 1681) and played an active role in the educational and ecclesiastical affairs of the Greek community in Venice. In 1703 Meletios was made the Metropolitan of Athens, a post he held until his death in 1714. In addition to his famous *Geographia Palaia kai Nea*, Meletios was also the author of works on medicine, astronomy, and theology including the often reprinted *Ekklesiastikes Historias* (1700).

31. Publisher's dedication, *Geographia Palaia kai Nea*. This element of the work was also highly praised by Konstantas and Philippides in the *Geographia Neoterike*. Meletios is mentioned twice in this later work, especially in the section on Iannina. "Iannina is famous for its schools," the writers explain, " which don't flourish now as they did earlier, and for the learned men that over time have come from there, amongst whom Meletios must have the first place, because he labored to benefit his nation, if the learned men of our race who came after him had imitated his example we would likely be in a better condition today." Konstantas and Philippides, *Geographia Neoterike*, 126.

32. Meletios, *Geographia Palaia kai Nea*, Preface.

33. Beginning his education at the Patriarchal Academy of Constantinople (1680-1), Notaras continued on to Padua where he studied theology, philosophy, medicine and even law. Notaras studied at Padua from 1697-1700. The eclectic nature of his studies combined with the fact that he did not take a doctoral degree from Padua leads one of his biographers to suggest that his intention was simply to acquire a sound background in the current state of knowledge. Stathos, *Chrysanthos Notaras*, 82-3. He was in any case cut out for another path. In 1707 Chrysanthos succeeded his uncle Dositheos as Patriarch of Jerusalem, a title he held until his death. Despite his ecclesiastical duties Notaras traveled widely throughout his life (including stays in Italy, Germany, Poland, France, Palestine and Russia) and wrote a great many works in addition to the *Eisagoge*. In addition to geography, Notaras wrote on theology, history, astronomy, law and mathematics. Stathos has made a valuable compilation of Notaras's vast writings, both published and unpublished, in *Chrysanthos Notaras*, 171-204.

34. This was a common feature of later works, especially the *Odon Mathematikes*, which is almost wholly devoted to astronomy. This text is in fact highly indebted to the earlier *Eisagoge* of Notaras from which it draws heavily. Methodios Anthrakites and Balanos Vassilopoulos, *Odon Mathematikes*, Vol 3, (Venice, 1749). Theotokes and Moisiodax also wrote at length on these subjects. For the former see below, for the latter *Theoria tes Geographias*, (Vienna: Ioannes Thomas, 1781), Chapter 28.

35. But not very late at all in the context of Greek intellectual history. The geocentric view was still promoted by Theotokes in his work from 1774. Nikephoros Theotokes, *Stoicheia Geographias*, Edited and annotated by Anthimiou Gazes, (Vienna: Zosimadon, 1804), 31-41.

36. Kepler, Galileo, Brahe and Copernicus, who had proposed that the earth moves and thus put it "in the class of a planet," all appear in the text. However, Notaras concludes that the study of geography is made untenable by such a premise. Rather the "Ptolemaein system as much for its acceptance among the ancients and its advocacy by so many of the learned who have accepted it, and that it is so much too in agreement with the holy writings judges it to be most probably true, just as in the preceding chapter above it was accepted that the earth is in the center of creation, in such manner it is necessary for it to be accepted that it doesn't move." Chrysanthou Notara, *Eisagoge eis ta geographika, kai sphairika*, (Paris, 1716), 84-5. These arguments supported by reference to Isaiah, Ch 38, paragraph 8; Aristotle, "final chapters" of his Universe, Book II; and Plutarch's third book concerning the "the philosophers." Ibid 83.

37. Nor, again, of Meletios's who died fourteen years before in 1714. Notaras was however familiar with the *Geographia Palaia kai Nea* as it circulated apparently before publication in manuscript form. In addition the two men, both high clerics in the Orthodox Church, knew each other and conducted an important correspondence on ecclesiastical affairs. Nonetheless, the timing of Notaras's exposure to Meletios's geography and its possible influence upon him are hard to establish. Konstantinos Th. Kyriakopoulos, *Meletios (Metros) Athenon, Ho Geographos*, 2 Volumes, (Athens, 1990), I: 159-63, 369-385. Scholars estimate that Meletios wrote his geography in the 1690s. See for example, Kitromilides, *Neohellenikos Diaphotismos*, 127 and Kyriakopoulos, *Meletios*, I: 158.

38. Notaras was prone to refer to Ptolemy simply as the 'professor' (hefegeseos), *Eisagoge*, 143.

39. Ibid, 140, 162. Dominique Cassini (1625-1712), whom Notaras studied under at Padua and Paris may well have had the greatest influence on him. Stathes, *Chrysanthe Notaras*, 90. Kyriakopoulos's detailed analysis of the sources referred to in Meletios reveals 44 Ancient Greek writers, 22 "Latins," 53 Christian writers (mainly Byzantine Greeks), and 42 "Europeans." Kyriakopoulos, *Meletios*, I: 594-607. I can render no judgement at this time on the position of Notaras and Meletios on the famous battle then raging between the 'Ancients and Moderns.' The essential notes of this conflict were sounded in the passages from Moisiodax's *Ethike Philosophia* discussed in Chapter 3, however its wider influence upon the thought of the logioi has yet to be fully examined. Moisiodax sought, like the geographers above, to broaden the mental horizons of his readers, however it is probably unlikely that these older logioi went as far as he in declaring that modern learning had surpassed the ancient. For a general overview of the controversy, see Franklin L. Baumer, *Modern European Thought: Continuity and Change in Ideas, 1600-1950*, (New York: Macmillan, 1977), 117-137.

40. However Montesquieu's *The Persian Letters* (1721) introduced some of the problems that will occupy him most famously in the later works. In Chapter 31 for example he ponders the "history and origin of republics." There follow some interesting remarks about Greece and its ancient freedoms, the consequences of empire and despotism, etc. Montesquieu, *The Persian Letters*, translated and with an introduction by George R. Healy, (Indianapolis: Hackett, 1999), 221-4

41. Notaras, *Eisagoge*, 41. Nature in this sense (fysin) as physical or natural constitution.

42. Ibid, 41-42.

43. Similar observations appear in the later *Geographia Neoterike* where they are credited to Hippocrates e.g: "Hippocrates says that the places where the winters and summers are extreme, bring forth people who incline naturally to the arts and sciences; thus if the atmosphere/climate is always gentle, the inhabitants become slow-witted, dull, slothful; if always frigid, they have a thinness of organs and an energetic mind." *Geographia Neoterike*, 42. Koraes had written similarly of his Ionian homeland in the 'Memoir': "A most remarkable thing, which in a way confirms Hippocrates' doctrine concerning the influence of climate, is that in ancient Greece the sciences were born in Ionia and spread from it, and that their rebirth in Greece seems to follow the same course." Koraes, *Report on the Present State of Civilization in Greece*, 170.

44. Notaras, *Eisagoge*, 131. He notes later that these divisions are to be properly understood as belonging to a larger conceptual framework. The geographer, he goes on to explain, further divides the world into the categories of Ancient, Modern and Unknown. Like Meletios his discussion of the original division of the world and its peoples leans heavily on the Old Testament: "The Ancient world concerns Europe, Asia and Africa, which (as written) were divided among the three sons of Noah, and so fell to Joseph Europe, to Simon Asia and to Ham Africa." Ibid, 138. Note Meletios's introduction to France: "The first people who settled in France after the great flood, as with the other provinces of Europe, were the Celts, the most ancient people (ethnos), who were descended from the grandson of Noah...." *Geographia Palaia kai Nea*, 91.

45. Notaras, *Eisagoge*, 137.

46. Ibid, 137-8.

47. Ibid, 141.

48. Ibid, 142. Notaras cautions that the geographer has a "duty to speak on the known part of the world," and thus avoid outright speculation. Nonetheless his own work includes the occasional fanciful element, such as

his reference to "the Kingdom of Prestor John, the Catholic Emperor of Africa." Ibid, 150, 39.

49. Ibid, 142. The subject of navigation was especially fascinating to him and may serve in fact to indicate a source of geography's wider popularity, e.g., the excitement surrounding the discovery of 'new worlds.' Notaras actually ends the book with a lengthy essay on the history of boat-making and the exploits of the great European explorers from the age of discovery. Ibid 162. Here again was another spectacular demonstration of the moral and scientific virtuosity of European civilization.

50. Ibid, 147.

51. Ibid, 139.

52. Ibid, 142.

53. Ibid, 139.

54. Meletios, *Geographia Palaia kai Nea*, 417.

55. Nikephoros Theotokes, *Stoicheia Geographias*, 201-2. Theotokes's 'Greece' included the Peloponnesus, Epiros, "all of Macedonia" (appears to include Thrace), Crete and the Aegean Islands. The clearest, and most extensive, delineation of 'Greece' appears in the *Geographia Neoterike* as discussed below.

56. On this subject Ernest Gellner wrote: "There is reason to suspect that the original Greek national movement aimed not at a homogeneous modern nation-state, but rather at a reversal of ranks within the then Empire: in brief, to put the clock back and replace the Ottoman Empire by a new Byzantium."Gellner, *Nationalism*, 41. Gellner apparently refers here to the early visions of a 'liberated' Greece shared by Regas, the Philike Etairia, etc. His 'proof,' that the Greek Revolution of 1821 did not begin in Greek lands and was thus not a 'national' uprising, is however historically misleading. Ypsilantis's invasion of the Danubian Principalities was a sudden shift of course from the previously established plan which called for an opening of hostilities in the Peloponnesus. A revolutionary outbreak in the Principalities was intended to trigger a Turkish invasion and thus provoke a new Russo-Turkish war—an event, it was hoped, that would benefit the prospects of Greek independence. Ypsilantis's brother Nicholas was nonetheless sent to the Peloponnesus to lead a simultaneous uprising planned to further divide and confuse Turkish forces. One can find a useful introduction to this subject by E.D. Tappe, 'The 1821 Revolution in the Rumanian Principalities,' in *The Greek Struggle for Independence*, 135-137. It should be noted that Gellner was writing in defense of his own controversial theory of nationalism. However non-specialists tend to overlook another fact of great significance, and this is the dispersion of the Greek population throughout the region. It is somewhat inconceivable that Greek nationalists would have limited their vision of a 'new Greece' to the lands that became the original Kingdom; they were the poorest parts and contained less than a third of the Greek inhabitants of European Turkey. The Greek-Turkish population concentration was most heavily weighted here on the side of the former, but left out the important centers of Greek culture and commerce on the coast of Asia Minor (including Koraes's patrida Smyrna), the numerous and prosperous islands, and of course Constantinople itself, which had become the cultural capital of this highly dispersed Greek world. 'Imagining' the boundaries of a new Greek homeland was thus a far from simple task.

57. Meletios, *Geographia Palaia kai Nea*, 41.

58. Ibid, 444.

59. Ibid, 118.

60. Ibid, 244.

61. Ibid, 91.

62. Nikephoros Theotokes, *Stoichiea Geographias*, (Vienna: Zosimadon, 1804), 91. Theotokes was a little more selective however than Meletios in his praise. Some lands received a critical appraisal, such as his reference to the Portuguese as "merciless," and his condemnation of the "merciless and inhumane Inquisition" conducted by Spain. Ibid, 75, 80. Other states such as Russia are treated to the kind of praise that exceeds anything found in Meletios; a revealing insight into the enormous impression its power had made upon Greeks over the preceding decades. After lavishing space on the size and greatness of Russia, Theotokes described its people as "powerful, magnanimous, highly civilized, excellent soldiers, friends of the arts and sciences. Each day their scientists and artists, whose names were previously unknown, have been cutting their way forward from the times since Peter the Great." Ibid, 179. Peter was elsewhere hailed as "immortal in memory." Nor did Theotokes fail to recognize his own patron, the "glorious and esteemed" Katherine the II. Ibid, 178.

63. Meletios, *Geographia Palaia kai Nea* 304.

64. Ibid, 304/5.

65. Ibid, 305. The phrase "the Ellas of Ellados" is difficult to translate so I have left it in transliterated form. It can be read perhaps as "the very Greece of Greece."

66. Ibid, 305. Similar observations are made in the section on the Peloponnesus: "Here were born famous heroes, Agamemnon and Menelaos and others like them and the Peloponnesus shone brightly to all the world, before the Romans, as much as their work of war as their study of letters. They sent colonists abroad, but after the empire of the Romans, they began to decline in such and such ways and in the empire of the Turks, that light of the world was entirely extinguished in a wretched night of darkness..." 356.

67. Ibid, 40. On the subject of the Greek language he has some further interesting observations. "Greek is spoken in Greece," he writes, "in the islands, in Macedonia, in Thrace and in many other places. It clings but not exactly to the ancient dialect, whose corrosion commenced from the time that Greece fell in war against the other peoples, especially the Romans." Ibid, 40/41. Nonetheless he has written the geography in the "corroded" dialect as did Notaras. This is not true of his other works, such as the *Ekklesiastikes Historias*, which was written in the ancient dialect.

68. Ibid, 37.

69. Meletios writes of Charles I who "was dealt a mortal wound from an axe by his own people on January 30, 1649, losing at once his kingdom and his life. And then Britain changed from a monarchy to an aristocracy, lasting from the death of Charles and remained in this state ruled by Oliver Cromwell, not as a king, but as a Praetor or as an overseer (epistatis) until 1658." Ibid, 123.

70. This cultural connection is not to be understood as obtaining solely from a Christian identity as both Notaras and Meletios saw ancient Greek and Roman civilization as existing within the ancient geography of Europe. Notaras, *Eisagoge*, 142.

71. There is also a 'racial' or primordial aspect to his enquiry that derives from his intent to give a historical account of each region's inhabitants, e.g., where they came from, their contiguities with the past, etc. "Three races do the Greeks number," he writes, "the Dorians, Ionians and Aioleians, later Greece enclosed the Peloponnesus and similarly Epiros and all of Macedonia and finally it includes Crete and the remaining

Aegean Islands." Meletios, *Geographia Palaia kai Nea*, 304. This passage repeated almost verbatim in Theotokes, *Stoicheia Geographias*, 203. Albania is described by Meletios as the "western part of Macedonia," and named now after the inhabitants, who were not an Illyrian people, but "descended from the Celts, crossed over from Italy into Dyrraxion and spread malignantly (kakothen) out from there." *Geographia Palaia kai Nea*, 305/6. One notes Kosmas Thesprotos's epithet "They (the Albanians) are the Tartars of Greece," in his much later geography of Albania. Thesprotos, 'Perigraphe Geographike Albanias,' *Geographias Albanias kai Epeirou*, 15

72. Meletios, *Geographia Palaia kai Nea*, 233.

73. Ibid, 237.

74. Ibid, 237.

75. In this sense Meletios's assumptions, like those of Notaras, fit squarely into the geographical framework of his times. See Kyriakopoulos, *Meletios*, I: 507. The observations of a French historian serve to introduce the developing climate of opinion: "As contemporaries confronted issues of population and resources, they began to ponder questions of cause and effect: Rousseau did so in the *Social Contract*, for example, as well as Buffon in the *Epoques de la nature*, also Ramond, who explored the Pyrenees, and Volney, who analyzed the Middle East, traveled in America, and wrote *Ruines*. The new thinking drew on knowledge of familiar territory as well as far off lands, natural as well as human causes, and on the transformation of natural philosophy into a doctrine of political progress. Man discovered that civilizations are mortal (Montesquieu proved this in the case of Rome, Volney in that of the Middle East). At the same time, however, people wanted to believe that man's action on nature (from which sprang the need for knowledge) paved the way for future progress." Daniel Roche, *France in the Enlightenment*, translated by Arthur Goldhammer, (Cambridge: Harvard University Press, 1998), 25.

76. Roche, *France in the Enlightenment*, 18/19.

77. Theotokes, *Stoicheia Geographias*, 105.

78. Ibid, 145, 155.

79. Ibid, 155. Demetrios Darvares offered similar observations in the geographical section of a work from 1804: "The German is sincere, the Italian political, the Frenchman humourous, the Spanish prideful, the Portuguese serious, the Englishman haughty, the Dutchman thrifty, the Dane truthful, the Swede steadfast, the Russian faithful, the Turk barbarous and the Hebrew avaricious." Darvares, *Eklogarion Graikikon*, 22.

80. Konstantas and Philippides, *Geographia Neoterike*, 102/13.

81. Works on ethical or moral philosophy received a strong emphasis as well. The popularity of this genre speaks again of that earnest effort undertaken by the logioi to morally regenerate Greek society.

82. David N. Livingstone, 'Geographical Inquiry, Rational Religion, and Moral Philosophy: Enlightenment Discourses on the Human Condition,' in *Geography and Enlightenment*, edited by David N. Livingstone and Charles W. J. Withers, (Chicago: University of Chicago Press, 1999), 95.

83. Godlewska describes how "as understanding of both the nature and importance of differences between peoples (and to some extent societies) began to dawn, descriptive geography, its achievements and the problems it traditionally addressed, began to seem elementary." Anne Marie Claire Godlewska, *Geography Unbound: French Geographic Science from Cassini to Humboldt*, (Chicago: University of Chicago Press,

1999), 55. The author characterizes the French translation and republication of Strabo's geography in 1805 as an example of the reorientation that was taking place within the science. Originally written in the First century C.E. In terms that could well be used to describe the work of Montesquieu, Godlewska depicts Strabo's intent as seeking to explain "what lay behind the distribution and variety of human existence on the earth.... These were the product of historical contingency. Thus, the characteristics of a people - their knowledge, way of life, language and abilities—were the result not just of latitude but of many things: chance, habit, the qualities of the resources surrounding them, education, etc. These a geographer could study." Godlewska, 94. The 'French' translator of Strabo's work was, coincidentally, Adamantios Koraes. See Koraes, 'Autoviographia,' in *Ho Korais kai he Epoche Tou*, 243-4.

84. Ernst Cassirer, *The Philosophy of the Enlightenment*, 47. In similar fashion did Rousseau exclaim in his famous discourse of 1754: "O Man, to whatever country you belong and whatever your opinions, listen: here is your history as I believe I have read it, not in the books of your fellow men who are liars but in Nature which never lies. Everything which comes from her will be true..." Rousseau, *Discourse on Inequality*, 79.

85. It is important to note that a healthy opposition developed against the discipline's tendency toward deterministic reasoning. An important group of scholars, including Turgot (1727-1781), Volney (1757-1820) and Saint-Simon (1760-1825), were to draw, as one historian has written, different lessons from Lockean 'sensationalism.' It was not Locke's view, they argued, that the human mind was bound by the abundance or poverty of sense experience. The emphasis should rather be placed on "the dynamism of the human mind and its power to overcome, and ultimately to control, the forces of nature." Michael Heffernan, 'Historical Geographies of the Future: Three Perspectives from France,' in *Geography and Enlightenment*, 127. Herder also came to take a dim view of these innovations: "That there is a certain creation and influence by the clime, hence certain national and provincial vices, forces and virtues; that in some regions and climates some inclinations, like some plants, must develop only weakly and saplessly, but in others strive upwards with whole, full nature—I may presuppose this physics of history, science of the soul, and politics as conceded on the whole, although in individual detail there will be eternal uncertainty and confusion in the offsetting and addition of these operative causes with other ones, and hence in the whole application of this geography of humanity, because there are always too many and too dissimilar forces operating in proximity." Johann Gottfried Von Herder, 'This Too a Philosophy of History for the Formation of Humanity,' in *Philosophical Writings*, 269.

86. Regas published his second book *Phisikes Apanthisma* in Vienna in 1790, affixing to the final page a brief advertisement announcing his forthcoming translation of Montesquieu. The translation was apparently never finished. Vranousis, *Regas*, 35. Regas's plans may have been affected by the striking change in the political atmosphere in Vienna following the onset of the Napoleonic wars and the resulting Austrian aversion for things French. Regas was himself ultimately taken into custody by the Austrian police in 1798 and later handed over to Turkish authorities.

87. Nature intervening, of course, through famine or other calamities to reestablish the proper balance should population increase. Montesquieu, *Spirit of the Laws*, Volume II, Book 14, 8.

88. "Sometimes the climate is more favorable than the soil, the people multiply and are destroyed by famine: this is the case of China. Hence a father sells his daughter and exposes his children...For the same reason, the religion of the isle of Formosa does not suffer the women to bring their children into the world till they are thirty five years of age: the priestess, before this age, by bruising the belly procures abortion." Ibid, Volume II, Book 16, 10.

89. "Neither is there any city upon earth," he groused, "where faction and intrigue exert their baleful influence more perniciously to the peace of the people than in this wretched town, insomuch that it may with truth be asserted that even in the most flourishing times of the Republic the spirit of party was not more prevalent than

it now is in the present deplorable dejection of the state." Lord Charlemont, *Travels in Greece and Turkey*, 113.

90. Ibid, 113/114. The Greek earth "had not lost the gifts of nature," he continues. "Why then should not the inhabitants retain their native genius? Want of cultivation in the one, and want of education in the other, will constantly disguise and deform, but cannot obliterate the natural characters of either." Ibid, 113.

91. Montesquieu, *The Spirit of the Laws*, Volume II, Book 18, 11. John Breuilly has noted the same tendencies in the thought of Herder for whom "conquest is regarded as the disruption of the natural development of a particular society." Breuilly quotes a key passage from Herder to illustrate: "Nature produces families; the most natural state therefore is one people (volk) with a natural character." What can be more 'unnatural' therefore than the 'enlargement of states' and the blending together of "different human species and nations under one sceptre." Cited in John Breuilly, 'The Sources of Nationalist Ideology,' in *Nationalism*, 117. See also Herder on cultural 'unity' in, *Philosophical Writings*, 297.

92. Montesquieu, *The Spirit of the Laws*, Volume II, Book 19, 11/12.

93. Ibid, Volume II, Book 28, 24.

94. Lord Charlemont, *Travels in Greece and Turkey*, 114.

95. There is evidence to suggest that *Anastasius* enjoyed a relatively wide European readership. Shelley mentioned the novel in the prologue to his *Hellas*. It even appeared on Count Metternich's reading list: "Do you know an English novel called *Anastasius*?" Metternich asked a colleague in a letter from 1821. "In it there is a description of the Greek character ... which is very good and accurate. You will find there Capo d'Istria word for word, exactly as he is..." Cited in E.D. Tappe, 'The 1821 Revolution in the Rumanian Principalities,' 142. Metternich's reference to his enemy Capo d'Istria (Kapodistrias) in the context of the novel's portrayal of the 'Greek character' suggests his delight over what he took to be a negative depiction. Other readers, including Shelley, had a different reaction. The author himself exhibited strong philhellenic sentiments and described his intention in the Foreword to furnish readers with an account of the "ever interesting regions, once adorned by the Greeks and now defaced by the Turks." Thomas Hope, *Anastasius, or, Memoirs of a Greek; Written at the close of the Eighteenth Century*, 3 Volumes, (London: John Murray, 1820), I: vi. There is probably some significance in the name Hope chose for the main character, e.g, 'Anastasius' or 'resurrection.'

96. Ibid, I: 79-80.

97. We note below Montesquieu's comments from 'Of the Principle of Democracy': "The politic Greeks, who lived under a popular government, knew no other support than virtue," he wrote. "The modern inhabitants of that country are entirely taken up with manufacture, commerce, fineries, opulence and luxury... When virtue is banished, ambition invades the minds of those who are disposed to receive it and avarice possesses the whole community." Montesquieu, *The Spirit of the Laws*, Volume I, Book 3, 21.

98. It has been my object here to offer only a few examples from the sizeable literature that exists on this subject. Useful surveys of this literature can be found in Olga Augustinos, *French Odysseys: Greece in French Travel Writing from the Renaissance to the Romantic Era*, (Baltimore: Johns Hopkins Press, 1994); Steven Larrabee, *Greece Observed: The American Experience of Greece, 1775-1865*, (New York: NYU Press, 1957); and David Roessel, *In Byron's Shadow, Modern Greece in the English & American Imagination*, (Oxford: Oxford University Press, 2002).

99. Apostoles Vacalopoulos, *The Greek Nation, 1453-1669*, 30. Regarding the verities of Ottoman rule and

its affect on native custom, Charlemont again provides interesting testimony. He was disappointed for example on arriving on the island of Chios to find the local maidens adorned in drab and unflattering dress. The cause was eventually revealed: "We were indeed told that the fear of the Captain Pasha prevented us from seeing the women on festival days in their best apparel, lest by appearing too rich they might be accordingly plundered." Lord Charlemont, *Travels in Greece and Turkey*, 34.

100. "This was the type," Vacalopoulos writes, "branded with infamy, bereft of any trace of manliness or dignity, which the Greek still calls to mind." Vacalopoulos, *The Greek Nation, 1453-1669*, 30. Despite the awful depictions of Greek society encountered in the sources from these years, there was too a strong current of sympathy. "Si vous faittes la paix je suis bien sur qu'elle sera tres glorieuse...Mais que deviendront mes pauvres Grecs?" Voltaire wrote Catherine II for example on the occasion of the Russo-Turkish War of 1768. His fear nonetheless that the Empress would make a hasty peace and leave the country to its fate—"Mais comment maintenir la force de ce decret s'il ne reste de troupes en Grece?"—were soon realized. Voltaire, *Correspondence*, edited by Theodore Besterman, (Geneva: Institut et Musee Voltaire, 1962), LXXVI: 46-47, LXXV: 129-130. These sentiments, aided by the translations of Voulgaris cited earlier, made Voltaire a man of some repute in Greece. See Demaras, 'Ho Voltairos sten Ellada,' in *Neoellenikos Diaphotismos*, 145-146. Even Pringos, was moved to say a word or two of appreciation for the "naturalist" Voltaire on hearing in 1772 that "he had written something against the Turks." Skouvaras, *Ioannes Pringos*, 188.

101. The authors of the geography were cousins born three years apart, Philippides in 1755 and Konstantas in 1758. Starting out from their village of Mylies in Thessaly where they gained their early education and joined the Church the two men followed a path that typifies the career of the eighteenth century logios. Both were ordained by 1779, Philippides as a monk and Konstantas as a deacon. There followed studies in the Ionian Islands and the Academy at Mount Athos. By 1780 both were in the Principalities, where they taught in the Jassy and Bucharest academies and came into the circle of the established logioi of these cities. From here they embarked on their journeys to the West. Konstantas worked in Vienna and later studied for a short time at Padua. Philippides' travels included Paris, Vienna and Leipzig. It was when back again in Jassy, in 1819, that he joined the Philike Etairia.

102. Much in the way that the larger Enlightenment had. See again Cassirer, *The Philosophy of the Enlightenment*, 3-5.

103. Konstantas and Philippides, *Geographia Neoterike*, 76/77. The authors appear to be referring to *The Spirit of the Laws*, Volume I, Book 21, Chapters 21 to 23.

104. These remarks would seem to apply equally well to the Vlach Hellenizers discussed in Chapter Three; they too had sought to escape the ignominy attached to their native tongue by adopting one of a 'higher rank.'

105. Konstantas and Philippides, *Geographia Neoterike*, 77.

106. Ibid, 135. One notes the possible connection here with Montesquieu. Of course, as noted in Chapter 3, many Orthodox churchmen had come to take a dim view on the monasteries and monks of the northern regions, as Konstantas and Philippides go on to say, "...it seems to me that nearly no one of merit goes in to those monasteries." Ibid, 135.

107. Ibid, 37. The authors do not identify here the European and ancient geographers in question. Note: the authors spoke in the first person throughout the text.

108. Ibid, 37.

109. Ibid, 65. The authors conclude their description of Corinth by lamenting "now only the ancient name

with its prestige remains, along with a few ruins in which appear its ancient luminosity, of the rest however it is a wretched city situated near a few others more wretched still." Ibid, 66.

110. Ibid, 46.

111. Theotokes, *Stoicheia Geographias*, 66.

112. Ibid, 201. As noted above this work was written by Theotokes in 1774 for use in his teaching duties in Jassy, but not published until 1804 (thirteen years after the publication of the *Geographia Neoterike*). It is possible, even probable, however that Konstantas and Philippides were familiar with the work given their periods of residence and teaching in the Principalities. Note finally that Moisiodax had acknowledged the harsher realities of Turkish rule in the earlier *Ethike Philosophia*, a condition that he believed could only be ameliorated through education, for it is by reforming himself that the slave "lightens the weight of tyranny."

113. Konstantas and Philippides, *Geographia Neoterike*, 47-49.

114. Ibid, 49/50.

115. Ibid, 55.

116. What "they did" was suffer a bout of that fatal "stasis." Ibid, 56.

117. "Living as they do in such a place, and preferring it over every other for their freedom, they have become accustomed to it (piracy) and have made it into a kind of art, which doesn't cause them a moment's thought or attack of conscience. Everyone condemns them for this, save one who thinks knowingly of their environment, who realizes their intention to remain there frying themselves up on the rocks, wouldn't make a critical tongue against them; we shouldn't condemn he who is forced by circumstances to excuse in his mind such wickedness; let's condemn what we do without having the need of the Maniotes." Ibid, 57.

118. Ibid, 57.

119. Ibid, 57/58.

120. Ibid, 38.

121. Meniates, 'Peri Fthonou,' in *Skouphos, Meniates, Voulgares, Theotokes*, 224.

122. The linkage of history and geography served for example to depict the ancient and modern Greeks as sharing a common homeland. This idea was represented in the figure of mother Hellas, as portrayed in the popular culture of these times. She was not, significantly, 'ancient Greece,' but was the land from which the Greeks, ancient and modern sprang; all were the offspring of a common geography, a common mother. Unmistakeable notes here of 'primordial' rhetoric.

123. Indeed this is the intent of that later work of Psalidas and Thesprotos, *Geographia Albanias kai Epeirou.*

124. These impulses were equally visible in the work of Plethon, the late Byzantine figure discussed in Chapter 2. Plethon's desire to restore to prominence the ancient elements of Greek culture and identity apparently led him also to an appreciation for geography. Plethon wrote commentaries on Strabo and produced some geographical works of his own based on Ptolemy. See Woodhouse, *George Gemistos Plethon, The Last of the Hellenes*, 180.

125. Giorgios Tertsetes, 'Apospasmata trion agnoston Logon,' in *Ho Giorgios Tertsetes kai ta evriskomena erga tou*, edited by Ntinos Konomos, (Athens: Library of the Boule of Greece, 1984), 480.

126. Note references to this figure in *Melissa*, *Rossanglogallos*, and Koraes's 'Salpisma Polemestirion' as surveyed in the previous chapter. "Greece calls out to you," wrote Regas himself in his Thourios, "she yearns for you, suffers for you, she appeals for your aid with a motherly voice." 'Thourious,' *Regas*, 393.

127. Alexander Ypsilantis, 'Proclamation of February 4, 1821,' in Richard Clogg, editor and translator, *The Movement for Greek Independence 1770-1821: a collection of documents*, (London: Macmillan, 1976), 202.

VI. Conclusion

Wounded national feeling—this scarcely needs saying—breeds nationalism...[1]

The term 'national problem' has been used throughout this study to help characterize a tradition of Greek thought raised upon the premise of cultural decline. The roots of these ideas lead back to the events surrounding the fall of Constantinople, although there is reason to suspect that intellectuals of earlier eras had begun to despair of these problems as well. Even scholars of Byzantine times, Steven Runciman once wrote, "found that it added to their prestige and the prestige of their people if they emphasized their descent from the venerated Greeks of old, whose language they spoke and whose works they never ceased from studying."[2] These Byzantine scholars made use of the Hellenic past much in the manner of the Enlightenment figures discussed here. Of course the discomfort that earlier scholars were beginning to experience was destined to be more sharply felt by their descendants. Those of later times came not from Byzantium, but a world fallen entirely into decay and increasingly associated with barbarism. If self worth is conditioned by group identity, then the ruin of modern Greece made even more vivid the predicaments of these later emigres.

The charge of barbarism posed a dilemma, nonetheless, that did not always resolve itself in a heightened sense of national activism. Some of the figures in this study, Vlachs, Bulgarians and Greeks alike, sought relief from their predicament by blending into their adopted societies. The strong archaizing tendency in the Greek Enlightenment represents a similar if more ambitious form of cultural escapism; it sought to negate the present and reinvent the nation on the model of those noble Hellenes who grace the pages of history.

Most scholars would likely agree that the importance of the Greek Enlightenment does not lie in the originality of its thought, but in what it may have to tell us about thought and history.[3] I have approached the Diaphotismos therefore as part of a larger historical discourse, and intended to show how certain themes and imagery moved through time and (social) space. This method emphasizes the unity and contiguity that are among the Greek Enlightenment's most salient features.[4]

The basis of the Diaphotismos's unity was the inspiration Greek thinkers derived from the 'national problem,' a view that George Henderson came to hold, but perhaps too late in his studies to develop in depth: "One would have to say," he concluded, "that throughout the 17th, 18th, and 19th centuries the Greeks preserved and exploited a sense of apartness, indeed of uniqueness, and that of all the conditions making possible the educational revival this was the most basic."[5] As these tentative comments suggest, Henderson had some difficulty in accounting for the driving force behind the "revival" he had taken pains to describe. Henderson ultimately found his answer in what he vaguely called a "sense of apartness." Koraes had apparently come to the same conclusion. "A national vanity," the logios declared in his famous address of 1803, served to inspire a notion of cultural legacy and mission in the Greeks throughout the centuries of Ottoman rule. This vanity, he wrote, "ridiculous in its motives but salutary in its effects, rendered the Greeks as proud of their origins as would be somebody who was the descendant, in direct line, of Miltiades or Themistocles."[6] The present study has attempted to provide a fuller picture of the national self-consciousness alluded to by these authors and the role it played in Greek intellectual history.

Beginning with the fall of Constantinople but focusing mainly on the seventeenth century, the second chapter surveyed the sources and early symbolism of the emerging national discourse. Images appeared in the writings of Argyropoulos, Skouphos and the students of the Flaggineio Schole that expressed a sometimes melancholy, sometimes defiant consciousness of national degeneration, along with dreamy reveries over a time when Greece was an object of admiration in the world.

These early modern examples of Greek thought have hopefully served to put the arguments of contemporary scholars into greater historical context. Benedict Anderson, for example, credited the rise of Greek national consciousness to the activities of eighteenth century European philhellenes. These recreated in their works a "glittering" world that fired the imagination of emigre Greeks and inspired dreams of cultural revival. "In the last quarter of the century," he wrote, "this 'past' became increasingly accessible to a small number of young Greek-speaking Christian intellectuals, most of whom had traveled outside the confines of the Ottoman Empire."[7]

The present study has clarified some important matters of Greek intellectual history addressed in this passage. The 'past' that Anderson speaks of had never disappeared of course from Greek letters. Having been raised in the grand tradition, the seventeenth century writers surveyed here produced pedagogical works of their own that held close to the hallowed saints and sages of the Hellenic pantheon. These range in variety from Patousas's tranquil *Egkyklopedia*, to Skouphos's polemical *Rhetorike*, a text that also contained a forceful plea for deliverance. Koraes himself, whose *Report on the Present State of Civilization in Greece* was the only source cited by Anderson, was exposed to this tradition in Smyrna as a boy.[8] The same would have held true for nearly all the emigre Greek scholars of this study—they came to complete their educations in the West not begin them. This was a historical process, furthermore, that Koraes's generation appeared at the very end of, not the beginning, as Anderson's comments might lead one to infer.

Perhaps this study has also indicated the larger implications of the Greek preoccupation with the past that Anderson and other scholars speak of. By continuing to study the ancient masters, Greek culture had long nourished the assumptions surrounding its former grandeur, and perhaps too the sad distance separating contemporary Greeks from their predecessors. Nor does Anderson take into account the 'dark' side of philhellenism, as encountered in the texts of Holderlin and others. However these factors were influential in shaping the content of the Diaphotismos and imbuing virtually all reflection on Greek life with mingled notions of pride and infamy. This theme was perhaps most strikingly revealed in the language dispute.[9]

What I have termed the mature Diaphotismos was addressed through a study of the figure and writings of Iosepos Moisiodax. Moisiodax's first work, the *Ethike Philosophia*, brought into view the heavy influence that the Enlightenment was coming to exert upon the Greek intelligentsia. This work was also characterized by an unflinching consciousness of the plight of Greece that was especially remarkable for its open acknowledgment of the criticisms leveled at the nation from Europe. Exposure to the West and to the prevailing opinions concerning 'Greece' that circulated in these lands served as a potent force in the popularization of the 'national problem' and the questions surrounding it.

But if such dismal lessons in the state of world opinion could prove a fertile source of mission, they could lead as well to evasion. The Vlach-logioi Moisiodax, Daniel and Darvares illustrate how the association of self worth and national identity could result in a kind of ethnic flight. Greek emigres were prone to similar acts of this kind. The Vlach-Hellenizers also provide important insights into the source of the archaism that featured so prominently in the Greek Enlightenment. An equally intense example of cultural flight, this impulse was perhaps the most visible manifestation of the motives and aims of the enlightenment project: it sought to banish the poor figure of the contemporary Greek from existence and replace him with a more suitable one from the past.

'Suitable,' of course, being a statement of value adduced in large part by the level of admiration an object engendered from Europe.[10]

The social dispersion of the discourse, accompanying important structural changes within the Greek East, was a key topic of the fourth chapter. Settling on the diaspora merchant, Ioannes Pringos, we saw how the 'national problem' had become much more than an internal matter of the logioi. Pringos's vehement reactions to the contempt that Greece elicited from the West and the intense sense of mission this inspired in him, depict in vivid fashion the mingling of self worth and identity that this 'problem' was given to arouse.

The figure of Pringos also served to demonstrate how events had conspired to raise into existence a new class of Greek merchant, and one exposed by vocation to the kind of predicaments experienced by the logoi. The fact that these two disparate groups should come to participate and collaborate so closely in the Diaphotismos says much about the influence of the emigre experience on the rise of the 'national problem.' As the 'emigre class' grew so did it serve to renew, widen and reinforce the cultural understanding of the 'national problem' in Greek society.

Pringos's writings provide historians finally with a valuable insight into how native works and ideas were dispersed within Greek society, and the influence they exerted. It was to the native tradition after all that Pringos often turned when moved to articulate his anger or despair. His recitation of phrases that he had learned from older sources reveals the internal transmission of language and imagery that is so essential to any understanding of the Diaphotismos's unity. The most visible instance of this transmission was the supplication for deliverance that Pringos borrowed from Meniates—one that Meniates himself had taken almost verbatim from Skouphos.

Modern historians have written of nationalism as a "pirated" idea and applied this approach to the Greek independence movement. Among these have been Elie Kedourie, whose words fell like a wrecking ball on the assumptions of the earlier 'primordialists.' According to Kedourie, "nationalism is a doctrine invented in Europe at the beginning of the nineteenth century."[11] For all the merits of Kedourie's scholarship, questions arise nevertheless over his reluctance to recognize the existence of native discourses that, however socially circumscribed, exerted a considerable influence of their own upon the thought of Eastern intellectuals. This essential element was not overlooked by Runciman, as we saw above. On one hand the old gods of the Hellenic tradition never disappeared from Greek pedagogy. It was through this same channel that early modern Hellenic literature was later to pass. The Greeks certainly made great use of Western ideology to clarify and refine their thought. But the impulse behind these appropriations—the question that Henderson struggled with above—is largely absent from Kedourie's analysis. One hardly ever finds the native quotient that the intellectuals of his works bring to the East-West exchange; these 'exchanges,' if they can be called such, are made in fact to flow in one direction only.[12] And yet the addition of a national element to the original European message complicates the neat, 'history as the movement of ideas' approach to this subject taken by some scholars. As elsewhere, a general failure to fully imagine the lives of the intellectuals who inhabit their studies is perhaps the greatest source of error in the accounts of Kedourie and Anderson.

Unfamiliarity with the native sources surfaces again as a consistent weakness in Gellner's treatment of Balkan independence movements. Recognizing that industrialization could not be used to explain the origins of Greek nationalism, he offered up something even more colorful. "It so happened in the Balkans," Gellner declared, "that the overlords were Muslim and the peripheral wild men were Christians." This "accidental convergence," he continued, sufficed to "endow a peripheral dissidence, practiced by tribesmen and bandits, with a kind of doctrinal content."[13]

Of course the "doctrinal content" came not at all from the wild men of the Balkan hinterlands, but no matter. What Gellner implied was that these early revolutionary outbreaks were simply not expressions of 'nationalism.' Speaking apparently of Regas, he observed that "there is reason to suspect that the original Greek national movement aimed not at a homogeneous modern nation-state, but rather at a reversal of ranks within the then Empire: in brief, to put the clock back and replace the Ottoman Empire by a new Byzantium."[14]

A revived Byzantium was in fact quite often what Greek nationalists had in mind, whether in name, or in the form of some other sprawling multi-ethnic entity consolidated around Greek culture. Such grand programs do indeed violate the precepts of nation-state doctrine, but should this be cause to further muddy our conception of what constitutes nationalism? Regas may even have expressed the 'logic' of ethnic aggrandizement in its most elemental form. More importantly, the dispersion of the Greek population throughout the eastern Mediterranean foiled any simple conceptualization of a 'nation-state.' To imagine a nation-state in this context, would have been to imagine as well a colossal project of ethnic "cleansing," something the early sources do not verify. The process of ethnic partition in the Balkans was often guided instead by the tempest of violence that accompanied each outbreak of war, consequences largely unforeseen by men like Regas. Chaim Kaufmann has alluded to the operation of this very process when commenting on more recent cases of ethnic strife.[15]

Regas's portrait of a liberated, yet ethnically diverse Greece departed not at all from ones that had appeared in the sources preceding him, and this for obvious reasons. It is not easy to see, given the fact that the most desirable parts of the 'Greek' world contained large numbers of other groups, what alternative form of territorial organization Greek 'nationalism' could have taken. The point is that the absence of a definite 'nation-state' in early modern Greek thought should not, in itself, lead us to label the national consciousness of this era as 'pre-modern,' or form hasty judgements about the cultural assumptions of the people of the time.

The fourth chapter also indicated how the popularization of the 'national problem' came to influence the development of the Philike Etairia. This influence was apparent in the organization's literature, rituals and the extent to which it possessed an ideology. The acts of mimicry undertaken by the Society's members appear to represent the desire to portray themselves as the redeeming sons and especially the 'merchant benefactors' so greatly celebrated by the Diaphotismos. Indeed the frequent appeals that one conduct himself as a 'father of the race' are fitting testimony of the traditional values of this society and how they could serve to motivate men to action. The fact that many of the Etairia's early members, to say nothing of its founders, were failed merchants suggests therefore a possible revolutionary linkage between self worth and nationalism.

This chapter also attempted to demonstrate the remarkable extent to which the 'national problem' had been ritualized in Greek culture by the end of the eighteenth century. We noted in this case how certain ideas had been 'vulgarized' into a set of stock images, and the remarkable degree to which these images resonated throughout Greek society. The occasional allusions in this study to the existence of a 'culture of self-contempt' describes how notions of national degeneracy and infamy had become so widespread a fixture of Greek discourse in the decades preceding the revolution.

The closing survey of Neohellenic geography attempted to show how internal and external sources of influence collaborated in refining the ideas associated with the 'national problem' over the full course of the eighteenth century. The emphasis on geography in the Greek Enlightenment is itself a conspicuous fact. The popularity of this science derived in some part from its unique value as a medium for depicting the problems that occupied Greek thinkers. This phenomenon helps to illustrate the selective appropriation of ideas, methods and in this case fields of knowledge, that accompanied the encounter between East and West over the course of the Enlightenment. It was in the geographical works, finally, that the national problem—its source, dimension and increasingly, its remedy—could be explored in depth.

The rise of the West played a heavy role in how the Greeks came to see themselves. This old element of the national discourse was strikingly illustrated in the first works of geography surveyed through to the late ones. In time the mission of renewal ultimately became a political rather than merely a cultural one, however this transition has to do with more than ideology. As noted in the fourth chapter, this final stage in the development of Greek thought was the work of European history as much as European ideas.

The Greek scholars surveyed in these pages had acquired a new vocabulary over the course of the eighteenth century to aid them in framing the problems confronting 'the nation'. But what did this nation consist of? Where did it lie and what were its boundaries? To answer such questions, they adhered mainly to native traditions of thought, a process that is revealed most strikingly in Regas's mythical Hellenic Republic of 1797. Here one finds a constitution of French origin superimposed upon that vast spatial entity spoken of by Skouphos and the geographers. Although clearly a product of national sentiment, it was not a nation-state, as Gellner was right to object. But here again the Republic may offer a revealing portrait of its time, indicating not only the aspirations of individuals like Regas, but their assumptions too regarding how they might be realized. Assumptions, it must finally be said, that were shortly to be undermined and, at last, overthrown by events.

Notes

1. Berlin, *Three Critics of the Enlightenment: Vico, Hamann, Herder*, 205.

2. Runciman, *The Great Church in Captivity*, 120.

3. Although, it is also worth noting, that as a specimen of 'nationalist' literature the Diaphotismos represents a unique resource that has yet to be fully appreciated and exploited by historians.

4. This approach departs from the one taken in Kitromilides's *Neoellenikos Diaphotismos*, which remains a valuable survey of the subject from the standpoint of thinkers and texts. Such surveys have performed the necessary service of freeing the Diaphotismos from the hold of Koraes—the source of many errors and misjudgements in Western historiography.

5. Henderson, *The Revival of Greek Thought 1620-1830*, 10.

6. Koraes, *The Present State of Civilization in Greece*, 158. "This vanity," he continued, "together with the

difference in religion and habits and the treatment which the Greeks received from the hands of their conquerors, resulted in the fact that a large part of the nation always looked upon itself as prisoners of war and never as slaves." Ibid.

7. Anderson, *Imagined Communities*, 72.

8. It was in fact to learn the ancient tongue—an essential fixture of the grandeur associated with the past, and thus too a means for drawing near it—that the young Koraes was inspired to excel in his lessons. (His mother had even acquired a tincture of ancient Greek during her studies as a youth). Koraes, 'Autoviographia,' in *Ho Koraes kai he Epoche Tou*, 236-7. It was in Smyrna too, while still an adolescent, that Koraes had bested his cousins in the race to inherit his grandfather Rysios's fine library of Greek and Roman classics. The studious Rysios, it appears, was something of a logios himself. Ibid, 28.

9. As for Anderson's celebrated linguistic thesis, it would take a sublime observer indeed to ascertain the influence of 'print capitalism' in the intense debates surrounding the language question.

10. The legitimating power accorded to Europe served to stir up resentment within intellectual circles throughout the ensuing history of the independent Greek state; it has in fact never completely dissipated. Note the following passage from a late nineteenth century text by Argyres Ephtaliotes (1849-1923): "...And now, let me ask you, privileged children of Greece, that go to Europe at great expense. Why don't you make each year and painlessly a trip to our islands, in order to see all these and other more interesting and beautiful things, and to know them and to love them as your own, which they are, and not to drain all your funds only in running to foreign parts, and not seeing how the greatest nations in this Europe of yours are those which admire their own, these rustic things that you regard as insignificant, and which some day the Franks will start to come to in crowds to walk among and to say how they yet live the beauties and delights of the Odyssey and then we will love them ourselves out of imitation, and not from our own whim!" Argyres Ephtaliotes, 'Nesiotikes Istories,' in *Psychares, Ephtaliotes, Palles, Vlastos*, edited by Stavros Thrasyvoulos, (Athens: Vasike Vivliotheke, 1956), 187-8.

11. Elie Kedourie, *Nationalism*, (London: Hutchinson, 1966), 9. Kedourie further characterized nationalism as the product of an attitude perhaps even more than an idea. Nationalism is a "variant," he wrote in a later piece, of an "ideological style of politics" that "originated in Europe and owed its popularity to the prestige of the West." Kedourie, *Nationalism in Asia and Africa*, New York: Meridian Books, 1970, 45. As these passages attest, Kedourie's theory dwells on the primacy of 'ideas and imitation'—a process whose 'legitimacy' he is given to doubt. Kedourie inferred that as foreign ideas they are not a genuine expression of the people who adopt them. In this sense they mask more subtle motivations. Kedourie once described Koraes for instance, not without justice, as an example of the "radical and far reaching character of the revolt against tradition" promoted by Western culture. *Nationalism in Asia and Africa*, 38. These motivations may suffice for intellectuals, but what of their wider dispersion? "National revival has been such a global phenomenon," Raymond Pearson for example has written, "that its attribution solely to the machinations of inventive, disaffected intellectuals lacks conviction." Pearson, 'Fact, Fantasy, Fraud: Perceptions and Projections of National Revival,' 48. In one of his most recent works Smith questioned many of the same assumptions: "What does it mean to say that the nation is a social construct and consists largely of invented traditions? Why do elites select this particular construct? Why does this type of discourse resonate with 'the masses'?" Anthony D. Smith, *Nationalism and Modernism*, (London: Routledge, 1998), 129.

12. An interesting comparative source for the questions raised here is Benjamin Schwartz's *In Search of Wealth and Power, Yen Fu and the West*, (Cambridge: Harvard University Press, 1964). Yen Fu was a late nineteenth century Chinese intellectual whose experiences and thought bear similarities to the Greek logioi of this study. According to Schwartz, Yen Fu manifested "the beginnings of a phenomenon which was to occur again and again among 'overseas students' in subsequent generations. Sent abroad to study some specific field of 'practical' knowledge, the most gifted seldom found themselves in a proper state of mind for unrelieved

attention to their chosen field of professional study. The enormously unsatisfactory general condition of China, contrasted with the wealth and power of the host country, inevitably turned their attention to general problems." Ibid, 28.

13. Gellner, *Nationalism*, 41-2.

14. Ibid, 41.

15. Such events, he argues, indicate how "restoring civil politics in multi-ethnic states shattered by war is impossible, because the war itself destroys the possibilities for ethnic cooperation." Chaim Kaufmann, "Possible and Impossible Solutions to Ethnic Civil Wars," *International Security*, Vol 20, No. 4 (Spring 1996), 136.

Appendix

Three Supplications: Skouphos [Texne Rhetorike, 1681], Meniates [Euaggelismon, 1688] and Pringos [Chroniko, 1768]

"Enough, righteous Judge, enough. Until when (os pote) must the thrice-wretched Greeks have to find themselves in the bonds of slavery, and with the infamous foot of the Barbarian Thracians (Turks) stepping on their necks? For how long must such an illustrious and noble race be forced to do obeisance to a godless touloupani atop the royal throne, and those cities(xoras), in which caused to bring forth to sight that Sun, and You the invisible, in human form sprung forth, under the half moon to be ruled? Recall, Theanthropic Jesus, that the Hellenic Race represented the first that opened its arms in order to embrace your divine Gospels; the first, that threw down the idols, and hanging on the Cross worshiped you as God; the first, that resisting the tyrants, that with such terrors sought to uproot from the world the Faith, and from the hearts of Christians your divine Name. Ah, recall, I beseech you, that you are not only Judge, but father, and that you punish, but don't destroy your children. Undoubtedly the sins of the Greeks moved your righteous anger, undoubtedly also in the

"Until when (os pote), immortal Virgin, must the thrice wretched race of the Greeks find themselves in the bonds of such unbearable slavery? Until when will it step upon its noble neck the barbarian Thracian? Until when must they be ruled under the half moon those cities (xorais) in which was caused to spring forth into human form, from your divine womb, the mystical Sun of righteousness? Ach! Virgin! Recall that in Greece before all the other places (topon) was lit the life-giving light of true faith, the Greek Race represented the first that opened its arms and embraced the holy Gospels of your only born Son. The first, that resisting the tyrants, that with such terrors sought to uproot from the hearts of the faithful your hallowed Name... Restore to it its former honor, raise it from the dunghill of slavery onto the throne of royal authority, from the bonds to the scepter, from captivity to kingdom...From Crete

"Why should we be under the Turk, why should we be slaves and not have as these people a kingdom and freedom? Merciful master, you who freed the Israelites from the slavery of the Pharaoh, free us too the orthodox christians from the Turk...O God become merciful toward us and let the race free itself from the Hagarene, o God move the heart of the Russian Emperor, who is of our faith, to free us from the heavy and unbearable yoke of the unjust, the predatory, the faithless Turk, in order that the security of the Christianity be increased. Yes master o lord become merciful. Until when (os pote) must the half moon rule over and dominate the city of Constantine? From 1454 (sic) until now it has been 314 years. Enough my Lord, long has your anger lasted, haven't the sins yet been exhausted for you to free us, my Lord? We turned to anger your benevolence and for this you put us into the subjugation of this savage wild animal of furnace of the same lawlessness they forged the lightning bolts that strike them from the face of the earth, You, who are entirely compassionate, absolve, and extinguish this rage in the ocean of your infinite mercy. As you are compassionate make it so with your divine power for them to leave the yoke of such Barbarian captivity; as charitable, and generous retributor, opening the treasures of your divine blessings, raise again to their former glory the Race, and from the dunghill in which it sits, give to it the scepter and the Kingdom. And if my calls don't move your pity, then let the tears that run from my eyes, and if these are not enough, then the cries of your Saints, who call out to you from all the parts of wretched Greece. From Crete cries Andreas and asks that you exterminate the Hagarene wolves from that Kingdom, in which from Constantinople cries out a Chrystotomos; and Katerina from Alexandria, the Ignations cry from Antioch, the Polycarpians from Smyrna, the Dionysians from Athens, the Spiridons from Cyprus from your high charity hope the Greek cities and all of Greece for deliverance."[1]

cries Andreas, from Cyprus cries Spyridon, from Antioch cries Ignatios, from Athens cries Dionysios, fom Smyrna cries Polycarpos, from Alexandria cries Katerine. From Constantinople cries Chrysostomos and showing you the awful tyranny of the godless Hagarene, hope from your high charity, the Greek Race delivery... And if these our cries don't move you to pity, then let them move you these bitter tears that fall from my eyes. And if yet these too are not enough, let them move you the cries of your Saints, that call out ceaselessly from all the parts of thrice-wretched Greece..."[2]

the disrespectful Hagarene. My Lord, nourish in the hearts of the Christian kings to unite to expel this bloodthirsty wolf, this insatiable animal, of which to life it is like a pig, in feeding and luxury in injustice with its tribute taking, weight upon weight in order to diminish us, in order to destroy us. Destroy him, my Lord, let your anger pass on to these, from where it came. Raise up, my Lord, another Alexander, as he who ousted the Persians from Greece, so too this tyranny to expel, to light up again the Christian faith in the places of Greece as it was before..."[3]

Notes

1. Skouphos, 'Texne Rhetorike,' 118-119.

2. Meniates, *Didachais*, II: 151-2.

3. Andriotes, 'To Chroniko tou Amsterdam,' 852.

Bibliography

Primary Sources

Anonymou tou Ellenos. *Hellenike Nomarchia, etoi logos peri Eleftherias*. Edited by Tasos Vournas. Athens: Aphon Tolide, 1982. Reprint of 1806 Edition.

Anthrakites, Methodios and Vassilopoulos, Balanos. *Odon Mathematikes*. Vol. 3. Venice, 1749.

Bartholdy, J. L. S. *Voyage en Grece, 1803-1804*. Translated into Modern Greek by Phontas Kondyles. Nea Epythraia: EKATE, 1993.

Bentham, Jeremy. 'Securities Against Misrule and Other Constitutional Writings for Tripoli and Greece,' from *The Collected Writings of Jeremy Bentham*. Edited by Philip Schofield. Oxford: Clarendon Press, 1990.

Bianu, Ioan and Hodos, Nerva, eds. *Bibliografia Romaneasca, Veche 1508-1830*. Vol. 2. Bucharest: Atelierele Socec & Co., 1909.

Clogg, Richard, ed. and translator. *The Movement for Greek Independence 1770-1821: a collection of documents*. London: Macmillan, 1976.

Crusio, Martino. *Turcograecia*. Modena: Editrice Memor, 1972. Reprint of 1554 Edition.

Darvares, Demetrios. *Alethes hodos eis ten eudaimonian*. Vienna: Georgio Vendote, 1796.

______. *Cheiragogia eis ten kalokagatheia*. Athens: Syllogos pros ton diadosin ton Hellenikon grammaton, 1876. Reprint of 1790 Edition.

______. *Eisagoge eis ten Hellenike Glossan*. Vienna: Georgio Vendote, 1798.

______. *Eklogarion Graikikon*. Vienna: Georgio Vendote, 1804.

______. *Megale Katechisis, etoi orthodoxos christianike Didaskalia tes Anatolikes Ekklesias*. Vienna: Georgio Vendote, 1805.

______. *Sophias Apanthisma*. Athens: Syllogos Pros Diadosin ton Hellenikon Grammaton, 1873. Reprint of 1811 Edition.

______. *Syntomos Iera Historia tes Ekklesias tes Palaias kai Neas Diathekes*. Vienna: Ioannou Karolou Sxouenderou, 1800.

Daskalakes, Apostoles Basileiou, ed. *Keimena-pegai tes Historias tes Hellenikos Epanastaseos*, Vol. 1. Athens: Typois Adelphon, 1966.

Demaras, Konstantine, ed. *Ho Koraes kai he Epoche Tou*. Athens: Vasike Vivliotheke, 1974.

______, ed. *Ho Rossanglogallos*. Athens: Poreia, 1990. Reprint of 1805(?) Edition.

Diderot, Denis. *Encyclopedia*. Translated and with an introduction by Nelly S. Hoyt and Thomas Cassirer. New York: The Bobbs-Merrill Company, Inc., 1965.

Eliou, Philippos E., ed. *Prosthekes sten Hellenike Vivliographia*. Athens: Neohellenikes Erevnes, 1973.

Fragkiskos, Emmanuel, ed. *Ta Hellenika Proepanastika Periodika*. Index. Athens: Kentron Neohellenikon Erevnon, 1971.

______, ed. *Ta Hellenika Proepanastika Periodica*. Vol 2. Hermes o Logios, 1811-1821. Athens: Kentron Neohellenikon Erevnon, 1976.

Gazes, Anthimios – Barbie du Bocage – Philippides, Daniel. *Allelographia*. Edited and with an introduction and commentary by Aikaterina Koumarianou. Athens: Estras, 1966.

Herder, Johann Gottfried Von Herder. *Philosophical Writings*. Translated and edited by Michael N. Forster. Cambridge: Cambridge University Press, 2002.

Hermes ho Logios, Vol. 1-11, Vienna, 1811-21.

Holderlin, Friedrich. *Hyperion and Selected Poems*. Translated by William R. Trask and adapted by David Schwarz. New York: Continuum, 1990.

Hope, Thomas. *Anastasius, or, Memoirs of a Greek; Written at the close of the Eighteenth Century*. Vol. 1-3. London: John Murray, 1820.

Katartzes, Demetrios. *Ta Evriskomena*. Edited by Konstantine Demaras. Athens: Hermes, 1970.

Koch, Adrienne and Peden, William, eds. *The Life and Selected Writings of Thomas Jefferson.* New York: The Modern Library, 1972.

Kodrikas, Panayiotes. *Melete tes Koines Hellenikes Dialektou.* Paris: Patrinou & Postolaka, 1818.

Kolokotronis, Theodore. *Memoirs from the Greek War of Independence 1821-1833.* Translated by E.M. Edmonds. Chicago: Argonaut Publishers, 1969.

Konstantas, Gregorios and Philippides, Daniel. *Geographia Neoterike.* Edited by Aikaterina Koumarianou. Athens: Hermes, 1988. Reprint of 1791 Edition.

Koraes, Adamantios. *Hapanta.* 2 Volumes. Athens: Vires, 1969.

______ and Petros, Stamates. *Grammata apo to Amsterdam.* Edited and with an introduction by Philippos Eliou. Athens: Hermes, 1976.

______. *Politika Phylladia, 1781-1831.* 11 Volumes. Athens, 1983.

______. *Lettres Inedites de Coray a Chardon de la Rochette.* Paris: Firmin-Didot, 1877.

Kosma tou Aitolou. *Didachais.* Edited by Ioannou B. Menounou. Athens: Tenos, 1979.

Laios, Georgios, ed. *Anekdotes Epistles kai Engrapha tou 1821.* Athens: Diphos, 1958.

Leake, William. *Researches in Greece.* London: John Booth, 1814.

______. *Travels in Northern Greece.* Amsterdam: Adolf M. Hakkert, 1967.

Locke, John. *Second Treatise of Government.* Indianapolis: Hackett, 1980.

Lord Charlemont. *The Travels of Lord Charlemont in Greece and Turkey.* Edited by E.J. Finopoulos and W.B. Stanford. London: Trigraph, 1984.

Meletios. *Geographia palaia kai nea.* Venice: Nikolaos Glykeis, 1728.

Melissa, Vol. 1-3, Paris, 1819-21.

Meniates, Elias. *Didachai.* Edited by Anthimios Mazarakes. Athens: Prometheus, 1925.

Mexas, Valerios G. *Hoi Philikoi.* Athens, 1937.

Moisiodax, Iosepos. *Apologia.* Edited by Alkhes Aggelou. Athens: Nea Hellinike Vivliotheke, 1976. Reprint of 1780 Edition.

______. *Theoria tes Geographias*. Vienna: Ioannes Thomas, 1781.

Montesquieu, Baron de. *The Persian Letters*. Translated by George R. Healy. Indianapolis: Hackett, 1999.

______. *The Spirit of the Laws*. Translated by Thomas Nugent with an introduction by Franz Neumann. New York: Hafner Press, 1949.

Notaras, Chrysanthou. *Eisagoge eis ta geographika, kai sphairika*. Paris, 1716.

Patousas, Ioannes, ed. *Anthe Eulaveias*. Edited and with an introduction by Athanasios Karathanases. Athens: Hermes, 1978. Reprint of 1708 Edition.

______. *Enkyklopaideia philologike, eis tessaras tomous dieremene*. Edited by Spyridon Vlantes. Venice: Nicholas Glykei, 1819. Reprint of 1710 Edition.

Petropoulos, Demetrios, ed. *Hellenika Demotika Tragoudia*. Athens: Vasike Vivliotheke, 1958.

Philemon, Ioannes. *Dokimion Historikon peri tes Hellenikes Epanastaseos*. 4 Volumes. Athens: P. Soutsa, 1859-61.

______. *Dokimion Historikon peri tes Philikes Hetaireias*. Nafplion, Th. Kontaxe, 1834.

Plethon, George. *Nomon Syggrafes, Ta Sozomena (Traite des Lois, Recueil Des Fragments)*. Edited and with an introduction by C. Alexandre, with French translation by A. Pellissier. Amsterdam: Adolf M. Hakkert, 1966.

Psalidas, Athansios and Thesprotos, Kosmas. *Geographia Alvanias kai Epeirou*. Iannina: Society for Epiriot Studies, 1964.

Rousseau, Jean-Jacques. *A Discourse on Inequality*. Translated and with an introduction by Maurice Cranston. London: Penguin Books, 1984.

______. *The Government of Poland*. Translated by Willmoore Kendall. Indianapolis: Hackett, 1985.

Sideres, Giannes, ed. *Neohelleniko Theatro (1795-1929)*. Athens: Vasike Vivliotheke, 1958.

Sakellarios, George. *Archaiologia Synoptike ton Hellenon*. Vienna: L. Polyzones, 1796.

Shelley, Percy Bysshe. *The Complete Poetical Works of Percy Bysshe Shelley*. Edited by Thomas Hutchinson. London: Oxford University Press, 1952.

Skouphos, Fragkiskos. *Patriotica kai Ethica*. Edited and with an introduction by Kostas Kairofelas. Athens: Syllogos pros diadosin Ofelimon Vivlion, 1940.

Tatakis, Basile N., ed. *Skouphos, Meniates, Voulgaris, Theotokes*. Athens: Vasike Vivliotheke, 1953.

Tersetes, Giorgios. *Ho Georgios Tersetes kai to evriskomena erga tou*. Edited by Ntinos Konomos. Athens: Library of the Parliament of Greece, 1984.

Theotokes, Nikephoros. *Stoicheia Geographias*. Edited and annotated by Anthimiou Gazes. Vienna: Zosimadon, 1804.

Velaras, Ioannes. *Stoicheia helleno-alvanikes grammatikes kai helleno-alvanikai dialogoi*. Edited by Titos G. Giochalas. Thessaloniki: Institute for Balkan Studies, 1985.

Voltaire. *Correspondence*. Edited by Theodore Besterman. Volumes LXXV- LXXVI. Geneva: Institut et Musee Voltaire, 1962.

Voulgaris, Eugenios. *Propheteke epistole pros tous orthodoxous christianous*. Athens: Orthodoxou Typou, 1969. Reprint of 1756 Edition.

______. *Stochasmoi eis tous parontas krisimous kairous tou kratous tou Othamanikou*. Reprint. Athens: Vivliophilika Tetradia Ergasias, 1996.

Vranousis, Leandros, ed. *Hoi Prodromoi*. Athens: Vasike Vivliotheke, 1955.

______. *Regas - erevna, synagogi kai meleti*. Athens: Vasike Vivliotheke, 1953.

Xanthos, Emmanuel. *Apomnemonevmata peri tes Philikes Etairias*. Athens: Hetaireia Historikon Ekdoseon, 1956.

Secondary Sources

Aggelos, Alkhes. *Hoi logioi kai ho Agonas*. Athens: Syllogos pros ton Diadosin Ophelimon Vivlion, 1971.

______. "Pos e noellenike skepse egnorise to 'Dokimio' tou John Locke." *Angloellenike epitheorese* 7 (1954): 128-49.

Anderson, Benedict. *Imagined Communities*. New York: Verso, 1991.

Andriotes, N., "To Chroniko tou Amsterdam." *Nea Estia* 10 (1931): 846-53, 914-20.

Augustinos, Olga. *French Odysseys: Greece in French Travel Writing from the Renaissance to the Romantic Era*. Baltimore: Johns Hopkins Press, 1994.

Audales, Athanasias. *He Egkyklopaideia Philologike tou Ioanne Patousa*. Athens: Library of Historical Studies, 1984.

Bailkey, Nels M., ed. *Readings in Ancient History*. Lexington: D.C. Heath and Company, 1976.

Batalden, Stephen K. *Catherine II's Greek Prelate, Eugenios Voulgaris in Russia, 1771-1806*. Boulder: East European Monographs, 1982.

Baumer, Franklin L. *Modern European Thought: Continuity and Change in Ideas, 1600-1950*. New York: Macmillan, 1977.

Becker, Carl L. *The Heavenly City of the Eighteenth-Century Philosophers*. New Haven: Yale University Press, 1965.

Bell, David A. *The Cult of the Nation in France: Inventing Nationalism, 1680-1800*. Cambridge: Harvard University Press, 2001.

Berkowitz, Leonard, "On the Formation and Regulation of Anger and Aggression: A Cognitive-Neoassocianistic Analysis." *American Psychologist* 45 (1990): 494-503.

Berlin, Isaiah. *Three Critics of the Enlightenment: Vico, Hamann, Herder*. Princeton: Princeton University Press, 2000.

Bien, Peter. *Kazantzakis and the Linguistic Revolution in Modern Greek Literature*. Princeton: Princeton University Press, 1972.

Bruess, Gregory L. *Religion, Identity and Empire: A Greek Archbishop in the Russia of Catherine the Great*. Boulder: East European Monographs, 1997.

Cassirer, Ernst. *The Philosophy of the Enlightenment*. Translated by Fritz C.A. Koelln and James P. Pettegrove. Princeton: Princeton University Press, 1979.

Chaconas, Stephen George. *Adamantios Korais, A Study in Greek Nationalism*. New York: Columbia University Press, 1942.

Charilaos, Neophytos. *Ho Neophytos Doukas kai he symvole tou sto Neohelleniko Diaphotismo*. Athens: Kyvele, 2002.

Chickering, Roger. *We Men Who Feel Most German*. Boston: George Allen & Unwin, 1984.

Clogg, Richard, ed. *Balkan Society in the Age of Greek Independence*. Totowa: Barnes & Noble Books, 1981.

______. "The 'Didaskhalia Patriki' (1798): an Orthodox Reaction to French Revolutionary Propaganda." *Middle Eastern Studies*, V (1969): 87-115.

______, ed. *The Greek Struggle for Independence*. London: Archon Books, 1973.

Cohler, Anne M. *Rousseau and Nationalism*. New York: Basic Books, 1970.

Douglas Dakin. *The Greek Struggle for Independence*. Berkeley: University of California Press, 1973.

Demaras, Konstantine. *A History of Modern Greek Literature*. Translated by Mary P. Gianos. Albany: State University of New York Press, 1972.

______. 'Eisagogika ste melete tes sylloges Anthe Eulaveias,'in *Mnemosynon Sophias Antoniade*. Venice: Library of the Hellenic Institute of Venice of Byzantine and post-Byzantine Studies, 1974.

______. "Katartzes." *Epoches* 12 (1964): 88-104.

______. *Neohellenikos Diaphotismos*. Athens: Philippos Eliou, 1977.

Dizikirikes, George. *Ho Neohellenikos diaphotismos kai to Europaiko Pnevma, 1750-1821*. Athens: Strates G. Filippotes, 1984.

Eade, J. C. and Sussex, Roland, eds. *Culture and Nationalism in Nineteenth Century Eastern Europe*. Columbus: Slavica, 1985.

Fanon, Frantz. *The Wretched of the Earth*. Translated by Constance Farrington, New York: Grove Press, 1963.

Finlay, George. *History of the Greek Revolution and the Reign of King Otho*. London: Zeno, 1971.

Forster, Robert and Greene, Jack P., eds. *Preconditions of Revolution in Early Modern Europe*. Baltimore: The Johns Hopkins Press, 1970.

Frangos, George. "The Philike Etairia 1814-21: A Social and Historical Analysis." Ph. D. dissertation, Columbia University, 1971.

Gallant, Thomas. *Modern Greece* London: Arnold, 2001.

Geanakoplos, Deno. *Interaction of the "Sibling" Byzantine and Western Cultures in the Middle Ages and Italian Renaissance (330-1600)*. New Haven: Yale University Press, 1976.

______. *Greek Scholars in Venice*. Cambridge, Massachusetts: Harvard University Press, 1962.

Gedeon, Manuel. *He pnevmatike kinisis tou genous kata ton IH kai ITH aiona*. Edited by Alkhes Aggelou. Athens: Hermes, 1976.

Gellner, Ernst. *Nationalism*. New York: New York University Press, 1997.

______. *Nations and Nationalism*. Ithaca: Cornell University Press, 1983.

Gkiolias, Markos. *Ho Kosmas Aitolos kai he Epoche Tou*. Athens: Tymphestos, 1972.

Godlewska, Anne Marie Claire. *Geography Unbound: French Geographic Science from Cassini to Humboldt*. Chicago: University of Chicago Press, 1999.

Goodman, Dena. *The Republic of Letters*. Ithaca: Cornell University Press, 1994.

Gourgouris, Stathis. *Dream Nation: Enlightenment, Colonization and Modern Greece*. Stanford: Stanford University Press, 1996.

Hall, John, ed. *The State of the Nation: Ernest Gellner and the Theory of Nationalism*. Cambridge: Cambridge University Pres, 1998.

Henderson, George Patrick. *The Revival of Greek Thought 1620-1830*. Albany: State University of New York Press, 1970.

Horowitz, Michael. *Ethnic Groups in Conflict*. Berkeley: University of California Press, 1985.

Hroch, Miroslav. *Social Preconditions of National Revival in Europe*. Translated by Ben Fowkes. New York: Columbia University Press, 2000.

Hupchick, Dennis P., ed. *The Pen and the Sword: Studies in Bulgarian History by James F. Clarke*. Boulder: East European Monographs, 1988.

Hutchinson, John and Smith, Anthony D. Smith, eds. *Nationalism*. Oxford: Oxford University Press, 1994.

Hutton, James. *The Greek Anthology in Italy to the Year 1800*. Ithaca: Cornell University Press, 1935.

Iorga, Nicolae. *Byzantium After Byzantium*. Translated by Virgil Candea. Iasi: The Center for Romanian Studies, 2000.

Kaltchas, Nicholas. *Introduction to the Constitutional History of Modern Greece*. New York: Columbia University Press, 1940.

Karathanases, Athanasios E. *He Phlangineias Schole tes Venetias*. Thessalonike, 1975.

______. *Hoi Hellenes logoi ste Vlaxia (1670-1714)*. Thessalonike: Institute for Balkan Studies, 1982.

Kasines, K.G. *He Rhetorike ton Didachon tou Meniate*. Athens: Syllogos Pros Diadosin Ofelimon Vivlion, 1998.

Kaufmann, Chaim. "Possible and Impossible Solutions to Ethnic Civil Wars." *International Security* Vol 20, No. 4 (Spring 1996): 137-175.

Kaufman, Stuart. *Modern Hatreds, The Symbolic Politics of Ethnic War*. Ithaca: Cornell University Press, 2001.

Kazantzakis, Nikos. *Anaphora ston Greko*. Athens: Eleni Kazantzakis, 1982.

______. *Taxidevontas*. Athens: Eleni Kazantzakis, 1969.

Kedourie, Elie. *Nationalism*. London: Hutchinson, 1966.

______. *Nationalism in Asia and Africa*. New York: Meridian, 1970.

Kelly, J.N.D. *Early Christian Doctrines*. London: Continuum, 2000.

Kimmelman, Michael, "El Greco, Bearer of Many Gifts." *New York Times* October 3, 2003, B31, 35.

Kitromilides, Paschalis. *Enlightenment, Nationalism, Orthodoxy: Studies in the Culture and Political Thought of Southeastern Europe*. Hampshire: Ashgate, 1994.

______. *Iosepos Moisiodax, Hoi syntetagmenes tes Balkanakes Skepses ton 18o aiona*. Athens: Morfotiko Idroma Ethnikes Trapezes, 1985.

______. *Neohellenikos Diaphotismos*. Athens: Morfotiko Idroma Ethnikes Trapezes, 1999.

______. *The Enlightenment as Social Criticism: Iosopis Moisiodax and Greek Culture in the Eighteenth Century*. Princeton: Princeton University Press, 1992.

Kohn, Hans. *Nationalism: Its Meaning and History*. New York: D. Van Norstrand, 1971.

Koliopoulos, John S. and Verenis, Thanos M. *Greece, The Modern Sequel*. New York: New York University Press, 2002

Kondyles, Panagiotes. *Ho Neohellenikos diaphotismos: hoi philosophikes idees*. Athens: Themelio, 1988.

Konstantakopoulou, Angelike. *He Hellenike Glossa sta Valkania (1750-1850), To Tetraglosso Lexico tou Daniel Moschhopolite*. Iannina: University of Iannina, 1988.

Kordatos, Ioannes. *He Koinonike Symasia tes Hellenikes Epanastaseos tou 1821*. Athens, 1924.

______. *Historia tes glossika zetema mas*. Athens: Boukoumanis, 1973.

Kourilas, Eulogios. *He Moschopolis kai he Nea Akademia avtes*. Athens: Phoinekos, 1934.

Kristophson, J., "Das Lexicon Tetraglossen." *Zeitschrift fur Balkanologie* 10 (1974): 1-128.

Kyriakopoulos, Konstantinos Th. *Meletios (Metros) Athenon, Ho Geographos*. Athens, 1990.

Lambropoulos, Vassilis. *Literature as National Institution: Studies in the Politics of Modern Greek Criticism*. Princeton: Princeton University Press, 1988.

Larrabee, Steven. *Greece Observed: The American Experience of Greece, 1775-1865*. New York: NYU Press, 1957.

Lederer, Ivo J. and Sugar, Peter F., eds. *Nationalism in Eastern Europe*. Seattle: University of Washington Press, 1969.

Livingstone, David N. and Withers, Charles W., eds. *Geography and Enlightenment*. Chicago: University of Chicago Press, 1999.

Lord Acton. 'Nationality' in *Selected Writings of Lord Acton:, Volume I: Essays in the History of Liberty*. Indianapolis: Liberty Fund, 1985.

Machiavelli, Nicolo. *The Prince*. Translated by W.K. Marriott. Chicago: Encyclopaedia Britannica, 1952.

Malcolm, Noel. *Bosnia*. New York: New York University Press, 1996.

Mazarakes, Anthimios. *Viographiai ton endoxon andron tes nesou Kephallenias*. Venice: Phoinekos, 1843.

Mazower, Mark. *The Balkans*. New York: Modern Library, 2002.

Michalopoulos, Phanes. *Kosmas hos Aitolos*. Athens: 1940.

______. *Moschopolis: Hai Athenai tes Tourkokratias, 1500-1769*. Athens: Ekdoseis Perigegetikes Lexsies, 1941.

Mouzelis, Nikos. *Modern Greece, Facets of Underdevelopment*. London: Macmillan, 1978.

Nkatsopoulos, Stavros, ed. *Moschopolis*. Iannina: Idrema Voreioepeirotikon Erevnon, 1979.

Nikarouses, A., "Ho Regas, he schole kai he vivliotheke tes Zagoras." *Deltion tes Historikes kai Ethnologikes Etaireias tes Ellados (nea seira)* V I (1928): 53-88.

Outram, Dorinda. *The Enlightenment*. Cambridge: Cambridge University Press, 1995.

Paparregopoulos, Konstantine. *Historia tou Hellenikou Ethnous*. Volume 15. Athens: Kaktos, 1993.

Papodopoulos, Athanasios. *Epidraseis tes Texne Rhetorikes tou R. Skouphos epi ton Didachon tou Elia Meniates*. Athens: Keimena kai Meletai Neohellenikes Philologias, 1965.

Pearson, Raymond, "Fact, Fantasy, Fraud: Perceptions and Projections of National Revival." *Ethnic Groups* 10 (1993): 43-64.

Petropulos, John A, ed. *Hellenism and the First Greek War of Liberation (1821-1830): Continuity and Change*. Thessaloniki: Institute for Balkan Studies, 1976.

Phasoulakes, Sterios, ed. *Praktika Synedriou 'Koraes kai Chios.'* Athens: Omereion Pnevnatikon Kentron, 1984.

Porter, Roy and Teich, Mikulas, eds. *The Enlightenment in National Context*. Cambridge: Cambridge University Press, 1981.

Protopsaltes, Emmanuel G. *He Philike Hetaireia*. Athens: Academy of Athens, 1964.

Roche, Daniel. *France in the Enlightenment*. Translated by Arthur Goldhammer. Cambridge: Harvard University Press, 1998.

Roessel, David. *In Byron's Shadow, Modern Greece in the English & American Imagination*. Oxford: Oxford University Press, 2002.

Rogers, G.A.J., ed. *Locke's Philosophy, Content and Context*. Oxford: Oxford University Press, 1994.

Runciman, Steven. *The Great Church in Captivity*. Cambridge: Cambridge University Press, 1968.

Schmidt, James., ed. *What is Enlightenment*? Berkeley: University of California Press, 1996.

Seferis, George. *On the Greek Style*. Translated by Rex Warner and T.D. Frangopoulos. Boston: Little Brown & Company, 1966.

Schwartz, Benjamin. *In Search of Wealth and Power, Yen Fu and the West*. Cambridge: Harvard University Press, 1964.

Skouvaras, Vaggeles. *Ioannes Pringos: He Hellenike paroikia tou Amsterdam*. Athens: Historikes kai logographikes etaireias ton Thessalon, 1964.

Smith, Anthony. *Nationalism and Modernism*. London: Routledge, 1998.

______. *Theories of Nationalism*. New York: Harper & Row, 1971.

Stathos, Penelope. *Chrysanthos Notaras*. Athens: Syndesmou ton en Athenais Megaloscholiton, 1999.

Stavrianos, Leften S. *The Balkans since 1453*. New York: New York University Press, 2000.

Stergelles, Aristeidis P. *Ta demosieumata ton Hellenon spoudaston tou Panepistimiou tes Padouas ton 17o kai 18o aiones*. Athens: Parnassas, 1970.

Stoianovich, Traian, "Factors in the Decline of Ottoman Society in the Balkans." *Slavic Review* XXI (1962): 623-32.

______. "The Conquering Balkan Orthodox Merchant." *Journal of Modern History* (1960): 234-314.

Tatakis, Basile N. *Byzantine Philosophy*. Translated and introduced by Nicholas J. Moutafakis. Indianapolis: Hackett, 2003.

______. *Gerasimos Vlachos, ho Kres*. Venice: Library of the Hellenic Institute of Venice of Byzantine and post-Byzantine Studies, 1973.

Thrasyvoulos, Stavros, ed. *Psychares, Ephtaliotes, Palles, Vlastos*. Athens: Vasike Vivliotheke, 1956.

Todorova, Maria. *Imagining the Balkans*. Oxford: Oxford University Press, 1997.

Tziovas, Dimitris, ed. *Greece and the Balkans, Identities, Perceptions and Cultural Encounters since the Enlightenment*. Hants, England: Ashgate, 2003.

Vacalopoulos, Apostoles. *The Greek Nation 1453-1669*. Translated by Ian and Phania Moles. New Brunswick: Rutgers University Press, 1976.

Valeta, G., "Nektarios Terpos: Ho agnoemenos megalos ethnophotistes, prodomos tou Kosma Aitolou (1690-1740)." *Nea Hestia* 89 (1971), 577-581.

Vallianatos, E.G. *From Graikos to Hellene: Adamantios Koraes and the Greek Revolution*. Athens: Academy of Athens, 1987.

Vournas, Tasos. *Philike Etairia*. Athens: Afon Totide Solomos, 1982.

Wohl, Robert. *The Generation of 1914*. Cambridge: Harvard University Press, 1979.

Woodhouse, Christopher M. *George Gemistos Plethon: The Last of the Hellenes*. Oxford: Clarendon Press, 1986.

______. *Modern Greece*. London: Faber and Faber, 1986.

______. *The Philhellenes*. London: Hodder and Stoughton, 1969.

Index

E

F

G

H

I

J

K

L

M

N

O

P

R

S

T

V

W

X

Y

Z